In this book Dr. Sheade provides a comprehensive and practical presentation of equine-assisted counseling. She delineates important constructs of the horse-human relationship and thoroughly explains how relational approaches with equines are effective interventions for human-client healing and recovery. Among the many topics covered she includes examination of theoretical approaches, descriptions of counseling strategies and techniques, and discussions of research, ethics, and practice logistics. I highly recommend this book to any current or aspiring practitioner of equine-assisted counseling.

—**Cynthia K. Chandler, EdD,** author of
Animal-Assisted Therapy in Counseling

Equine-Assisted Counseling and Psychotherapy is a comprehensive practitioner's guide that covers foundational basics and evidence-based strategies for intentionality and effectiveness in equine-assisted interventions. Sheade covers essential, species-specific knowledge about equines that all equine practitioners must know, and includes crucial aspects of safety and welfare for the humans and animals involved. Further, readers will find an in-depth discussion of the elements of a successful human-animal relationship required for all professionals integrating animals into human healthcare or social service professions. It is a natural follow-up to Chandler's *Animal-Assisted Therapy in Counseling* for those interested in developing the equine-specific knowledge, skills, and attitudes after mastering the competencies required for providers working with all species of animals. I look forward to incorporating this text into my own courses on animal-assisted interventions in counseling.

—**Leslie A. Stewart, PhD, LPC,** associate professor in the
Department of Counseling at Idaho State University

Equine-Assisted Counseling and Psychotherapy

Equine-Assisted Counseling and Psychotherapy offers a comprehensive guide to the practice of working with equines in a psychotherapeutic setting.

Chapters provide a research-informed approach to integrating the contributions of horses and other equines into mental health services. With a focus on equine welfare, the book uses a relational approach to explore a broad range of topics including documentation and treatment planning, work with clients across the lifespan and with diverse needs, complexities related to horses in the therapeutic relationship, as well as ethical, legal, and best-practice considerations.

Mental health and equine professionals will come away from the book with a strong understanding of both the theoretical and practical aspects of equine-assisted counseling.

Hallie E. Sheade, PhD, LPC-S, RPT-S, founded Equine Connection Counseling to provide equine-assisted counseling and psychotherapy. She is a registered play therapist and has worked with equines for over thirty years.

Equine-Assisted Counseling and Psychotherapy

Healing Through Horses

Hallie E. Sheade

NEW YORK AND LONDON

First published 2021
by Routledge
52 Vanderbilt Avenue, New York, NY 10017

and by Routledge
2 Park Square, Milton Park, Abingdon, Oxon, OX14 4RN

Routledge is an imprint of the Taylor & Francis Group, an informa business

© 2021 Hallie E. Sheade

The right of Hallie E. Sheade to be identified as author of this work has been asserted by her in accordance with sections 77 and 78 of the Copyright, Designs and Patents Act 1988.

All rights reserved. No part of this book may be reprinted or reproduced or utilised in any form or by any electronic, mechanical, or other means, now known or hereafter invented, including photocopying and recording, or in any information storage or retrieval system, without permission in writing from the publishers.

Trademark notice: Product or corporate names may be trademarks or registered trademarks, and are used only for identification and explanation without intent to infringe.

Library of Congress Cataloging-in-Publication Data
Names: Sheade, Hallie, author.
Title: Equine-assisted counseling and psychotherapy : healing through horses / Hallie Sheade.
Description: New York, NY : Routledge, 2021. | Includes bibliographical references and index.
Identifiers: LCCN 2020013231 (print) | LCCN 2020013232 (ebook) | ISBN 9781138571099 (hardback) | ISBN 9781138571112 (paperback) | ISBN 9781351257565 (ebook)
Subjects: MESH: Equine-Assisted Therapy—methods | Counseling—methods | Horses | Bonding, Human-Pet
Classification: LCC RC489.H67 (print) | LCC RC489.H67 (ebook) | NLM WM 450.5.A6 | DDC 616.89/1658—dc23
LC record available at https://lccn.loc.gov/2020013231
LC ebook record available at https://lccn.loc.gov/2020013232

ISBN: 978-1-138-57109-9 (hbk)
ISBN: 978-1-138-57111-2 (pbk)
ISBN: 978-1-351-25756-5 (ebk)

Typeset in Baskerville
by Apex CoVantage, LLC

This book is dedicated to all of the equines who have been my friends, partners, and co-therapists, with a special dedication to Cowman, who first sparked my excitement about the power of the human-equine bond. This book is also dedicated to the clients who give me the honor of walking with them along their journey.

Contents

Preface	xi
Acknowledgments	xiv
About the Author	xv

1 Partnering With Equines in Equine-Assisted Counseling
  and Psychotherapy   1

2 Nature of Equines   13

3 Philosophical Domains in Relational Equine-Partnered
  Counseling   23

4 Counseling Environments in Equine-Assisted Counseling
  and Psychotherapy   50

5 The Treatment Team in Equine-Assisted Counseling and
  Psychotherapy   58

6 Facilitating Relational Equine-Partnered Counseling   75

7 Integration of Counseling Theory in Equine-Assisted
  Counseling and Psychotherapy   89

8 Practice of Equine-Assisted Counseling and
  Psychotherapy Across the Lifespan   102

9 Counseling and Psychotherapy Formats in
  Equine-Assisted Counseling and Psychotherapy   112

10	Implementing Equine-Assisted Counseling and Psychotherapy With Different Client Populations	118
11	Ethical Considerations in Equine-Assisted Counseling and Psychotherapy	142
12	Risk Management Considerations in Equine-Assisted Counseling and Psychotherapy	167
13	Program Design in Equine-Assisted Counseling and Psychotherapy	175
14	Research Issues in Equine-Assisted Counseling and Psychotherapy	182
	References	186
	Index	213

Preface

Like many others in the field of equine-assisted activities and therapies, the impetus for me was a childhood love of horses. As a child, I found myself forming deep, meaningful connections with horses both in the saddle and on the ground. One particular horse named Cowman set me on the path to partner with equines for healing. Even at twelve years old, I was fascinated by the interspecies connection between myself and Cowman. More so than riding him, I loved spending time in his stall. I made the decision then that I wanted to better understand the human-animal bond. That desire is what led me down the path that I am on today, including the writing of this book. In a way, I have come full circle—starting with my deepening relationship with Cowman, and now helping others to experience the same through equine-assisted counseling and psychotherapy (EACP).

In large part, this book is based on my experiences over the last ten years in the field and more than 6,000 hours of EACP sessions provided through my practice. However, my intent was not to just convey my beliefs based on my own experiences alone, but also to support these beliefs based on current research on equines and on counseling and psychotherapy, and the integration of the two. In writing this book, I felt my twelve-year-old self waking up again in excitement as I researched the various topics. Every article or book that I read fed that curiosity to learn more about the human-animal bond. My hope is that reading this book will do the same for you.

Since first becoming involved in the field, I have witnessed EACP grow by leaps and bounds. Every week, I receive inquiries from both clients seeking services and therapists and equine professionals wanting to learn how to provide services. Given the increasing number of calls that I receive and my practice's ever-growing waiting list, it is clear that there are many clients looking for an alternative to office-based treatment. Many of these clients have felt uncomfortable or dissatisfied with the results of traditional therapies and therefore have sought out EACP.

My approach to EACP is inherently relational in nature. That does not mean that all clients have "warm and fuzzy" relationships with the equines. I believe that we are all in relationships with everyone we encounter, both human and

xii Preface

animal. These relationships may be long-lasting bonds and friendships, or fleeting interactions. I believe there is much we can learn by engaging in relational ways with equines that can help us establish and strengthen our relationships with each other. It is important to note that while there are many approaches to EACP, the approaches that I use in my practice and that I promote in this book are Relational Equine-Partnered Counseling (REPC) and Equine-Partnered Play Therapy (EPPT).

Belief in the inherent sentience of equines is integral to these approaches. In reflecting back on my relationship with Cowman, the twelve-year-old me felt a deep connection with him, almost like a sense of magic. During my studies and in researching this book, I have come to better understand this "magic" and how it may be explained in part by our shared basic mammalian needs for physical safety and emotional security through our relationships with others. As a result of this belief, it is important to me that equine welfare is a top priority in caring for our therapeutic partners and that we model this caring for our clients.

As there are many approaches to EACP, some may take a different view of the REPC and EPPT practices and assumptions that I've outlined in this book. In my research, I came across several studies on equine behavior and psychology that challenged some of what I thought I knew about equines and our interactions with them. These findings really opened my eyes to things that I never considered before. That being said, I realize that some may take exception to these findings and what they may mean about these relationships. I encourage you to reflect on your relationships with equines, both past and present, as you develop your own identity and philosophy in your practice as an EACP facilitator. I hope this book will serve as a resource to do so.

In researching this book, I was struck by several things. I was especially struck by the continued scarcity of EACP outcome research with regard to specific clinical client populations. I was also struck by the lack of consistent terminology across research studies. Many studies used the blanket term "equine-assisted activities and therapies" to describe treatment without defining or describing what the treatment actually consisted of and who facilitated it. This made it impossible to distinguish between studies that examined the effect of horsemanship-based activities from those that examined a true psychotherapy intervention. For that reason, several studies have been left out of this book, as I could not determine the true nature of the treatment provided. It is apparent that there is much work to be done in clarifying not only terminology for the broad field of equine-assisted activities and therapies, but also the scope of and competencies required for each one. As this book is focused on EACP, contributions from other types of interventions such as therapeutic riding or equine-assisted learning have been purposely minimized. In my opinion, each of those interventions could warrant an entire book of their own.

Finally, there are a number of client stories interwoven throughout the various chapters of the book to better illustrate the content discussed. These stories illustrate the use of my EACP approaches, REPC, and EPPT. None of these stories are reflective of a single client. In every case, the stories are an amalgamation of various clients and similar therapeutic patterns. All identifying information, including the names of the equines involved in the sessions, has been changed.

Acknowledgments

First and foremost, I would like to acknowledge the hundreds of equines that have played a part in my journey and in teaching me to understand the power of the human-equine bond. A few of the equines who have had the most impact on my development as a counselor practicing equine-assisted counseling and psychotherapy include Coalie (my first lesson pony), Gator, Cowman, Asia, Redford, Star, and Coco. These equines have each taught me different lessons at different times in my own life. I would also like to thank my childhood riding instructor, Mary Goldman, for nurturing my interest and excitement about horses and the relationships that we can form with them.

I have had the privilege of studying under the very talented counseling faculty members at Georgia State University and the University of North Texas (UNT) Counseling departments. I especially would like to thank my UNT advisor and mentor, Dr. Cynthia Chandler, for all of her guidance and encouragement. I also received invaluable mentorship from talented therapists in the field of equine-assisted counseling and psychotherapy, especially the late Brooke Pitts (Knox), Dr. Priscilla Faulkner, and Dr. Marilyn Sokolof. Finally, I would like to acknowledge the therapeutic riding centers and equestrian facilities who provided me with a place to grow my skills and build my practice, especially The Ranch at Windy Point.

I would also like to express my gratitude to my father, Ron, for his continual support and the countless hours that he "works" in retirement to help manage the business aspects of my practice. My father has always encouraged me to follow my passion and has supported me wherever it led. I would like to thank my mother, Gina, for enrolling me in riding lessons and always supporting my dreams, and my sister, Becca, for never complaining on all the car trips back and forth from the barn as kids. I would also like to express gratitude to my in-laws, David and Ann, for their support and encouragement.

Finally, I would like to thank my husband, Paul, for his boundless love and encouragement. He works tirelessly to take care of me and our one-year-old daughter, Sari, enabling me to serve my clients and grow within my profession. I am so glad to have a partner who shares my love of horses and helping people, and I can't wait to see where our dreams will take us.

About the Author

Dr. Hallie E. Sheade's relationship with equines began at two years old when she was the only child in her play group who wanted to go on the pony ride at a local state fair. From then on, she was fascinated with horses. At age five, her parents enrolled her in riding lessons near their home in the suburbs of Chicago, Illinois. Within a few years, Dr. Sheade was spending all of her free time at the barn, taking lessons and doing barn chores in exchange for riding time. After graduating in 2003 from Adlai E. Stevenson High School in Lincolnshire, Illinois, Dr. Sheade moved to Miami, Florida where she competed on the University of Miami equestrian team and trained horses for a local shelter. After graduating with a bachelor of science degree in psychology and biology, Dr. Sheade moved to Atlanta, Georgia where she completed a master of science degree in professional counseling at Georgia State University. While in Atlanta, Dr. Sheade earned certification as a Professional Association of Therapeutic Horsemanship International (PATH Intl.) Registered Therapeutic Riding Instructor in 2008. While completing her M.S., Dr. Sheade taught therapeutic riding lessons for children and adults with disabilities.

Still eager to learn, Dr. Sheade moved to Denton, Texas to study with Dr. Cynthia Chandler, a world-renowned expert in animal-assisted therapy in counseling. While working on her dissertation, Dr. Sheade established Equine Connection Counseling (ECC), an equine-assisted counseling and psychotherapy (EACP) practice. After graduating with a Ph.D. in counseling in 2015, Dr. Sheade continued to build her practice. In 2017, Dr. Sheade and her husband, Paul Ziehe, established S.T.E.P.S. With Horses, a nonprofit PATH Intl. Member Center to increase client access to services and expand the types of services available.

Dr. Sheade is a licensed professional counselor (LPC-S) and registered play therapist (RPT-S) in the state of Texas. She is also a PATH Intl. certified therapeutic riding instructor (CTRI) and equine specialist in mental health and learning (ESMHL). She continues to see clients, supervise graduate interns, and offer professional trainings in EACP. As a result of her work in the field of EACP, Dr. Sheade received the 2013 PATH Intl. Marjorie V. Kittredge Equine Facilitated Psychotherapy and Learning National Conference and Annual

Meeting Scholarship and the 2015 Outstanding Practitioner Award from Chi Sigma Iota, an international honor society in counseling. Dr. Sheade is also actively involved in the development of the EACP field by presenting at professional conferences, serving as a committee member on PATH Intl.'s Health and Education Advisory Committee, and becoming a PATH Intl. Faculty Candidate for the Equine Specialist in Mental Health and Learning Workshop.

For more information about Dr. Sheade or about training and consultation services, please visit www.equineconnectioncounseling.com.

Chapter 1

Partnering With Equines in Equine-Assisted Counseling and Psychotherapy

Humans have always had an innate fascination with other living things. The earliest cave paintings depict various animals including horses (Olmert, 2009). Humans have interacted with animals in various capacities both in the role of prey evading predators by staying in the trees and later as predator hunting other animals for food. Although theories abound regarding the evolution of human intelligence and transition from prey animal to predator, many theories indicate that humans' propensity for observing animals may have led them to observe the behavior of large predators and begin by scavenging the remains of the large predators' hunts. Even the earliest humans appeared fascinated with animals and may have observed them for both strength and spiritual guidance, and to learn pragmatic survival skills. It is believed that humans first formed symbiotic relationships with wolves, ultimately leading to the domestication of today's dogs. Each had something to offer the other—in exchange for security and companionship, the wolf gained a new type of pack. A pack that was willing to share the spoils of each hunt. The earliest indication of a close, bonded relationship between a human and a dog was found in the remains of an Israeli burial approximately 12,000 years ago, in which a human skeleton and dog skeleton were found buried together (Davis & Valla, 1978).

Our early human ancestors used the equine for one main reason—survival. It is believed that horses may have been domesticated multiple times by different groups. Furthermore, there are many competing theories regarding the domestication of horses. One of the earliest indicators of domestication is an increased variation in coat colors as early as 5500 BCE as a result of selective breeding associated with horses in the Eurasian steppes (Ludwig et al., 2009). It is believed that the first group to domesticate horses was the Botai people of the northern steppe of Kazakhstan. Evidence of their husbandry from the fourth millennium BCE includes leather equipment, milking tools and milk residue in pottery, corrals, and skeletal evidence of bitting, indicating a significant relationship between the Botai people and their horses (Gaunitz et al., 2018; Outram et al., 2009). As the Botai people are believed to be hunter-gatherers turned pastoralists, they are likely to have domesticated horses through the "prey pathway" in which horse husbandry arose from efforts to not deplete the horse as a food source from over-hunting (de Barros Damgaard et al., 2018).

2 Partnering With Equines

In light of new genetic findings, researchers have suggested that the horses of the Botai may not in fact be the ancestors of modern horses. The only horses considered to be truly "wild", the Przewalski's horses, show genetic evidence of links to the Botai horses; however, modern domesticated horses do not show such ancestry. Due to both human and equine genetic findings, it is believed that other cultures also domesticated horses independently of the Botai, leading to domestication of the ancestors to modern-day horses. There are several theories regarding the ancestors of modern-day horses due to gaps in the research identifying additional groups of domesticated horses. The high amounts of mitochondrial DNA diversity found in modern horses indicates that horses may be have been domesticated more than once by different groups (Vila et al., 2001). These secondary domestication centers are believed to be in in Eastern Europe, the Pontic-Caspian Steppe, Eastern Anatolia, Iberia, Western Iran, or the Levant (Gaunitz et al., 2018; Lira et al., 2010; Shev, 2016). The domestication of horses by these groups may have also followed a different domestication pathway, the "direct pathway", in which experienced farmers first hunted the horses and later initiated horse husbandry so as to not deplete the stock of available animals for food and to create a secondary resource in the form of use for milk, hide, and transportation (Zeder, 2012, p. 245). It is believed that donkeys, descended from the Nubian wild ass, were domesticated in Africa by the direct pathway also, the farmers in this case seeking their assistance in carrying heavy loads longer distances. Unlike other domesticated animals such as pigs and dogs, there are no observable differences in the appearance of wild horses and domesticated horses, leading researchers to rely on archaeological evidence of domestication such as the presence of manure and corrals (Zeder, 2012). These ancient cultures primarily used one of two approaches to domestication and training of equines based on the establishment of either a dominant human-equine relationship or cooperative human-equine relationship. Cooperative relationships were rooted in the culture's desire to understand equine behavior to form a mutually satisfying relationship.

The domestication of horses has had a tremendous impact on the shaping of all aspects of modern society. Partnership with horses enabled the transmission of language, culture, and trade across areas previously inaccessible on foot (Gaunitz et al., 2018). Evidence of horses being used for riding is demonstrated in the dental patterns of horse bones found in the Botai region (Anthony & Brown, 2011). It is likely that horses were first ridden to hunt wild herds of horses for food and increase effectiveness of livestock management for cattle and sheep. As both mobility and livestock herd sizes increased, herding social economics and political power associated with possessing a larger herd likely followed. This societal change may have led to tribal raiding beginning in 4000 BCE followed by the birth of organized cavalry in 1000 BCE, thus forever changing the nature of warfare (Anthony & Brown, 2011). Cultures which had integrated horses and riding were tremendously successful in warfare and conquest, easily overpowering societies which lacked horses (Outram et al., 2009).

Evidence of horse-drawn chariots based on burial evidence from the Sintasha culture in 2100–1700 BCE shows additional benefits for an edge in warfare (Anthony & Brown, 2011).

Healing and the Human-Equine Bond

As the use of horses expanded to new people and cultures, horses were no longer regarded solely for utilitarian purposes but also for spiritual guidance and healing. Hippocrates may have been one of the first to document the health benefits of riding horses (Riede, 1987). Xenophon, an ancient Greek general and philosopher, also touted the benefits of riding horses to heal physical ails. In addition, the horse also served as a symbol of transcendence (Hamilton, 2011). The ancient Egyptians conveyed the bond between horses and humans through hieroglyphics by depicting an intertwined rope between a horse and a person (Hamilton, 2011). Other cultures also looked to horses for spiritual guidance, including the Celtics, various Native American tribes, Bedouins, and Mongolians. Some of these cultures appreciated the horse for enhancing their own self-awareness and viewed their horses as extensions of themselves (Hamilton, 2011). Many biblical and mythical stories across the religious traditions of Christianity, Judaism, Hinduism, Islam, ancient Greek, Roman, and Nordic mythology feature horses as a central part of the stories. In Jewish scripture, horses were often represented as highly regarded heavenly creatures helping the Jewish people to win un-winnable battles. In the book of Zechariah, horses are represented as guardian angels to the world. In the Hindu story of Vishnu, a horse is referenced in saving the world (Howey, 1923).

Horses were not the only animals recommended for healing physical and psychological suffering. The concept of partnering with animals to promote healing in people dates back to the time of the ancient Greeks (Grier, 1999). Living with companion animals (i.e., pets) imparts numerous physical and psychological benefits. Researchers have documented the benefits of bonding with animals to promote resilience and coping during difficult life experiences (Walsh, 2009). In the early to mid-1900s, middle-class Americans began to focus on the role of animals in teaching children self-awareness, empathy, and socialization. It was believed that interacting with animals both in nature and as companion animals enabled children to learn valuable skills that would later assist them in developing positive familial and societal relationships. These experiences were believed to be even more important in training children who had demonstrated cruel behavior to become functioning members of society (Grier, 1999).

Sigmund Freud was one of the earliest proponents of including animals in psychotherapy. Although he initially included his dog, Jofi, in sessions for his own comfort, Freud soon noticed that his patients also seemed more comfortable and talkative in the chow's presence. He noted that the dog provided a source of safety and acceptance for clients in distress (Fine, 2010). Boris

Levinson was one of the earliest therapists to call for the specific integration of animals in psychotherapy in 1961. Levinson advocated for the benefits of including pets as catalysts in speeding up the psychotherapy process, facilitating engagement with withdrawn clients, and helping children to experience healthy relationships (Levinson & Mallon, 1997). Interest in and momentum for including animals in psychotherapy began to really take off in the 1970s (Rice, Brown, & Caldwell, 1973). Corson and Corson began using Levinson's techniques at Ohio State University and conducted some of the earliest research on the inclusion of animals in psychotherapy (Levinson & Mallon, 1997). Pet Partners (formerly known as the Delta Society) was established in 1977 in order to study the effect of the human-animal bond. This organization later became the first group to establish standardized guidelines on providing animal-assisted activities and therapies (Pet Partners, n.d.).

Neurobiology of the Human-Equine Bond

People have much in common with equines. We are both social animals who rely on our families and herds for safety, protection, support, and comfort. We, like other mammals, also share the brain structures (e.g., amygdala and hypothalamus) and neurochemicals (e.g., dopamine, oxytocin, endorphins, and serotonin) responsible for emotion, social connection, and empathy (Panksepp, 1998). As positive social interaction with others in our own respective species results in the activation of our brain's reward system and release of endogenous opioids and dopamine, it is likely that humans and equines experience a similar effect when involved in positive social interaction with each other (VanDierendonck & Spruijt, 2012). The human-equine bond may be rooted in mammalian attachment in which both human and equine experience a reciprocal emotional bond (Payne, DeAraugo, Bennett, & McGreevy, 2016). Researchers have demonstrated that equines can recognize and will respond differently to familiar people in comparison to unfamiliar people by using vocal, visual, and olfactory cues (Lampe & Andre, 2012; Proops & McComb, 2012). These factors combined may help us to connect with equines on an interspecies neurological level and form the foundation of the human-equine relationship.

As prey animals, equines are highly attuned to reading body language in both equines and in other species, such as humans. Equines read and react to tension in human body language in the same manner that they would respond to perceiving physical tension in an equine herd member (Goodwin, 1999). Equines and humans co-evolved to better understand each other and communicate more effectively. Much of this understanding is first communicated through touch (Scopa et al., 2019; Lagarde, Peham, Licka, & Kelso, 2005). It is likely that the relationship was strengthened by the empathic communication that accompanied riding activities. Chardonnens (2009) described Brühwiller Senn's (2003) idea of the empathic reciprocity that occurs between horse and rider in learning to read and respond to each other's posture, breathing, and movement to work together. This experience likely played a crucial role in the strengthening of the emotional components of the human-equine bond.

Equines are also capable of reading and responding to different human emotions (Hama, Yogo, & Matsuyama, 1996) and facial expressions (Smith, Proops, Grounds, Wathan, & McComb, 2016). Additionally, equines may use human odor to interpret positive and negative emotions in people. In a preliminary study, Lanata and colleagues (2018) found that horses experienced changes in their autonomic nervous system resulting in increased arousal in response to smelling human odors in response to the emotions of fear and happiness, indicating that a transfer of emotions likely takes place from humans to horses. Equine ability to read and respond to human emotion has likely played a large role in the establishment of human-equine relationships for both work and pleasure.

Researchers have found numerous physiological and neurobiological benefits for humans as a result of ongoing interactions with animals, like those that occur by having companion animals. These benefits include improved cardiovascular health such as lower resting heartrate and blood pressure and decreased state anxiety (Barker, Knisely, McCain, Schubert, & Pandurangi, 2010; Levine et al., 2013; Shiloh, Sorek, & Terkel, 2003). Odendaal (2000) and Odendaal and Meintjes (2003) found that when people stroke dogs, both the people and the dogs experienced increases in social connection hormones such as oxytocin and the people also experienced decreases in stress hormones such as cortisol. Hama and colleagues (1996) found that both people and equines have demonstrated physiological indicators of relaxation when interacting in a positive manner. After reviewing literature on the physiological effects of social support through interaction with animals, Virués-Ortega and Buela-Casal (2006) suggested that these positive effects may be due to stress-buffering resulting from receiving noncritical social support from animals as well as relaxation as a result of classical conditioning.

Benefits of Including Equines in Counseling and Psychotherapy

There are numerous benefits to including equines in counseling and psychotherapy. Equines naturally embody many of the facilitative factors identified by researchers for client improvement and client satisfaction in counseling, namely acceptance and empathy (Lambert & Barley, 2001). In their interactions with people, equines are naturally nonjudgmental and accepting of most people contingent on their ability to feel safe and secure around those people. An equine will not judge a client for how they are dressed, the negative thoughts that play in the client's mind, or the trauma that they may have experienced in the past. Instead, the equine will respond to the client in the present moment, helping a client to feel emotionally safer and less guarded and therefore more open. Equines also possess inherent empathic understanding as they are capable of reading and interpreting the client's many nonverbal cues such as

6 Partnering With Equines

body language and physiological changes. As equines communicate primarily through body language and facial expressions, that is also the primary way that they seek to understand people (Hill, 2006; Smith et al., 2016). Through observation, the equine can understand some of the client's inner world. Additionally, it is likely that equines are also capable of sensing the client's physiological changes in breathing, heart rate, and hormones, furthering the equine's understanding of the client's present experience (Lanata et al., 2018). The equine's subsequent behavioral feedback in response to these cues communicates this empathy to the client and enables the client to feel understood.

These facilitative factors inherently possessed by equines also enable clients to establish relationships through which they can learn positive relationship skills such as communication skills, social skills, assertiveness, empathy, and boundary-setting. These benefits have also been widely documented by professionals and researchers (Carlsson, Ranta, & Traeen, 2014; Chandler, 2017; Rothe, Vega, Torres, Soler, & Pazos, 2005; Smith-Osbourne & Selby, 2012; Vidrine, Owen-Smith, & Faulkner, 2002). The relationship with equines can become a microcosm of the client's world and patterns of interacting with other people. Through the process of building and testing the boundaries of this relationship, the equine will respond to the client with immediate, honest, and nonjudgmental feedback. Oftentimes, the client will be much more receptive to this feedback coming from an equine than another person. The equine's feedback towards specific choices and behaviors that the client may engage in during the session enables the client to gain a greater sense of personal responsibility for their actions and decision-making skills. Additionally, clients become better at self-monitoring and more deliberate and intentional in their behaviors and communication. In this way, the client-equine relationship serves both as a lab in exploring different ways of relating and later as a template for forming healthy relationships.

Learning to communicate with and gain cooperation from an animal as large as an equine can greatly empower a client while doing wonders for their self-esteem, self-efficacy, and self-confidence (Burgon, 2011; Chandler, 2017). In order to gain this cooperation and trust from the equine, the client must learn emotional regulation and to become authentic and congruent. Through this process, the client gains a stronger sense of self. Oftentimes, the equines will disconnect emotionally or even physically by moving away from clients who are not authentic. Clients will quickly learn that unhealthy patterns of relating such as aggressiveness, passiveness, or avoidance will not work with the equines. As interaction with the equines can be highly motivating, clients may feel safer to disrupt unhealthy patterns, work through barriers, and be authentic with others. As the client-equine relationship grows, many clients begin to express interest in caring for the equine by asking to clean stalls or engage in other "barn chores" independent of hands-on interaction with the equine. These requests often reflect a greater sense of belonging and connectedness in the client's belief about their own abilities to contribute positively to others and the world around them.

The presence of the equine can help clients feel less anxious about the counseling process itself and may enable them to be more open (Kaminski, Pellino, & Wish, 2002; Sobo, Eng, & Kassity-Krich, 2006). This openness can help to build strong rapport between the client and treatment team, and help the client feel safer to process upsetting thoughts, feelings, and experiences. The presence of the equine helps the client to stay grounded and engage in deeper processing levels and experience greater improvements. By stroking the equine, the client is likely to gain physiological benefits such as a decreased release of stress hormones and increased social connection hormones (Cole, Gawlinski, Steers, & Kotlerman, 2007; Odendaal, 2000). Through the relationship with equines, clients have the opportunity to process and express themselves nonverbally through touch and physical contact (Sexauer, 2011). Furthermore, the client can express and receive affection from the equines to connect, self-soothe, and self-regulate. Finally, the presence of the equines can increase client engagement in the counseling process by piquing interest and activating different parts of the brain through the novelty of the experience and physical engagement in the process, thus creating a more lasting positive impact.

The presence of the equines can also help to facilitate and strengthen the therapeutic alliance (Carlsson et al., 2014; O'Callaghan & Chandler, 2011; Wesley, 2012). Observation of the treatment team's interactions with the equines can help the client develop trust in seeing the "humanness" of the treatment team. The client is afforded the opportunity to witness how the treatment team will respond to an unruly equine, model healthy communication and boundaries, and cope with unexpected events in the session. On the flip side, the therapist has a unique opportunity to witness how the client responds in real-world situations and relationships outside of the relationship with the therapist. This observation can help the therapist to determine how the client responds to stressors and other unexpected events, as well as evaluate the client's tolerance for discomfort. Through these observations, the therapist can evaluate the client's progress through changes in the relationship with the equines and help the client to apply and evaluate new skills in the moment. The presence of the equines can also influence the client's receptivity to the overall counseling and psychotherapy process. In my equine-assisted counseling and psychotherapy practice, I often find clients to be more motivated to attend and perceive less stigma about attending compared to some colleagues' experiences in office-based practices. I am not alone in my experience. Increased client motivation when participating in equine-assisted counseling and psychotherapy has been widely documented by many other researchers and clinicians (Carlsson et al., 2014; Chandler, 2017; Karol, 2007; Vidrine et al., 2002).

Partnering With Equines Versus Other Common Therapy Animals

I believe that equines impart unique benefits in comparison to other common therapy animals such as dogs and cats. In my experience, being with equines

8 Partnering With Equines

tends to provoke a strong initial response by most clients. Many people across cultures have specific feelings and beliefs about horses. Throughout history, literature and art have portrayed romantic notions of horses' power, strength, grace, and beauty. Many clients come to psychotherapy with preconceived thoughts and feelings associated with equines, regardless of their level of previous exposure. Some clients come to psychotherapy with feelings of fascination and awe towards equines. Other clients come with feelings of anxiety, fear, or intimidation as a result of negative past experiences with equines. Overall, most people have less exposure to equines than they do to dogs and cats, therefore making their interaction with equines more unique. For clients who have had equines in their lives, the equine becomes a source of comfort and safety to counteract the anxiety of beginning psychotherapy.

Other factors that differentiate the experience of working with equines from working with other common therapy animals include equines' large size and mentality as a prey animal. The large size of the equines provides opportunities for clients to overcome fears and learn new ways to communicate in order to get the partnership of such a large animal. Even a miniature horse may weigh 200 pounds and outweigh most large dogs. For many clients, working with a large animal can enable them to feel a range of emotions, from safety and security to anxiety and intimidation. Learning to work with such as a large animal can result in increased feelings of empowerment, assertiveness, accomplishment, confidence, and self-esteem (Chandler, 2017). Clients who may be used to communicating in maladaptive ways with others by using force or coercion may find these strategies ineffective when working with an equine.

Unlike dogs and cats, the equine has a prey animal mentality. Therefore, the equine possesses a very different "operating system" or basic understanding of itself and the world around it than humans, dogs, and cats. Equines also have different motivations in their interactions with humans than predators such as dogs and cats do (Payne et al., 2016). The main priority to an equine is to feel safe and comfortable in its herd and environment overall. Therefore, many equines are slower to approach and build trust with a human due to fears about their own safety in the interaction. The equine is highly aware of and attuned to its surroundings at all times—including the people in its environment. In addition, equine are astute readers of body language, as the majority of their communication happens through body language. Not only do equines read the body language of other equines to understand them and communicate, equines continuously read human body language as well. Therefore, working with equines requires people to not only be aware of themselves and own their body language, but also observant of the equine's body language. Learning to read equine body language combined with learning to understand the equine prey animal mentality enables psychotherapy clients to work towards developing high levels of empathy and self-awareness. Additionally, as equines live in herds for increased safety, additional opportunities are presented for clients to observe, experience, and process the social dynamics among the equines in the context of living in social group with others of the same species. Finally, unlike most predators who tend to be driven by rewards (e.g., food or attention), equines tend to be driven to engage in actions that remove pressure and/or discomfort (Hamilton, 2011).

Benefits for the Equine by Participating in Equine-Assisted Counseling and Psychotherapy

Participation in equine-assisted counseling and psychotherapy can also be good for the equines themselves and improve their overall quality of life. In fact, it is essential that programs are structured in such a way that the equines do benefit from participation (Hatch, 2007). Often the equines experience the session as enjoyable and communicate a desire to participate. Positive changes in the equines participating in equine-assisted counseling and psychotherapy have been reported at every facility where I have practiced. One program reported that horses who had previously refused to be haltered in the pasture and ran away in response to seeing the halter began to willingly stand and be haltered. A donkey at another facility, who had been badly neglected prior to being cared for by the current owners, used to run at the sight of people approaching. After a few months of participating in equine-assisted counseling and psychotherapy sessions, this donkey began to connect with specific clients and approached them during sessions. Less than a year later, the same donkey became the "pasture greeter" and approached most clients as soon as they entered the pasture. Finally, a therapeutic riding program reported noticing less stress behaviors in the horses during lessons after the horses began participating in equine-assisted counseling and psychotherapy when they were not in lessons. I believe that it is very likely that, like canines, equines experience positive physiological benefits from interacting with people (Odendaal & Meintjes, 2003). Furthermore, the positive nurturing and low-pressure interactions that equines experience with many clients in session can repair the equines' negative experiences with other people and in other working contexts. This idea is supported by findings from Lynch, Fregin, Mackie, and Monroe (1974) indicating that equines may demonstrate positive physiological responses while being pet by a person. These interactions enable the equine to have more freedom and autonomy to express themselves. The equines can build trusting relationships on their terms with people and have the freedom to express themselves in an environment where they will be heard and respected.

History of Equine-Assisted Activities and Therapies

The accomplishments of Lis Hartel, an equestrian paralyzed below the knees from complications related to polio, are regarded as the catalyst for the development of today's field of equine-assisted activities and therapies (EAAT). Hartel successfully competed in dressage at the 1952 Helsinski Olympics and later in the Melbourne Games. Her success spurred interest in horseback riding for people with disabilities (PATH Intl., 2018a; Times Staff and Wire Reports, 2009). From this interest, the first two therapeutic horseback riding centers were established in the United States: The Community Association of Riding for the Disabled and the Cheff Center for the Handicapped. As interest and excitement for the field continued to grow, the North American Riding for the Handicapped Association (NARHA) was established in 1969 to establish programming and standards for horseback riding for individuals with disabilities. In 2011, the organization changed its name to the Professional Association of Therapeutic Horsemanship International (PATH Intl.) to better reflect its growth and expansion in the industry. Today, PATH Intl. not only provides certification and safety standards for therapeutic horseback riding programs, but also for programs for hippotherapy, equine facilitated psychotherapy, equine facilitating learning, therapeutic driving, and interactive vaulting. Equine-assisted counseling and psychotherapy (EACP) has been used to treat a wide variety of mental health concerns such as trauma, anxiety, depression, eating disorders, grief, oppositional behavior problems, autism, and others (Trotter & Baggerly, 2019a, 2019b).

In 1996, the Equine Facilitated Mental Health Association (EFMHA) was established by Barbara Rector, Boo McDaniel, and a group of other PATH Intl. (formerly NARHA) members interested in creating standards, ethics, and definitions for the practice of equine facilitated mental health. Rector was one of the first to formally begin the practice of equine facilitated psychotherapy and learning to address mental health and wellness. Her work with Adventures In Awareness and emphasis on the power of equine sentience to promote healing has had a lasting effect on the field (Hallberg, 2008; Rector, 2005). Starting first as a subsection of PATH Intl., EFMHA has accomplished much in the way of creating best-practice guidelines and later a formalized Equine Specialist in Mental Health and Learning workshop and certification to train equine professionals on best practices for EACP. EFMHA formally integrated with PATH Intl. in November of 2010 (NARHA, n.d.). It is important to note that although PATH Intl. provides certification for equine professionals and standards for practice, they do not offer a structured EACP model. As the field continues to develop, there is growing interest in the field. The American Counseling Association established the Human-Animal Interactions in Counseling Interest Network and created competencies for the practice of animal-assisted therapy in counseling (Stewart, Chang, Parker, & Grubbs, 2016). Chandler (2017) developed a guiding theory for the human-animal relationship. Many colleges and universities, such as University of North Texas, Carroll College, Oakland University, Prescott College, University of Denver, and Texas Tech University, offer training programs in animal-assisted therapy in counseling (Chandler, 2017). As interest in partnering with equines with mental health treatment grows, more organizations and models for practice are being developed both in the United States and worldwide. There are many different approaches for partnering with equines in EACP. There are several models developed for partnering with equines exclusively such as Relational Equine-Partnered Counseling, Equine-Partnered Play Therapy, PATH Intl.'s Equine Specialist in Mental Health and Learning curriculum, the Equine-Assisted Growth and Learning Association, Eponaquest Approach™, EQUUSOMA™, Adventures in Awareness, Natural Lifemanship, EquiLateral, HEAL Model™, Human-Equine Relational Development, and many others. You can find a reference for Schlote's (2018a) comprehensive resource of the many different approaches to EACP in the Resources section at the end of this book. Throughout this text, I will highlight the integration of my approaches—Relational Equine-Partnered Counseling and Equine-Partnered Play Therapy—with case examples, best practice guidelines, client conceptualization, and specific intervention approaches in the practice of EACP.

Terminology in Equine-Assisted Activities and Therapies

As previously noted by Schlote (2009), lack of consistent terminology continues to be an ongoing problem in the field. The term "equine therapy", despite being widely used, can be a vague and misleading term used in reference to a variety of interventions. These interventions include therapy for people involving equines, services involving equines that do not qualify as therapy, and even therapy for equines provided by people. My preference is to avoid use of this term to avoid confusion and, instead, use specific terms such as "therapeutic horseback riding" or "equine-assisted counseling" to better assist consumers in understanding and identifying the proper service to meet their needs. PATH Intl. (2019) issued a statement strongly discouraging individuals who are not licensed healthcare professionals (and who do not provide services qualifying as medical therapy) from using the term "therapy" in any written literature, program names, and/or marketing. PATH Intl. (2019) advocated for the importance of reducing public confusion related to the services offered and competence of practitioners as the rationale for this recommendation.

PATH Intl. (2018a) created terminology to help clarify the different purposes of the different types of equine-assisted activities and therapies (EAAT). However, there is still much public confusion and incorrect usage of even these terms by professionals and researchers. At the time of publication, PATH Intl. had initiated a task force that is actively working on clarifying and redefining terms for the field. Based on the PATH Intl.'s current terminology, EAAT services can be categorized into equine-assisted *activities* (services facilitated by equine professionals intended to promote overall well-being to individuals with physical and psychological challenges) and equine-assisted *therapies* (services facilitated by a licensed healthcare professional and equine professional intended to meet specific treatment goals for physical and psychological conditions).

Equine-Assisted Activities

Therapeutic Horseback Horsemanship and Riding: an *activity* facilitated by qualified riding instructors intended to promote overall physical and psychological well-being by providing a safe, basic horsemanship or riding lesson.

Therapeutic Driving: an *activity* in which qualified driving instructors teach individuals with physical, cognitive, or emotional disabilities to learn to drive equines from a carriage seat.

Interactive Vaulting: an *activity* facilitated by qualified vaulting instructors that blends dance and gymnastics through a series of different movements on or with the horse.

Equine-Assisted Therapies

Hippotherapy: physical, speech, or occupational therapy facilitated by an appropriately credentialed healthcare professional and equine professional to utilize the equine's movement in meeting specific functional or treatment goals.

Equine-Assisted Counseling and Psychotherapy (EACP) (also known as Equine Facilitated Psychotherapy): mental health or substance use treatment facilitated by an appropriately credentialed healthcare professional and equine professional to meet specific treatment goals through interaction with horses. It is important to note that EACP is not a standalone clinical framework. Instead, therapists should integrate best practices in counseling and psychotherapy into the delivery of EACP (Ferruolo, 2015).

In this book, my preferred term is equine-assisted counseling and psychotherapy (EACP). The word "equine" encompasses not only the inclusion of horses, but also other equines such as ponies, donkeys, and mules. The term "assisted" recognizes the contribution of the equine in assisting the treatment team's facilitation of the psychotherapy process. The use of this term acknowledges the equine's importance while also emphasizing the need for the presence of a credentialed treatment team to facilitate the process (C. Chandler, personal communication, 2013). Finally, the inclusion of the terms "counseling" and "psychotherapy" enables mental health professionals identifying with various fields such as counselors, psychologists, social workers, psychiatrists, marriage and family therapists, psychiatric nurse practitioners, and others to be included in providing the service and use their preferred term. (It is important to note that, in many places, the terms "counseling" and "psychotherapy" are not regulated and can be utilized by anyone regardless of level of education and/or licensure.) Only licensed mental health professionals (or appropriately credentialed interns under the supervision of a licensed professional) should provide EACP. Of course, requirements to practice counseling and/or psychotherapy can differ across different countries. Therefore, therapists seeking to practice EACP should ensure that they are following the laws of their specific country for requirements to practice. (See Chapter 5 for more information on recommended education, training, and credentials.)

Chapter 2

Nature of Equines

The fossil record for the evolution of horses and other equines dates back 55 million years ago. Of all animals, the horse's fossil record is one of the most complete records for macroevolution (Bokor, Broo, & Mahoney, 2016). Horses are members of the order Perissodactyla, which includes all species of equids as well as rhinoceroses and tapirs. The hallmark trait of this group of mammals is having an odd number of toes. Today's equid family not only includes domesticated horses and donkeys but also six other wild species of asses and zebras, all of which have a single toe on each foot. Despite their (mostly) large size today, the earliest ancestors of today's equines were much smaller and approximated the size of a small dog. Modern-day equines are believed to have evolved in North America and spread outward until becoming extinct in North America about 10,000 years ago in response to climate changes. Domesticated horses were later reintroduced to North American during the Spanish conquest (Orlando, 2015).

Like humans, equines are mammals and share much in common, from our brain structures to the importance of our social relationships with others. However, unlike people (who are predators), equines are prey animals. This identity influences equines' "operating system" or how they see, interpret, and respond to their environment. Their identity as a prey animal also influences the development of their five senses and associated morphological structures to provide them with the best chances for survival. Finally, individual equines vary in personality and behavior based on their unique life experiences and genetics.

Emotions in Equines

There is some controversy surrounding the assignment of emotions in non-human animals. World-renowned ethologist Dr. Marc Bekoff (2007) maintained that, despite skepticism, animals do in fact experience emotions. He differentiates emotions from feelings. Bekoff (2007) described emotions as arising from physical reactions that influence behavior to respond to external events whereas feelings arise from thoughts and influence our interactions with others. Given that equines are mammals, like people, we share many similarities in

14   Nature of Equines

anatomical structures, physiology, and behaviors in response to certain stimuli. Therefore, we can infer that although equines cannot articulate their emotions like people, they do have emotional states (Bekoff, 2006; Paul, Harding, & Mendl, 2005). Additionally, just like people, different equines may express emotion in different ways (Bekoff, 2007).

Equines interpret and respond to the world and others based on this emotional energy (Hamilton, 2011). Equines living in herds rely on transmission of positive emotions to promote group cohesion and negative emotions such as fear to predator detection (Hall, Randle, Pearson, Prenshaw, & Waran, 2018). This tendency is supported by the fact that equines tend to show right-brain dominance, the hemisphere which is the home to emotion (Johnson et al., 2019). In interactions with other equines, people, and other animals, equines observe scent, pheromones, facial expressions, eye movement, and gaze to infer emotions in others (Bekoff, 2007). It is likely that they also perceive other physiological markers such as heart rate, breathing rate, and possibly the presence of certain neurochemicals relating to stress and social connection.

Darwin (1890/2009) identified six basic emotions universal to all animals: anger, surprise, happiness, sadness, fear, and disgust. Bekoff (2007) defined Darwin's six basic emotions as primary and proposed that animals also experience secondary, more complex emotions involving higher brain processes. These emotions can stem from the primary emotions such as empathy, compassion, jealousy, embarrassment, longing, and regret. Unlike humans, equines cannot filter or hide their emotions, although the expression of their emotional states associated with certain experiences such as pain or discomfort may be different than those of people or other animals (Bekoff, 2007; Broom, 2007). In contrast to people or dogs who may verbalize in response to pain, equines may not due to their nature as a prey animal and avoidance of drawing attention to themselves (Broom, 2007). It is important to be aware that even if equines respond differently to emotions, it does not mean that they are not still experiencing them. In fact, the best way to recognize equine emotions is to attend to changes in body posture or tension, movement, facial expressions, eye size and movement, and vocalizations. Most people possess the inherent capacity to observe and intuit what emotion an animal is experiencing even if they are untrained in that particular species (Bekoff, 2007). However, the ability to identify an equine's emotions is not the same as understanding the specific meaning of a behavior and therefore it is still essential to become well-versed in reading and interpreting equine behaviors in order to practice equine-assisted counseling and psychotherapy.

According to Paul and colleagues (2005), emotional states are comprised of physiological, behavioral, cognitive, and subjective components. Mendl, Burnman, and Paul (2010) described equine emotion as characterized by two dimensions: arousal (calm versus excited) and valence (positive versus negative). Emotions serve an adaptive purpose for both people and equines. An emotional response to a stimulus helps us to stay out of harm's way and encourages us to approach positive or rewarding stimuli (Elliot, Eder, & Harmon-Jones, 2013). From there, we can infer an equine's feelings and expectations about a particular stimulus (or person) based on whether the equine decides to approach, avoid, retreat, or turn away. However, it is important to note that, at times, prey animals may approach a potential "predator" to gather more information if they are unsure about the risk posed by the potential predator (Fishman, 1999). Additionally, the equine's vocal cues, ear positioning, and facial expressions will also communicate their emotions (Paul et al., 2005; Wathan, Proops, Grounds, & McComb, 2016). Just as with people, equines' emotions influence their thought process and, in turn, their thoughts influence their emotions (Hausberger et al., 2019).

Equine "Operating System": The Prey Animal

I like to use the term "operating system" to describe the differing ways that prey animals and predators see and operate in the world. Just as the ultimate goal of all computers is information processing, the ultimate goal of all animals is to survive to live another day. However, the ways that prey and predator go about meeting this ultimate goal differ, just like Microsoft and Apple have different operating systems with the ultimate goal of information processing. Although there are many similarities, there are also distinct differences. The identity of the equine as the "quintessential prey animal" influences everything about the equine's life experience from their form, senses, social structure, and behaviors (Hamilton, 2011, p. 4). At the end of the day, the equine's ultimate goal is to not get eaten, followed by the desire to feel safe and comfortable. In contrast, predators are less concerned with fear of being eaten and more focused on gaining rewards or "the spoils of the hunt." The equine's high level of emotional attunement and skill in communicating nonverbally likely arose as a survival mechanism directed primarily by the right brain hemisphere. In contrast, people became the "Super-Predator" by increasing our reliance on left-brain skills such as language development, planning, and building (Hamilton, 2011, p. 5). However, through this process, the right brain hemisphere lost ground, resulting in the loss of much of our emotional attunement skills (Hamilton, 2011). These differences in operating systems can create incompatibilities that often result in difficulties for equines and humans to connect and feel safe with each other. Understanding and responding to the equine as a prey animal is the best way to overcome these difficulties and form mutually satisfying relationships.

As a prey animal, equines have a heightened awareness of what is happening around them on all sides. They live in herds to "crowd source" this awareness and decrease their chances of being eaten by a predator. Furthermore, equines prefer to move patiently and intentionally in the world as opposed to rushing, which can signify the presence of a predator and is linked to the fear emotion. This understanding is important to keep in mind as a person's frustration, elevated energy, or efforts to "hurry" an equine can lead to a heightened anxiety

16 Nature of Equines

and fear in the equine. Furthermore, equines tend to move towards things at a curve or angle rather than a straight line like a predator. When learning something new, equines can learn with less repetition than predators. Furthermore, equines are more motivated by a release of pressure than a reward. An equine's primary response to something unfamiliar is to perceive it as a potential threat and initiate survival efforts (Hamilton, 2011). As a prey animal, the equine's main defense is flight (Goodwin, 1999). Even the placement of the equine's eyes on the side of their head is indicative of being a prey animal. In contrast, people and other predators literally "see" the world in a completely different way given our forward-facing eyes. However, that is not the only difference between us. Predators also tend to use much more verbal language to communicate than prey animals who try to stay quieter and less detectable to potential predators.

The Five Senses

Equines have some of the largest eyes of all mammals. Equines rely on visual cues and have excellent eyesight that is believed to be better than that of dogs or cats (Wathan, Burrows, Waller, & McComb, 2015). Although equine and human eyes share many similarities, they also differ in significant ways. Equine eye placement on the sides of their head enables them to have a greater field of vision in order to detect movement and potential predators (Saslow, 2002). Equines use both monocular vision, in which two separate images are created, and binocular vision, in which two separate pictures are superimposed to create a single three-dimensional image. Equines use binocular vision when they are able to move their heads and necks freely. As equines get closer to an object, they process it through monocular vision and therefore need to see it with each eye. In total, with unrestricted movement, equines have an almost 360-degree field of vision. It is important to be aware that equines have blind spots that are directly behind, directly in front (under the nose or in front of the forehead), and on their backs near the withers (Hill, 2006). It is likely that equines have dichromatic color vision and are skilled with depth perception and judging distance. Their vision is likely superior to humans in low-light conditions (Murphy, Hall, & Arkins, 2009). Additionally, equines use visual cues to identify and recognize familiar humans (Lampe & Andre, 2012; Proops & McComb, 2012) and other equines (Proops, McComb, & Reby, 2009).

Equines have excellent hearing. Although their ear structures are similar to those of other mammals, equine ears have more mobility than other domestic animals. Equines likely have superior auditory abilities in comparison to people as they can hear higher pitches and lower frequencies. In addition, they can hear sounds from a much further distance than a person. Equines use auditory cues to evaluate potential threats (Hill, 2006) and to recognize familiar people and equines (Lampe & Andre, 2012). When an equine hears an unfamiliar or potentially threatening sound, they often appear to "freeze" and become extremely focused on listening until they determine the sound to be insignificant. Furthermore, the positioning of the equine's ears can provide clues on what they are attending to and what direction it is in (Wathan & McComb, 2014).

Equines also possess a superior sense of smell in comparison to people. In fact, their sense of smell is so acute that they can detect changes in water based on scent (Hill, 2006). Equines breathe into each other's nostrils to gain valuable information about each other. Oftentimes, efforts to smell hormones in urine, sweat, or other bodily fluids can provoke the flehmen response, in which the equine curls the upper lip back to try to get a deeper scent by pushing the scent deeper into the nostrils (Hill, 2006). Additionally, equines can experience emotional transmission through scent, as different human emotions (e.g., happy or angry) produce different physiological responses in equines that appear to be consistent with the emotion in the scent presented (Lanata et al., 2018). Equines take a great interest in smelling manure of other equines and likely use this information to identify individual herd members and to detect the presence of equines with whom they have a history of agonistic interactions (Krueger & Flaunger, 2011). Using scent to identify individual herd members may have been generalized to also recognize familiar humans using olfactory cues (Lampe & Andre, 2012). Like other mammals, taste is closely connected to sense of smell. Equines have a natural affinity for salty foods and learn to enjoy sweeter foods later in life. They are more disinclined towards bitter or sour tastes (Hill, 2006).

Tactile communication is essential in equine and other mammalian social bonding. Equines are sensitive to touch, even one as a light as a fly. In fact, equines often respond reflexively to flies who land on them by contracting muscles in their skin to move the fly (Hill, 2006). Equines use their vibrissae (i.e., whiskers) surrounding their eyes, nose, and mouth to determine if their head or nose can fit into a small space to avoid getting stuck (Hill, 2006). These vibrissae are believed to be so sensitive that clipping or cutting of the whiskers has been banned in Germany, Switzerland, and France (Eurodressage, 2019). Sensitivity to touch can vary by individual equine and across breeds. For example, cold-blooded breeds such as draft horses may be less responsive to touch in comparison to hot-blooded breeds such as Thoroughbreds (Hill, 2006) Historically, tactile communication has been a critical component of the human-equine relationship for both bonding and for utilitarian tasks such as riding. Grooming just above the withers (whether mutual grooming with other equines or by people) can trigger a calming, relaxation response in the equine receiving the grooming (Feh & De Mazieres, 1993). Equines use tactile exploration, such as with their lips, to explore and gain information about unfamiliar objects especially since they cannot see objects directly underneath their nose. They also use their hooves to inspect or dig by pawing (Hill, 2006). Equines are responsive to pressure whether it is applied directly using a hand on their rump

18   Nature of Equines

or shoulder or the pressure applied by the noseband of a halter when leading an equine (Hill, 2006).

Equine Social Behavior

Equines are highly social and live in groups for survival as prey animals. In both feral and domestic groups, herds are typically led by mares (female equines), not stallions (unaltered male equines). Mares tend to demonstrate more dominant and aggressive behaviors than stallions. It is interesting to note that aggressive behavior in stallions kept by humans may be more a function of the artificial nature of equine husbandry (e.g., kept individually in stalls or small pens) rather than increased aggression as an innate trait (Goodwin, 1999). Overall, domestic equines tend to demonstrate more aggressive behaviors than feral equines as a result of resources limitations (i.e., food, water, or space) or competition to access resources (Goodwin, 1999). Equines work to maintain harmony and stability in the herd in order to function efficiently to best protect herd members from potential predators. Furthermore, equines will actively work to reduce conflict in the herd and even intervene to disrupt conflict among herd members (International Society for Equitation Science, n.d.). I, myself, have witnessed this in session, both in observing conflict among equines and between session participants and equines. In one herd, Turbo, a Palomino gelding, frequently intervened when Rebel, a young Appaloosa gelding, became too excitable both with other equine herd members and with the human participants. On numerous occasions, Turbo has intervened and driven Rebel away from the session when Rebel starts to engage in high-energy pushy or mouthy behaviors. He will continue to keep Rebel at a distance until Rebel demonstrates behaviors believed to be calming signals, such as licking and chewing. Only then will Turbo allow Rebel to re-approach the herd and people in the herd.

Equines are also likely to form pair bonds with other herd members in order to experience increased social support. Domestic equines also form these bonds with other species such as goats, donkeys, and humans. Equines can also experience joy and sadness in their interactions with others. I have witnessed horses who appear to grieve and feel sadness following the death of a herd member. Others have also documented grief in equines such as donkeys (Bekoff, 2007).

Equines evolved to establish partnerships and understanding with other species in order to be more aware of potential predators and ensure survival. This trait is demonstrated in the mixed species groups of zebras, wildebeests, and other African ungulates which learn and respond to each other's predator warning signals (Goodwin, 1999). Therefore, forming relationships and learning to understand humans may be a natural extension of this innate tendency to relate to other species.

Equines build relationships based on affiliative interactions more so than agonistic (i.e., aggressive) interactions. Recent research indicates that herd decisions are not made solely by an established "leader" but as a group in which any equine can initiate herd activity such as moving to a new location. Equines with higher levels of "boldness" may be more inclined to initiate herd movement than "shy" equines. Furthermore, equines who are pair-bonded are more likely to move together (Hartmann, Christensen, & McGreevy, 2017). Equines engage in two types of leadership: social leadership and spatial leadership. Social leadership is identified as equines who take action to reduce conflict in the herd (e.g., Turbo's handling of Rebel's agonistic behaviors). Spatial leadership refers to the initiation and direction of herd members to move to a new location (International Society for Equitation Science, n.d.). Equines do establish dominance between members of the herd. However, dominance in not necessarily linear in the herd. Instead, most recent research indicates that equines relate to each other as individuals rather than establishing a rank order of all herd members (International Society for Equitation Science, n.d.). For example, although horse A may be dominant to horse B, and B may be dominant to C, C may still be dominant over A (Goodwin, 1999). The concept of dominance in equines may be overemphasized or misunderstood by humans in trying to integrate into equine social structures for training and handling purposes (Goodwin, 1999).

One of the ways that equines connect is through play. Starting as babies (i.e., foals), play provides valuable opportunities for social development. Play serves many functions in animals from learning social skills to building relationships. Just as in people, animal play is characterized by cooperation, fairness, trust, apology, forgiveness, and empathy (Bekoff, 2006). Even adult equines may engage in play to solidify relationships with other herd members or to relieve stress (Goodwin, 1999).

Equines relate to each other and to humans by reading and interpreting body language, especially in perceiving potential cues for alarm (Goodwin, 1999). As a highly social animal, equines have sophisticated methods of communicating with both equines and other animals (including people) through use of body language, scent, small movements of eyes, ears, and head, and vocalization (Lanata et al., 2018; Proops & McComb, 2010; von Borstel, n.d.; Wathan & McComb, 2014). Equines are capable of identifying different emotions in humans and equines using an interpretation of cues related to body language, body tension, facial expressions, and scent. By using body language, equines can transmit messages over considerable distance without making sounds that could alert a potential predator (Hamilton, 2011). Equines attend to ear positioning and facial expressions of herd members to detect potential predators, find food, and establish social bonds (Wathan et al., 2015; Wathan & McComb, 2014). The information gained from observing other herd members' facial expressions determines how best to respond to another herd member. Equines are more inclined to approach other herd members displaying positive or relaxed facial expressions and avoid members displaying agonistic facial expressions. Equines also demonstrate physiological indicators of increased arousal such as increased heartrate in response to a herd member's

20 Nature of Equines

agonistic facial expression (Wathan et al., 2016). Finally, equines also use different types of whinnies in response to different types of emotional arousal and valence to regulate social interactions (Briefer et al., 2015).

Equine Temperament and Personality: Interaction of Nature and Nurture

Whereas temperament is regarded as innate traits that we are born with that inform our nervous system responses, personality is regarded as temperament combined with traits that we acquire through life and experience (Sackman & Houpt, 2019). As fellow mammals, it is likely that equines share certain personality traits with people (Gosling & John, 1999). However, it is important to consider these personality characteristics in the context of the equine's "operating system" and how they may present differently than in individual people or equines. The emergence of equine personality traits is likely the result of an interaction of several factors such as genetics, early life experiences, training, housing, diet, and the skill of previous human handlers (Hausberger, Roche, Henry, & Visser, 2008; Sackman & Houpt, 2019; von Borstel, n.d.). Understanding equine personality and temperament can help predict the likelihood of the demonstration of certain behaviors and susceptibility to stress in individual equines (Visser et al., 2003). Individual equines show high levels of variation across certain personality characteristics such as level of fear or outgoingness. These personality traits are influenced by genetics, breed, and environment (Hausberger, Muller, & Lunel, 2011). In particular, fear reactions can be influenced by both breed (genetics) (Hausberger, Bruderer, Le Scolan, & Pierre, 2004) and past training and experiences with humans (von Borstel, n.d.).

Equines can inherit certain personality traits from their parents, just like people (Hausberger et al., 2008). According to McBride and Mills (2012), equines vary across three primary temperament dimensions: sensitivity to aversion (e.g., flightiness), sensitivity to reward (e.g., extraversion and exploratory behavior), and sociability and gregariousness. Other researchers have suggested six personality dimensions that equines can be evaluated on: dominance, anxiousness, excitability, protection, sociability, and inquisitiveness (Lloyd, Martin, Bornett-Gauci, & Wilkinson, 2007). An equine's sensitivity at a young age may be predictive of behavior as they grow older (McBride & Mills, 2012). In addition, an equine's genetic makeup can influence their level of stress tolerance, comfort with new situations, and propensity for developing stereotypies (i.e., stress-related compulsive behaviors) such as cribbing (Briefer Freymond et al., 2019; Hausberger et al., 2004).

It is important to keep in mind that every equine is unique and comes with their own set of life experiences. However, certain personality traits are often associated with specific breeds, which is likely a combination of selective breeding and the types of experiences that horses of different breeds may experience in a similar manner. For example, a Thoroughbred racehorse will have a different set of experiences than a Percheron draft horse. That being said, researchers have documented differences between breeds. Certain breeds, such as Thoroughbreds, Arabians, Welsh Cobs, and Warmbloods, are believed to be more reactive or nervous, and more inclined to develop anxiety-related or problem behaviors; whereas Irish drafts, Quarter Horses, drafts, paints, Appaloosas, and Highland ponies are the least nervous (Bachman, Audige, & Stauffacher, 2003; Lloyd, Martin, Bornett-Gauci, & Wilkinson, 2008; Sackman & Houpt, 2019). Thoroughbreds may be more disinterested in people than a French Saddlebred or Anglo-Arab (Hausberger et al., 2008). However, other researchers found Thoroughbreds and Arabians to be more sociable and inquisitive in comparison to Welsh Cobs, Quarter Horses, and Irish drafts (Lloyd et al., 2008; Sackman & Houpt, 2019). Quarter Horses are often perceived as more patient and obedient. An equine's propensity for learning new information may also be influenced by breed. For example, Quarter Horses have demonstrated an increased learning ability when compared to Thoroughbreds (Mader & Price, 1980). Hausberger and colleagues (2008) did not find any significant differences in equines' relationships with humans based on sex. Nervousness is also not associated with sex (Sackman & Houpt, 2019). However, male equines may focus longer on novel stimuli than female equines (Wathan et al., 2016). Despite the correlations indicated in these studies, it is important to view each equine as an individual rather than to make sweeping generalizations based on breed or sex.

An equine's personality is also influenced by "nurture", or early life and/or environmental experiences that shape their view of and functioning in the world. An equine's early life experiences with humans can influence their perception of humans and level of comfort with humans as they get older. An equine's prior training or "job" can influence their ability to learn new things and their comfort with separation from herd members (Hausberger et al., 2004). Negative early life experiences may increase reluctance to work with and form relationships with people later in life. Furthermore, equines who do not receive adequate socialization opportunities when young may demonstrate more aggressive behaviors towards people (Hausberger et al., 2008).

Equines also change as a result of age and experience. Equines' learning skills improve as they age (Mader & Price, 1980). Younger equines may need more time to process new information than older equines (Wathan et al., 2016). Younger equines are also more likely to show increased initial avoidance of unfamiliar stimulus but increased exploratory behaviors after determining the stimulus to no longer be a potential threat (Baragli, Vitale, Banti, & Sighieri, 2014). As equines get older, they are better able to cope with stressful situations by demonstrating less physiological reactivity and decreased behavioral indications of stress (Baragli et al., 2014). Exploratory behavior following initial avoidance likely helps equines to gain more information and experience about the world around them. As equines age, they develop greater capacity for emotional and behavioral regulation. However, it is important to note that just because older equines may not demonstrate behaviors indicative of stress does not in fact mean that they are not experiencing stress. For some equines, although they may be experiencing stress, they may learn to modify their behavior to avoid showing stress or as a result of learned helplessness (Hall, Goodwin, Heleski, Randle, & Waran, 2008).

Chapter 3

Philosophical Domains in Relational Equine-Partnered Counseling

There are many approaches to equine-assisted counseling (EACP), some of which view an equine as a tool to help reach treatment goals and others that view the equine's sentience as a critical component. The Relational Equine-Partnered Counseling (REPC) approach to EACP, which is featured in this chapter, is a relationship-focused approach of that takes the latter view (Sheade, 2019c). As such, the client's relationships with both the treatment team and with the equines are the centerpiece of this approach. We use the term "relationship" to loosely refer to any interaction or experience of interaction shared between two or more beings including people-people relationships, animal-animal relationships, and people-animal relationships. In this way, every interaction that we share with someone else constitutes its own relational experience. One of the best indicators of our overall mental health and functioning is the way we interact in relationships with others. Through the client's relationship and interactions with the equine(s), we are given a window into the client's relational world and overall mental health.

Hausberger et al. (2008) use Hinde's (1979) definition of relationship in understanding the human-equine relationship as "an emerging bond from a series of interactions" that is influenced in a positive or negative direction based on a pattern of interactions over time (p. 1). In the field of psychotherapy, Gelso and Carter (1985) defined the relationship as "the feelings and attitudes that counseling participants have toward one another, and the manner in which they are expressed" (p. 159). In accordance with this definition, everyone involved in REPC, including both human and equine, are considered "counseling participants". The value of including equines in the therapeutic relationship and emphasis on this relationship as a powerful vehicle for change is supported by industry leaders in animal-assisted therapy (Chandler, 2017; PATH Intl., 2017; Rector, 2005; Sokolof & Stuart, September 2000, personal communication).

The term "Equine-Partnered" refers to the collaborative relationship between the treatment team and the equine(s) involved in the counseling session. The choice of language is deliberate to convey the importance of a positive working relationship between the equine(s) and the treatment team, in which both

24 Philosophical Domains

play equally necessary and important roles in REPC. Furthermore, this term is intended to convey the importance of respect for the equine's sentience in responding to the client in a self-directed and authentic manner. In the REPC approach, it is critical to respect the equine's role as an active and equal participant in the client-equine relationship and reduce reliance on activities intended to deliberately control, overpower, or project onto the equine.

The REPC approach was developed to be an integrative trans-theoretical approach to counseling and psychotherapy in order to enable therapists of diverse clinical backgrounds to integrate the REPC approach into their practice. In REPC, we approach the client in ways that are congruent with how an equine may perceive the client. Therefore, therapists are encouraged to focus beyond the client's thoughts, feelings, and behaviors, and instead to also process the client's body language and somatic and other internal experiences. By focusing on a client's body language and somatic experiences, we allow the equine to contribute and relate to the client using the equine's experience and natural language. The approach is developmental, as the content and activities for each session are informed by the progress made in the previous session and guided by the nature of the client's relationship with the equine(s) over time. The REPC approach is informed by four philosophical domains: relational, experiential, neurobiological, and transpersonal. I discuss each in some detail in this chapter. At the end of this chapter, I include a section on general guidelines for REPC practice (Sheade, 2019c).

Relational Domain

Theoretical Basis of the Relational Domain

As humans, we are relational and social animals. We can have both personal relationships with those closest to us (our spouse, children, parents, neighbors, friends, etc.) and professional relationships (our boss, employees, teachers, colleagues, etc.). Even our interactions with other drivers on the road, the cashier at the grocery store, and computer technical support in another country can be considered relational experiences. The way that we interact with others can speak volumes about how we feel about ourselves, others, and our sense of overall well-being.

As fundamentally social beings, many times our personal relationships are inextricably connected to our health and well-being. The "need to belong" is a natural human tendency to seek and maintain social bonds (Baumeister & Leary, 1995, p. 497). From an evolutionary perspective, meaningful connections with others protected us and our offspring and enabled our species to survive, reproduce, and prosper (Cacioppo & Hawkley, 2009). The happiest people are the ones with full and satisfying social lives (Diener & Seligman, 2002). Having high levels of social support and perceived social connectedness can promote recovery from physical health and psychological disorders

(Cacioppo & Hawkley, 2003; Heinrichs, Baumgartner, Kirschbaum, & Ehlert, 2003; House, Landis, & Umberson, 1988). Furthermore, individuals with high levels of perceived social connectedness are better able to cope with stress, solve problems, and seek support when needed (Cacioppo & Hawkley, 2003).

In contrast, people who feel socially isolated or excluded are more likely to have difficulty maintaining relationships. Furthermore, they often view others as less trustworthy and more threatening (Cacioppo & Hawkley, 2009; Rotenberg, 1994). These individuals may look for ways to fill the void of social connection by holding on to nostalgic memories, becoming attached to television characters, anthropomorphizing pets, focusing on celestial or supernatural beings, or even feeling fondness towards technological gadgets (Cacioppo & Hawkley, 2009). There are noticeable differences in the physiology (e.g., brain activity and stress hormones) of people who are lonely in comparison to people who are not, including areas related to physical pain (Eisenberger, Lieberman, & Williams, 2003); critical thinking, sleep, and regulation (Cacioppo & Hawkley, 2009); appetite, pleasure, and happiness; and empathy (Cacioppo, Norris, Decety, Monteleone, & Nusbaum, 2009). There are also differences in mental well-being and health such as increased anxiety, sadness, loneliness, jealousy, and guilt (Baumeister & Leary, 1995); difficulty learning, paying attention, and regulating emotions; and engagement in destructive ways of communicating (Cacioppo et al., 2006). Certain mental health diagnoses are associated with loneliness such as depression, borderline personality disorder, schizophrenia, generalized anxiety disorder, obsessive compulsive disorder, and posttraumatic stress disorder (Ernst & Cacioppo, 1999; Shevlin, McElroy, & Murphy, 2014). Loneliness and social isolation are linked to early death, obesity, Alzheimer's disease, stroke, cancer, diabetes, heart attacks, suicide, substance use disorders, low self-esteem, and dropping out of school (Cacioppo & Hawkley, 2003; Cacioppo & Hawkley, 2009; House et al., 1988; Rotenberg, 1994).

The Therapeutic Relationship

There are different terms to refer to the therapeutic relationship in counseling and psychotherapy such as therapeutic alliance, working alliance, and helping alliance. Although these terms may have slightly different meanings, the terms are often used interchangeably. For the sake of clarity, I will use the term "therapeutic relationship" in this section.

The importance of the therapeutic relationship was first described by Sigmund Freud. He believed the client's unconscious processes and projections (i.e., transference) to be the core component of the psychotherapy process (Flückiger, Del Re, Wampold, & Horvath, 2018). Gelso and Carter (1985) identified three common components of the therapeutic relationship that span all theoretical orientations: the working alliance, transference and countertransference, and the real relationship.

26 Philosophical Domains

The working alliance refers to actual "work" that occurs in counseling and psychotherapy. The earlier that the working alliance is established, the greater likelihood of success in psychotherapy. Bordin (1979) believed the strength of the alliance to be directly correlated with the likelihood of success in therapy across all theoretical orientations. Bordin identified three core parts of the working alliance: goals, tasks, and bonds. First, the therapist and client must agree on therapy goals related to the client's primary concerns. Tasks refers to the collaboration and engagement between client and therapist, with each fulfilling their roles during the psychotherapy process. Finally, bonds refer to the nature of the relationship and overall trust between the client and therapist.

Transference was defined by Gelso and Carter (1985) as "a repetition of past conflicts (usually but not always beginning in early childhood) with significant others and that feelings, behaviors, and attitudes belonging rightfully in those early relationships are displaced" (p. 170). In the psychotherapy process, these unconscious or subconscious thoughts and feelings are projected onto the therapist. Transference is universal in all forms of psychotherapy, although the way in which the transference is addressed and managed will differ based on the therapist's theoretical orientation. The management of transference will impact both the process and outcome of psychotherapy. Countertransference refers to the therapist's reactions to the client based on the therapist's own personal experiences separate from the therapeutic relationship that activate the therapist's own internal conflicts. Just as with client transference, therapist countertransference is universal across all therapists and theoretical orientations (Gelso & Carter, 1985).

The "real relationship" is best understood to be the two-way exchange that occurs between therapist and client resulting from each's feelings, perceptions, attitudes, and actions (Gelso & Carter, 1985, p. 184). Both therapist and client participate in the real relationship through efforts to be genuine and open. This relationship transcends all theoretical orientations and plays an important role in the establishment of the bond in the working alliance. This relationship also includes the inherent power differential between the client and therapist, with the client seeking help and expected to be real and genuine and the therapist providing help while being genuine but also "at work" (Gelso & Carter, 1985, p. 191).

Subsequent research has affirmed the importance of the therapist-client relationship in counseling and psychotherapy. One of the largest predictors of a beneficial outcome is the client's perception of the therapeutic relationship (Barber, Connolly, Crits-Christoph, Gladis, & Siqueland, 2000; Hatcher & Barends, 1996; Lambert & Barley, 2001). Together, the combination of the therapist's possession of facilitative factors and the strength of the therapeutic relationship are the greatest predictors of client improvement (Lambert & Barley, 2001). Carl Rogers (2007), one of the field's most influential psychologists, identified three core conditions or attributes that the therapist must embody in interaction with the client to promote psychotherapeutic change—empathy, unconditional positive regard, and congruence. Empathy refers to the therapist's ability to understand the client's world from the client's perspective and communicate this understanding back to the client. Unconditional positive regard refers to the therapist's warmth and nonjudgmental acceptance of the client as a person. Finally, congruence refers to the therapist's ability to be genuine and authentic in therapeutic interactions with the client. Researchers have validated Rogers' beliefs in the importance of the therapeutic relationship and associated facilitative conditions (Kirschenbaum & Jourdan, 2005). Clients who recall a positive experience in counseling often cite the perceived positive attributes of the therapist as the key to successful treatment (Karver, Handelsman, Fields, & Bickman, 2006; Lambert & Barley, 2001).

Relationships in REPC

In REPC, the therapeutic relationship is extended to also include the equine(s) and equine specialist. Please see Chapter 1 for a review of the human-equine relationship as well as an interspecies neurobiological basis for the relationship. In this section, I limit my discussion to how the interrelationships formed in REPC relate to the Relational Domain. It is important to understand that all of the relationships occurring in any EACP session, regardless of approach, influence one another and the effects of each become intertwined.

The Equine

As one of the main goals of psychotherapy is to help clients feel safe to form relationships with others (Cozolino, 2016), equines can play a valuable role in this process by not only developing a direct relationship with the client but also by helping build trust between the client and human treatment team (Carlsson et al., 2014; O'Callaghan & Chandler, 2011; Wesley, 2012). The opportunity to witness the equines' behaviors towards the human treatment team can help the client determine if the treatment team is trustworthy. Like people, equines also need positive connections and relationships with others and will work to establish these relationships not only with other equines, but also with people. Equines naturally embody the facilitative core conditions required in psychotherapy, without the need for training (Chardonnens, 2009), and clients are likely to perceive these conditions in the equines and other animals (Jenkins, Laux, Ritchie, & Tucker-Gail, 2014). Equines are naturally empathetic and can recognize nonverbal indicators of what someone may be feeling or experiencing and respond accordingly (Goodwin, 1999; Hama et al., 1996; Lanata et al., 2018; Smith et al., 2016). Equines provide unconditional, positive, and nonjudgmental feedback as they respond to a client's present-moment actions. They are naturally congruent in that they are incapable of lying or deliberately

28 Philosophical Domains

trying to deceive. Finally, equines serve as a model for the need for positive social connection as they, too, experience negative effects when they cannot form or maintain social connections with other equines (van Dierendonck & Goodwin, 2005).

Equines are inherently (and unintentionally) nondirective in their work with clients, as they will offer an immediate response to the client but not deliberately try to lead or direct the client towards a specific therapeutic outcome, instead leaving room for the client to gain insight and take responsibility for their own therapeutic growth. In contrast to relationships with most people, clients can communicate with and be understood by equines in ways beyond talking, and thus, together they co-create a relationship based on touch and body language (Brandt, 2004). The equine's natural empathy enables them to respond to the client's present-moment experiences, not their words. Knowing that the equine does not have "an agenda" can help the client feel safer to explore without fear of judgment or penalty.

For most clients, the relationship formed with the equine(s) is special and meaningful. Some clients perceive this bond to be stronger and more real than the bond with therapist and equine specialist. Clients can experience some of the most crucial components to healing in their relationship with the equine— love and connection (Cozolino, 2016). As a result of this experience, clients can gain therapeutic insight through the relationship with the equines. Clients who have established unhealthy patterns of interacting with other people are likely to demonstrate these patterns in how they interact with the equine(s) as transference occurring between the client and the equine. Given the expressive and experiential nature of any form of EACP, it is likely to elicit more client transference than office-based approaches such as cognitive-behavioral therapy (Gelso & Carter, 1985). As the client-equine relationship develops, the client's positive experiences with the equine(s) become a template for improving their relationships with people.

The Equine Specialist

As discussed in Chapter 5, the primary role of the equine specialist is to ensure safety for all equines and humans involved in the session. However, the equine specialist and the client also form a relationship. In certain cases, the client may feel closer to the equine specialist than to the therapist. Additionally, the client is likely to transfer past experiences onto the equine specialist. In turn, the equine specialist is likely to experience countertransference reactions to the client. Due to the presence of the equine(s), with whom the equine specialist likely has a strong preexisting relationship with outside of the session, the likelihood of countertransference is higher. It is important that the equine specialist receives specialized training to learn how to appropriately form their own relationship with the client.

Experiential Domain

Theoretical Basis of the Experiential Domain

One of the most critical components of any type of counseling or psychotherapy is to promote client change through experience, as experience enables clients to gain deeper self-awareness and insight (Pos, Greenberg, & Elliott, 2008). Exploration of emotional experiencing results in greater insight and the creation of meaning (Bohart, 1993). Through experiencing, clients gain insight into their patterns of interacting with themselves, others, and the world.

The experiential approach in psychotherapy is rooted in humanistic, existential, and phenomenological philosophies and can be facilitated by therapists of different theoretical orientations. Some encourage clients to initiate new experiences, others encourage clients to explore existing inner experiences (Pos et al., 2008). It is important to attend not only to the client's psychological experiences, but also the client's somatic (bodily) and social experiences (Gendlin, 1973). The therapist should not only process the client's new insight and awareness, but also engage in dialogue to understand the process through which the client attained this new awareness (Pos et al., 2008).

Interaction With Equines as Experiential

Any interaction with equines is inherently experiential, as it engages all aspects of experiencing—feelings, thoughts, and somatic experiences. As prey animals, equines are present and focused in the moment. The ability to attend to and interpret the immediate responses of other herd members, as well as other species in their environment, is critical to equine survival (Goodwin, 1999). Past experience is used to inform how to best respond in the here and now. Equines also respond to clients based what they perceive from the client in the present moment and its meaning. For example, equines will read a client's body language, facial expressions, scent, and other physiological indicators to interpret the client's emotions and how to best respond (Goodwin, 1999; Hama et al., 1996; Lanata et al., 2018; Smith et al., 2016). However, it is also important to note that not only can equines recognize individual people (Proops & McComb, 2012), an equine's past experience with a specific person will inform their experience of and reaction to that person at a later time (Proops, Grounds, Smith, & McComb, 2018). Finally, equines notice when a client is not present in the here and now, and will respond differently to an attentive person versus and inattentive one (Krueger, Flauger, Farmer, & Maros, 2011).

The Experiential Domain in the REPC

The REPC approach acknowledges the importance of the client's experience in the present moment (during the session) as playing a major role in the client's

30 Philosophical Domains

healing and improved functioning outside of session. By promoting client experiencing, the client learns to become aware of, process, and accept their affective (i.e., emotional) experiences during the session. Through the experiences in relationship with the equine(s) and treatment team during the sessions, the client has opportunity to have experiences different from the ones encountered in regular day-to-day life. Through this process, the client can gain awareness of their present-moment experiences, find symbols or parallel interactions to represent experiences, reflect and make sense of the experiences, and live more authentically and functionally in the world (Pos et al., 2008).

Client growth occurs through the client's ability to experience the relationship with the equine(s) with emphasis placed on the client's autonomy in creating meaning from the experience and valuable opportunities provided for the client to experience change through experience (DeMayo, 2009). In order to effectively work with equines in any context, a person must be present in the here and now. As equines primarily communicate nonverbally, a person cannot rely on verbal language to understand the equine. Instead, they must work to understand the equine's behaviors in the context of what is presently occurring in the environment. Researchers have identified the positive impact of the here-and-now quality of EACP in promoting psychological benefits for clients (Chalmers, 2014; Gergley, 2012; Johansen, Arfwedson Wang, Binder, & Malt, 2014; Lee & Makela, 2015; McCullough, Risley-Curtiss, & Rorke, 2015; Schroeder & Stroud, 2015.

It is crucial that the treatment team create a safe and trusting relationship with the client and facilitate a safe, trusting relationship between the client and equine(s) (Pos et al., 2008; Zimring, 1994) to allow the client to gain the experiences that will lead to improvement. The client's level of emotional involvement (i.e., experiencing) in the session can influence the client's likelihood of improvement (Castonguay, Goldfriend, Wiser, Raue, & Hayes, 1996). Interaction with equines often elicits significant emotions from the client such as happiness, calm, fear, or anxiety. Furthermore, a client's emotional responses to talking about upsetting or traumatic past experiences will result in increased emotional experiences in session as well. Many clients have attributed this emotionality to the increased feelings of safety and comfort that they feel in the presence of the equine. By practicing grounding skills with the equine, a client can explore past experiences and associated strong negative emotions that may have previously been avoided. For example, in my work with Jessica, she often made negative self-statements. In those moments, her horse, Beauty, often abruptly left the session. When I encouraged Jessica to then check in with herself, she often realized that she was avoiding a painful memory in which she felt sad or rejected by her mother as a child. As she began to discuss the feelings and somatic experiences that Beauty may have noticed and responded to, Beauty returned to the session. In this way, Jessica was able to experience previously avoided feelings in a new, safer way.

In other cases, clients have the opportunity to practice new skills or ways of thinking through interaction with the equines. For example, Stacy struggled to communicate her needs to her friends and often found herself in risky situations once it was too late to avoid them. Her mother was frustrated with Stacy's continued "choices" to go to underage drinking parties. In talking with Stacy, she reported that she did not want to go to the parties but did not know how to "say no" to her friends. Her work with Blaze revealed parallels, as once Stacy would put the halter on, she would often find herself being led through the pasture by Blaze. Through this work, she began to understand the impact of her hesitation to assert herself to Blaze. She realized that, like with her friends, she feared Blaze becoming upset with her if she asked him to go somewhere that he did not want to go. As their sessions progressed, Stacy began to identify specific locations in the pasture where she wanted to go and practice communication skills to convey that information to Blaze. When Stacy felt sure in her decision, Blaze typically responded willingly to her requests. Stacy began to realize that Blaze would not get mad at her, and he had simply been taking the lead instead. As Stacy's confidence grew, she slowly began to try communicating with her friends in the same way. Through that process, Stacy was able to identify which friends were receptive to her efforts and which ones were not. Over time, Stacy began to focus more of her efforts on spending time with friends who cared and listened to her needs and found herself no longer getting into trouble and she experienced more satisfaction in her friendships overall.

Finally, the treatment team can facilitate activities to specifically encourage the client to practice attending to thoughts, feelings, perceptions, and somatic experiences. These activities can be accomplished in a number of different ways and can include mindfulness, relaxation, or intentional processing of activities such as grooming or leading. The therapist can direct processing to help the client gain insight into everything that they are experiencing in the present moment as well as attend to observations (both internally responses and external observations) of the equine in the session. I will often encourage clients to imagine how the equine would respond to them when they are outside of session to check in with themselves. This exercise helps clients tune in with their present moment experiences and identify present-moment thoughts, feelings, bodily sensations, and needs.

Interspecies Neurobiological Domain

Theoretical Basis of the Interspecies Neurobiological Domain

The ultimate goal of any form of counseling and psychotherapy is to change the brain and its functioning (Perry, 2009). Our brain is comprised of billions of neurons connected by synapses. Messages between neurons are communicated by neurotransmitters that provide information that influences our thoughts, feelings, behaviors, and nervous system activity. Genes and experience work together to impact the brain's functioning and our mental health. Memories are made up of thoughts, feelings, body sensations, and relational experiences resulting in certain neurons becoming interconnected and encoded in a shared neural net. Anytime we recall an event or memory, the potential exists for these aspects to become modified as a result of the brain's neuroplasticity, which subsequently allows us to change our response patterns. For example, recalling a traumatic event in a psychotherapy session where the client feels safe can result in a decrease of overall feelings of danger associated with the memory. Some believe that the mind results from the brain's neurophysiological processes and is best understood as a transfer of energy and information both within our own brains' processes and between our brain and others' brains when interacting with each other (Siegel, 2001). In this view, mind consists of our memories, consciousness, and self-awareness (Cozolino, 2016). Others view the mind as "nonlocal" in nature in which the mind is not limited to a specific point in time and space but separate from the material or physical world and our body within this world. In accordance with this view, the minds we perceive as own individual minds are transmitted through (but not produced from) the brain and are, in fact, part of a greater consciousness that transcends our individual selves (Beauregard, 2012; Dossey, 1989, 2015).

The brain is best described in two different ways: triune and hemispheric. The triune brain is comprised of three parts: brainstem, limbic, and cortex (Badenoch, 2008). The *brainstem*, also referred to as the "reptilian brain", is the oldest part of the brain and is responsible for maintaining bodily functions, meeting basic needs, and primitive emotion (Panksepp, 1998). The *limbic* region, also referred to as the "old-mammalian brain", is responsible for motivation, emotion, and social connection. The *cerebral cortex*, also referred to as the "neo-mammalian" brain, is responsible for cognitive processes such as logic, imagination, theory of mind, and reasoning. Different mammals have different degrees of sophistication of this brain region (Panksepp, 1998).

As both people and equines are mammals, they share similar brain organization. In a study of one horse, researchers found the horse demonstrated brain structure that may indicate enhanced cortical functioning in the form of heightened sensitivity in comparison to other mammals (Schmidt, Knemeyer, & Heinsen, 2019). Both people and equines have two brain hemispheres: left and right. In people, the right hemisphere is primarily responsible for emotion, attachment, emotional regulation, and sense of self as well as expression of emotions and social behaviors (Cozolino, 2016; Porges, 1995, 2011). Interpersonal attunement and nonverbal emotional sharing also occur through outputs of the right brain hemisphere (Siegel, 2001). The left hemisphere primarily houses abilities that develop later, such as language and rational thought followed by problem-solving and communication skills. It may also play a role in the development of self-awareness (Cozolino, 2016). As equines

Philosophical Domains 33

demonstrate right-brain dominance, especially when processing stressful experiences or social interactions (Johnson et al., 2019), it is likely that equines best relate to people via right brain processes.

Just like brain structures are organized similarly in equines and people, so is the mammalian autonomic nervous system. The mammalian nervous system is designed to promote survival in unsafe environments and restoration in safe ones. This system diverged from reptiles with the development of a social engagement system that enables mammals to self-regulate in response to social interaction. Mammals evaluate the safety of the environment by using neuroception. When interacting with familiar individuals, we read their facial expressions to determine the overall safety of the environment. If the environment is determined to be safe, mammals tend to become less defensive and experience decreased physiological arousal leading to state of calmness. In this way, mammals utilize others' assessment to self-regulate and reduce arousal and anxiety (Porges, 2011).

The role of interspecies neurobiology can be understood on the basis of two systems: the social response system and the stress response system (Chandler, 2017). As described in the section on the Relational Domain, we have seen that disconnection and loneliness can alter the functioning of a person's brain and how they respond to others and the world around them. According to Insel (1997), "abnormal social attachments characterize virtually every form of psychopathology" (p. 726). Social attachment in mammals, such as equines and people, serves to establish a sense of safety and reduce stress (Carter, 1998). Therefore, it is important to understand the chemistry, anatomy, and physiology of social bonds (Insel, 1997).

Oxytocin, a neuropeptide, may play a central role in behavioral regulation, social interaction, and engagement in prosocial behaviors (Kosfeld, Heinrichs, Zak, Fischenbacher, & Fehr, 2005), as well as the positive physiological effects of social interaction, connectedness, and perceived social support (Heinrichs et al., 2003). Oxytocin release may also be responsible for the development of increased client trust in the context of a safe and supportive therapeutic relationship (Kosfeld et al., 2005; Mikolajaczak et al., 2010). The release of social connection hormones, such as oxytocin, and subsequent increases in social behavior has been correlated with activity in the hypothalamic-pituitary-adrenal axis and is likely influenced by neurochemicals such as opioids, catecholamines, and serotonin. Endogenous opioids and catecholamines such as dopamine and norepinephrine likely play a role in initial bonding and positive social interactions in both people and equines (Carter, 1998; Van-Dierendonck & Spruijt, 2012). The importance of attachment and the role of oxytocin has also been implicated in the manifestation of different psychological disorders such as autism, social anxiety, obsessive-compulsive disorder (OCD), borderline personality disorder (BPD), depression, and schizophrenia (Bartz & Hollander, 2006). Additionally, early life stress is believed to impact the oxytocin-vasopressin stress response system and influence development of

34 Philosophical Domains

disorders such as posttraumatic stress disorder (PTSD) and BPD. Bartz and Hollander (2006) encouraged investigation of therapeutic benefits of oxytocin in treating these types of disorders.

Neurophysiological Benefits of Including Equines in Counseling and Psychotherapy

In both this section and the subsequent section, I attempt to integrate research and theory on equine behavior and physiology with research and theory on interpersonal neurobiology. My goal is to hypothesize a theoretical basis of neurobiological mechanisms underlying equine-assisted counseling (EACP) and then discuss how it applies to the REPC approach in EACP. However, there is very limited research on this topic. These hypotheses are based on my practical experiences, the available research, and theories put forth by others also seeking to better understand the physiological and neurobiological processes underlying the human-animal bond in animal-assisted interventions (Beetz, 2017; Chandler, 2017; Serpell, McCune, Gee, & Griffin, 2017). Given the rapid growth of EACP, it is my hope that research studies testing the validity of these hypotheses can be conducted in the near future. As a result, many of the inferences described in the following sections are theoretical.

Simply the presence of the equine(s) in session as a social support can facilitate numerous physiological benefits to the client. Most of my clients have reported feeling calmer and more at peace at the end of their first session. Researchers have found evidence of positive physiological and neurobiological changes that occur as a result of being in contact with animals. The release of oxytocin may be a key component in promoting positive psychophysiological change in clients participating in animal-assisted interventions (Beetz, 2017; Chandler, 2017). Odendaal (2000) and Odendaal and Meintjes (2003) found that interaction between humans and dogs led to positive hormonal changes such as increases in oxytocin and decreases in stress hormones such as cortisol. I believe that it is likely that similar effects would be found if these studies were to be repeated with humans and equines interacting in a positive manner. Additionally, both clients and equines may experience physiological changes indicative of reduced stress when participating in a shared activity (Yorke et al., 2013).

Halm (2008) summarized the results of several studies that indicated that the presence of a therapy animal can produce positive feelings and physiological changes consistent with a relaxation response. These studies illustrate the possible neurobiological and physiological benefits of having equines present in the session in order to reduce the client's anxiety about the counseling process. The release of oxytocin may facilitate adaptive social learning and relationship skills by increasing encoding for positive social cues (Guastella, Mitchell, & Mathews, 2008). Oxytocin may also increase client tolerance for processing stressful or traumatic experiences by modulating the nervous system's activity and inhibiting stress hormones, such as cortisol (Heinrichs et al., 2003). These effects may explain the finding that interaction with animals and spending more time with an animal that an individual has bonded with can lower physiological reactivity during a stressful situation (Allen, Blascovich, Tomaka, & Kelsey, 1991; Allen, Shykoff, & Izzo, 2001). It is likely that these findings apply to interactions with equines. It is my experience that when clients interact with equines, they are less guarded, have feelings of connectedness to the equine, and experience feelings of social support and mitigating anxiety. This observation may also be explained by the release of oxytocin and endogenous opioids, such as endorphins. These effects are likely magnified by physical contact with the equine, as clients who stroke an equine may perceive increased feelings of relaxation and decreased tension. This effect may be even more pronounced in clients who are experiencing more negative feelings at the start of the session (Hama et al.,1996).

The Interspecies Neurobiological Domain in the REPC Session

As highly social animals, both people and equines evolved to be attuned to others' inner experiences (Cozolino, 2016). Inner experiences like emotions are characterized by experiential, physiological, and behavioral responses (Mauss & Robinson, 2009). The ability to experience the transmission of positive and negative emotions is critical for equine herd cohesion and survival (Hall et al., 2018). It is likely that equines experience similar emotional recognition and transmission with clients and people in the session (Hama et al., 1996). As a result, equines may perceive changes in a client's sweating, brain states, or cardiovascular indicators such as heart rate, blood pressure, or heart rate variability to interpret and respond to the client's emotional state (Mauss & Robinson, 2009). Additionally, it is likely that equines also perceive and interpret a client's emotions based on behavioral indicators such as the client's vocal characteristics, facial expressions, and overall body language. Equines are capable of recognizing specific facial expressions not only in other equines but in humans as well. In fact, equines demonstrate differences in behavior and physiological arousal when exposed to human facial expressions indicative of positive emotions versus those indicative of negative emotions (Smith et al., 2016). This response may be, in part, due to similarities in the structure and form of facial expressions between equines and people (Wathan et al., 2015). Finally, equines are capable of detecting a client's level of attentiveness in the session and respond differently to clients who are attentive and inattentive (Proops & McComb, 2010). It has also been hypothesized that mirror neurons in people may play a role in in facilitating resonance, empathy, mutual understanding of the other's intent and emotions, and self-awareness (Acharya & Shukla, 2012; Badenoch, 2008; Cozolino, 2016). If true, this may also help explain how equines perceive and understand human emotion as well.

36 Philosophical Domains

Equines are likely to respond differently to clients based on specific client emotions experienced in session as a result of possible detection of physiological and behavioral indicators associated with specific emotions. As a result, equines may demonstrate behaviors associated with relaxation and lower physiological arousal when interacting with a client who feels calm and demonstrate behaviors associated with avoidance or physiological reactivity with a client who is nervousness or angry (Hama et al., 1996; Hartmann et al., 2017). Therefore, when working with clients in session, equines are likely to gravitate more towards calmness and may make efforts to release stress or tension, just as they would in trying to restore peace or harmony among other equines (Wilsie & Vogel, 2016).

As equines primarily respond to the client's "right brain" experiences, I encourage the treatment team to become "horse-like" in conceptualizing and processing with the client. To become horse-like, the treatment team should strive to notice and attend to the same changes and behaviors that the equines would also notice about the client. Such qualities include the client's nonverbal communication, somatic experiences, incongruencies, physiological changes, and tone and volume of the client's verbal communication. To become horse-like, the treatment team should work to be immediate and present, as equines are experts in the use of immediacy. Therapists who are uncomfortable or inexperienced in using immediacy often become overly focused on verbal dialogue and the client's cognitive thought patterns and beliefs. However, this focus often results in sessions that are disjointed and ineffective, as there is no bridge of shared understanding and communication between the treatment team and equines. While the equines are likely attending and responding to the client's right-brain experiences, the therapist in these cases is often focusing on the client's left-brain experiences. It is important that the therapist is able to find a balance in attending to both experiences.

In most of my sessions, I have observed changes in the equines' behavior in response to the client's changes in emotions and attentiveness throughout the session. I have observed a number of different equine behaviors, such as moving towards or away from the client, yawning, licking and chewing, stretching, or becoming pushy or nippy towards the client. These responses can provide valuable feedback to the client, which can be used to encourage the client's reflection on thoughts, feelings, and somatic experiences in the present moment. In this way, clients gain awareness into their level of presence in the session and any factors may be inhibiting their ability to be present.

For clients to progress in psychotherapy, they must have a secure relationship with the therapist (Cozolino, 2016). In REPC, some clients may feel safer to first establish this secure relationship with the equine before establishing it with the treatment team. As adult attachment style is influenced by infant attachment (Carter, 1998), it likely that a client will display a similar initial attachment style in the relationship with the equine and can work towards development of a secure relationship. As a secure attachment relationship with a human therapist can influence improved psychotherapeutic outcomes, it is anticipated that the establishment of a secure attachment relationship with the equines can also enhance outcomes (Bachi, 2013; Yang, 2017). Working with an equine who is present, attuned, and respectful can enable clients to feel safer to let down their guard. As the relationship grows stronger, the client is likely to feel safer to express negative or distressing thoughts and feelings. Therefore, the experience of a healthy attachment relationship with the equine can result in changes in the brain and thus influence positive changes in the client's relationships with others as well (Cozolino, 2016).

Clients can also practice new ways of relating to others through "experiments in living" with the equine (Cozolino, 2016, p. 112). Clients can gain awareness into parallels and patterns in their social interactions and practice new ways of relating. By first practicing with an equine with whom the client has a safe and trusting relationship, the client's amygdala activation and associated anxiety is lower, thus making it easier to try new ways of relating to others (Cozolino, 2016). The treatment team can help the client gain this awareness by encouraging the client to notice within themselves what an equine may notice. As clients achieve this heightened self-awareness, it will become easier to also tune into others' emotional states and develop empathy (Cozolino, 2016).

The treatment team can also facilitate calming and self-regulation activities designed with the intent of promoting specific neurobiological benefits for the client. For example, the therapist can lead the client in a mindful grooming activity with the specific intent to help the client downregulate anxiety and associated physiological arousal through muscle relaxation combined with stroking the equine. This activity may facilitate a decrease in stress hormones and an increase in social connection hormones in both the client and equine (Odendaal, 2000). During these activities, the equines will often provide ongoing feedback based on their perception of changes in the client's internal emotional state (Hama et al., 1996) and level of presence in the here and now (Proops & McComb, 2010). This feedback encourages clients to check in with themselves and work to understand what they are feeling instead of engaging in unhealthy reflexive, automatic behavior. This experience provides opportunities to reflect, reconsider, and redirect, which can ultimately change the brain's functioning (Cozolino, 2016).

By experiencing a safe relationship with the equine and learning calming skills, clients can also learn to inhibit fear responses and build new neural connections resulting in an increased capacity for emotional regulation (Cozolino, 2016). The equine's calm, quiet presence during the session may enable the client to internalize a sense of safety and facilitate reduced physiological arousal overall (Beetz, 2017; Porges, 2011). The treatment team can use this knowledge to create opportunities for clients to process trauma or other distressing experiences. As strong negative emotions arise in the session, I often see some equines leave the session and others approach. If the client has already established a close relationship with a particular equine, that equine tends to stay along with

38 Philosophical Domains

the other herd members who have approached. In the case of clients with trauma, the approach and subsequent staying of the equines can be very powerful. These clients often turn to the equine and began to self-soothe by petting or talking to the equine and thereby initiate self-regulation. It is likely that affect attunement and social referencing processes help the client to regulate their internal state based on the equine's own regulation processes (Siegel, 2001). Having a witness while we express thoughts, feelings, and experiences activates the social brain. The client can become better able to articulate experiences that were previously made up of images, bodily sensations, and emotions. They can also create a new memory of the story while observing someone else's reactions. Equines can be the ultimate witnesses in allowing people to express themselves freely without judgment and to feel safe and supported while doing so (Cozolino, 2016).

Finally, the treatment team can also provide psychoeducation to the client in order to help the client better gain insight into themselves on a neurobiological basis (Badenoch, 2008). For many clients, understanding why they respond to things in certain ways and identifying steps they can take to help themselves can help them feel empowered. For example, many of my clients have found it helpful to learn that equines notice changes in body and facial expression and can recognize positive versus negative emotions. With this information, the clients develop a structured way to check in with themselves by learning to evaluate their own body language when the equine provides feedback. The client can then connect this observation to internal experiences such as thoughts and feelings. For other clients, learning about the neurobiological basis behind why they feel more relaxed with the equines can help them identify other activities outside of session that may produce a similar response, thus expanding their repertoire of coping skills.

Spiritual Domain

Theoretical Basis for the Spiritual Domain

The spiritual domain recognizes aspects of the relationship between the equine and client that cannot be explained by behavioral or physiological theories. This domain encompasses what I like to call "things that happen in the pasture, that we see happen in the pasture, even if we don't have the 'science' to explain it . . . yet". The equine's physiological ability to detect and respond to emotions in the client is only half of the story. The other half, accounted for by the spiritual domain, is why equines care to provide the feedback in the first place. Why does the herd surround a vulnerable client? Why doesn't the equine just walk away from distressed client? These accounts are not just limited to equines in REPC sessions—there are countless stories of animals connecting with members of other species that seem counterintuitive or even counterproductive to their survival based on our existing knowledge and understanding

Philosophical Domains   39

of these animals (Bekoff, 2007). Finally, the spiritual domain is also influenced by biophilia, or humans' innate affinity for nature and the experience of calmness and tranquility that people experience by being in nature and interacting with animals (DeMayo, 2009; Kellert & Wilson, 1993; Lee & Makela, 2015). The role of nature is a critical component among many religious and cultural traditions. Many people also report experiencing spiritual or transformative experiences as a result of spending time in nature independent of engagement in specific religious or cultural practices (Jordan, 2013).

The spiritual domain enables us to experience openness in challenging and revising the assumptions that we have about our minds, brains, and bodies in both ourselves and in others. Beauregard (2012) and Dossey (1989, 2015) presented a scientific basis to challenge these assumptions and expand our understanding of the interaction of our minds and bodies beyond what we think we know, including about physical and psychological healing. This openness can have significant ripple effects in changing the way that we think, feel, and function in our bodies. It can also fundamentally change the way that we perceive and relate to others, including equines.

It is important to differentiate the term "spiritual" from the term "religious". Religious refers to the belief system of a specific group; spiritual refers to "the realm of the human spirit, that part of humanity that is not limited to bodily experience" (Scotton, 1996). Spiritual or transpersonal experience refers to human experience that transcends the bodily experiences or higher level of functioning of human consciousness. Transpersonal psychology has been influenced by prominent individuals in the development of the fields of psychology and psychiatry such as William James, Sigmund Freud, Carl Jung, and Abraham Maslow. Therapists can integrate transpersonal or spiritual elements into counseling and psychotherapy through use of meditation, mindfulness, guided imagery, and breath work (Scotton, Chinen, & Battista, 1996). Therapists can explore a client's sense of spirituality through discussions about meaning and purpose in the context of the client's existing spiritual belief system (Boorstein, 1997). Integration of these components in session should be approached cautiously and with the appropriate training, especially as it is likely to heighten the experience of transference and countertransference (Boorstein, 1997).

Integration of Spirituality and Equines

The spiritual connection between humans and equines dates back to antiquity and transcends various spiritual traditions (see Chapter 1). Many people have written about the spiritual, mythical, or transpersonal components of the human-animal connection throughout the course of time (Hausman & Hausman, 2003). Some emphasize the integration of spirituality with horse training approaches (Blake, 1975; Hamilton, 2011; Irwin, 2005). Others make specific references to spiritual aspects of relating to or communicating with equines using telepathy or extrasensory perception (Blake, 1975; Hamilton, 2011;

40 Philosophical Domains

Sheldrake, 1999). There are also individuals who integrate the spiritual experience of being with equines with interventions to promote healing (Broesma, 2007; Kohanov, 2001; McCormick & McCormick, 1997; Rector, 2005). Working with equines can shift our state of consciousness and help us to become more aware and attuned to both ourselves and others (Kohanov, 2001; Rector, 2005). Efforts to engage in mindful and meditative practices while in a relationship with the equine can result in increased awareness, regulation, and spiritual intelligence, and can improve the quality of the human-equine relationship (Irwin, 2005; Kohanov, 2001; Maziere & Gunnlaugson, 2015).

Interaction with equines can help people to engage in self-reflection by raising questions about their place in the world and facilitating movement towards wholeness (Skeen, 2011). In order to gain the trust and cooperation of equines, we have to step outside of the human language and enter into the world of the equine, one in which we are viewed profoundly differently than we often see ourselves. For many people, this experience alone can be transformative and life-changing. It can raise significant questions about our own identities and our place in the world, resulting in fundamental changes in not only how we operate in the world as individuals but also how we perceive and relate to others, including other people and animals.

The Spiritual Domain in the REPC Session

Acknowledgement of the spiritual domain in the REPC session enables the treatment team to affirm the external occurrences and the client's internal experiences. An example of an external occurrence would be when the herd (or members of the herd) spontaneously choose to surround a client who is having a deeply emotional experience. I have witnessed this occurring more times than I can count. One client, who we'll call Suzy, a 14-year-old, showed up for REPC feeling very stressed. She discussed feeling overwhelmed with school and trouble staying on top of her homework. As the session progressed, Suzy began to make indirect comments about stress at home. She slowly began to describe ongoing conflict with her father and feeling unloved by him. As she began to talk about her father, three mares within the herd slowly began to make their way over to Suzy. As she talked about feeling unloved, the three mares surrounded Suzy from all sides. Upon noticing this, Suzy began to cry while reaching out to pet the mares. She stated that she felt better that they understood and cared about her. In this example, there are two dimensions to consider. The first is the physical act of the mares choosing to approach and then surround Suzy. From my readings, I have not found any research documenting the phenomenon of equine herd members surrounding a distressed human. However, having witnessed this phenomenon numerous times with many different clients and many different herds, I can say with full confidence that equines can and often will perceive and surround a distressed person. What does this mean? We can make inferences about the equines' capability and intent to read and respond to human emotion, but cannot explain this behavior with certainty. My best guess would be that the equines are perceiving the human to be vulnerable and therefore more at risk for a potential predator. Surrounding the vulnerable human reduces the risk to human. In this type of interaction, the equines appear to be demonstrating empathy, or care for the client. However, that begs the next question. Why do the equines care in the first place? Dossey (1989, 2015) may offer an explanation in the theory of the nonlocal mind and of shared mind and consciousness. In accordance with this theory, the equines may have been demonstrating their capacity to not only access high levels of awareness and universal consciousness but also an ability to not only perceive others' internal experiences but also to influence others, both human and equine.

The second dimension pertains to the client's internal evaluation of the experience. In this particular case, the client reported that the equines "understood" and "cared" about her. Can we know with certainty that the equines truly "understand" and "care"? No, we cannot. On the flip side, can we say that they do not "understand" and "care"? Also no. What's most important is the client's experience and interpretation of meaning from the experience. The treatment team should both facilitate and honor the client's own creation of meaning.

Another example of this phenomenon is that of clients who have reported to experience the equine speaking directly to them. (It is important to note that none of the clients have ever reported hallucinations, delusions, depersonalization, or derealization.) I once worked with Angela, an adult female survivor of childhood sexual abuse. She had worked with her horse, Jake, for several months. One day, during an especially difficult session, Angela suddenly stated that she had "heard" Jake tell her that she could "do this". Angela reported feeling immensely comforted and reenergized by this experience and began to process her trauma in detail—something that she had been unable to do until that point. In examining Angela's report of Jake "speaking" to her, we can consider a number of different possibilities including that Jake did, in fact, "speak" to Angela. Alternatively, Angela could have been interpreting her own consciousness as Jake's voice. Others may interpret Angela's experience of hearing Jake's voice as that of a higher power. It could also be a reflection of a possible shared consciousness experience (Dossey, 1989, 2015). What's most important is the positive effect it had on Angela and her own meaning from the experience. For some clients, the integration of equine-assisted interventions within the client's existing spiritual framework can allow for a transformative experience of spiritual exchange. These experiences can honor the client's unique spiritual identity and worldview in ways that office-based therapies may be unable to do (Dell et al., 2011).

REPC General Guidelines

Equine Sentience

Animal sentience is best be defined as "the ability of animals to feel and experience emotions such as joy, pleasure, pain and fear" (Proctor, Carder, & Cornish,

42 Philosophical Domains

2013, p. 883). Broom (2007) described sentient animals as possessing "some ability to evaluate the actions of others in relation to itself and third parties, to remember some of its own actions and their consequences, to assess risk, to have some feelings, and to have some degree of awareness" (as cited in Broom, 2007, p. 100). Sentient animals also demonstrate flexibility in behavior when making decisions and responding intentionally to different people and things in their environment (Bekoff, 2007). Furthermore, sentient equines are likely to possess executive awareness of being able to assess, deduce, and plan (Broom, 2007). If you have ever seen equines around feeding time, you will notice that the equines may first observe the changing behaviors of both the humans preparing the feed and other equines who are aware that it is feeding time. In most cases, the equines will then exhibit behaviors indicative of this awareness such as pacing or lining up in front of the gate. By moving to be in proximity to the gate, the equines are demonstrating the capacity to plan for what is likely to occur next. Equines' ability to learn (i.e., training) is another indication of their sentience.

Renowned ethologist Dr. Marc Bekoff (2006) believes that animals have more in common with people than areas in which they differ. Charles Darwin (1890/2009) rejected the idea of a divide between humans and animals. Instead, Darwin promoted the notion that all animals (including humans) share the same experiences on an evolutionary continuum. Therefore, all animals experience similar thoughts, behaviors, and feelings that may vary by degree but not in kind. The topic of animal sentience remains one of great controversy. It brings up questions related to scientific methods and ways of knowing. It also can create great discomfort in blurring the distinctions that some ascribe between people and other animals by challenging long-held beliefs and raising questions about animal treatment and welfare.

Proctor (2012) traced the beginnings of the study of animal sentience to ancient thinkers such as Plutarch, Hippocrates, and Pythagoras. This notion continued from the Renaissance through the Enlightenment and the 19th century. During the Enlightenment, people began to question animal husbandry practices and developed a greater focus on animal welfare. In the 19th century, Darwin promoted his beliefs about animals' experience of pain, emotion, and self-consciousness. During the 20th century, interest in animal sentience waned with the advent of behaviorism, which disregarded subjective experiences such as sensation, feeling, though, and emotion in lieu of focusing on observable behavior (Duncan, 2006). Griffin (1976) initiated renewed interest in animal sentience (as cited in Duncan, 2006). Since then, much progress has been made in recognizing the sentience of animals worldwide. The European Union has recognized animals as sentient since the Treaty of Lisbon took effect in 2009. In 2012, a group of scientists issued *The Cambridge Declaration on Consciousness*, where they declared the following:

> Convergent evidence indicates that non-human animals have the neuroanatomical, neurochemical, and neurophysiological substrates of conscious states along with the capacity to exhibit intentional behaviors.

Philosophical Domains   43

Consequently, the weight of evidence indicates that humans are not unique in possessing the neurological substrates that generate consciousness. Non-human animals, including all mammals and birds, and many other creatures, including octopuses, also possess these neurological substrates.

(Low et al., 2012)

Bekoff (2013) and other scientists have maintained the existence of animal sentience for quite some time. Shared brain structures enable animals to experience much of what humans also experience (Bekoff, 2006). Many animals such as crows, fish, killer whales, and non-human primates can experience a wide range of emotions, culture, empathy, and morality. Bekoff (2006) noted that although anthropomorphism is important in understanding animals and providing a shared vocabulary to talk about animals, it must be used carefully and in consideration of an animal's specific species and biology. He suggested asking the question "what is it is like to be that individual?" to maintain the animal's point of view as a member of their species (p. 50). It is important to keep in mind that the skills we use to infer what an animal is feeling or thinking are not so different from the ones we use to infer the private thoughts and feelings of another person. This ability is crucial to empathy by helping to establish and maintain relationships and promoting compassion. For more detailed reading on this topic, see Bekoff (2006).

In summary, equines are regarded as sentient partners and therefore capable of being self-directed in providing natural and valuable feedback to the client (McLean & McGreevy, 2010). Therefore, in the practice of REPC, the core of which lies in the belief in animal sentience, the treatment team should never refer to the equine as a "tool" or use the term "use" to describe the equine's participation in the session. Statements such as "I 'use' horses in counseling" should be avoided. Use of these types of statements and terms minimize the equine's role as a sentient being and their contributions to REPC sessions. Instead, it would be appropriate to use statements such as "I work with horses in psychotherapy" or "I practice equine-assisted counseling". Similar sentiments and beliefs about the equine's role in psychotherapy are shared by other industry leaders such as PATH Intl. (2017).

De-Emphasis on Teaching Horsemanship and Riding

The REPC approach is intended to enable clients to engage in an experiential, discovery-based learning and growth processes. Therefore, teaching and evaluation of structured horsemanship and riding skills is discouraged, except in special cases. Such cases should be mutually agreed upon by both members of the treatment team and intended to maintain a safe environment or facilitate movement towards specific clinical goals informed by the therapist's clinical judgment. It is important to note that engagement in teaching or evaluation of horsemanship skills is likely to detract from the psychotherapeutic process. Furthermore, interventions involving more structured teaching of horsemanship skills or riding possess a heightened risk of impeding recognition of the equine's authentic feedback and ability to participate as a true partner (Carlsson, Ranta, & Traeen, 2015). For these reasons, REPC is intended to primarily be practiced on the ground. There are several reasons that REPC is primarily ground-based. The first reason relates to the fact that the equine simply cannot respond as naturally or organically when the client is mounted. For example, if an equine were to have a reaction to a client on the ground, the equine could walk away without any physical safety risks to client or equine. Imagine how that would go if an equine being ridden decided to leave the session! In addition, the equine's communication signals are not as clear when mounted, as the client's view of the equine's body language is restricted. Furthermore, the equine's signals may be diluted or confused due to the impact of tack worn for the mounted activity. Secondly, the primary focus of REPC is to meet specific mental health treatment goals, not to learn riding. However, if the client is mounted on the equine, they will require much more teaching and evaluation of riding skills to simply keep them safe while mounted. Finally, researchers have found that some equines may experience more emotional reactivity when being ridden (Hausberger, Gautier, Biquand, Lunel, & Jego, 2009). Therefore, it is possible that mounted work may add additional stress to the equine, interfere with the development of the client-equine relationship, and impact the equine's ability to provide feedback to the client.

Beyond a Mirror

Despite the equine's sensitivity to a client's emotional experiences and emotional transmission that may occur resulting from the equine's matching of the client's emotional experience, it is important to keep in mind that the equine is a unique individual, just as the client is. There are many EACP models and practitioners that use the term "mirror" to describe the equine's responses to the client. In my opinion, this term can fall short in communicating the equine's capabilities and role in the session. The equine is not simply a mirror that reflects back what the client is experiencing, but instead is a sentient thinking and feeling being responding in relation to the client (Wycoff, 2019). Instead, the equine is viewed as a sensitive participant in the session who is impacted by the client's emotional experience. Rather than focusing on what the equine is "mirroring" to the client, the treatment team in REPC should instead work to help the client develop self-reflection skills while processing their relationship with the equine to better understand both themselves and the equine in their shared relationship.

Use of Interpretation

In the REPC approach, interpretation of the equines' responses and behaviors should be used carefully and intentionally. Unlike other EACP approaches that

Philosophical Domains   45

prohibit use of interpretation, I believe appropriate use of interpretation of the equines' behaviors by a qualified equine specialist provides several benefits to both the equines and client. First, by interpreting the equine's behavior, the equine specialist respects the equine's sentience and contributions by giving him or her a voice in the session, rather than promoting the equine as a tool to be projected onto. Furthermore, as most clients are not equine experts, they do not possess the skill and experience to accurately understand equine body language or the prey animal worldview, at least not at the start of REPC. As the client develops this understanding through the psychotherapy process, they are better able to learn valuable relational and social skills such as communication, empathy, and compromise. Without the equine specialist acting as the equine's voice, the relationship can easily become one-sided and far from an ideal model that emphasizes mutually satisfying and healthy interpersonal relationships.

However, it is equally important that the equine specialist does not over-interpret and allows space for the client to explore and process their assumptions about the equine. Supporting the client in working towards a greater understanding of the equine as a unique individual can model healthy relationship development. If the client tends to misunderstand much of the equine's behaviors and intent, the client is also likely to misunderstand and misattribute intent in their interpersonal relationships. Over-interpreting can interfere with the client's development of greater self-awareness and new skills. The treatment team must seek balance between facilitating the client's process and respecting the equine as a sentient being and partner.

One example that I frequently share when teaching about REPC is how many clients initially interpret the meaning of the equine's back foot when cocked. In spite of the rest of the equine's body appeared relaxed, I have had countless clients notice the cocked hoof and, generally, immediately label the equine as "angry" or "about to kick." However, in most cases, the equine specialist that sees an equine displaying the body language described would be inclined to conclude that the equine is not upset and is comfortably resting. When a client perceives the equine as "angry", this presents a valuable opportunity for the client to explore, process, and gain insight into that assumption. In that moment, the client is only focusing on a single part of the equine, despite the rest of the equine's body language being wholly incongruent with the equine as "angry". In these moments, the treatment team can encourage the client to look at the rest of the equine's body language and state what they see. As the client begins to observe and label the equine's eyes as soft or closed or neck as relaxed, most revise their interpretation. The therapist can then proceed to process the interaction by discussing with the client how they arrived at their initial conclusion and their revised conclusion following more observations of the equine and the context. Had the equine specialist jumped to immediately correct the client's initial assumption, the client would have been robbed of this valuable clinical opportunity. Often clients who jump to conclusions about an equine's negative mood based on a small, single piece

46 Philosophical Domains

of information while ignoring the larger whole also do the same with people, resulting in significant interpersonal anxiety or conflict when the conclusions they draw are not reflective of the other person's actual thoughts, feelings, or intent. The processing that occurs in REPC can be generalized to discuss and improve relationships with other people. Both the client and equine benefit from sessions being facilitated in this manner. The client benefits from the opportunity to identify, challenge, and gain insight into unhealthy patterns and the equine benefits from being understood.

It is also important for the treatment team to consider a client's developmental level and/or cognitive capacity in deciding when and how to interpret experiences that occur in REPC. Young children, clients with cognitive disabilities, or clients who have experienced a brain injury may have a more difficult time learning to accurately understand the equine without assistance from the treatment team. For example, I once worked with a teenage boy named Scott who was attending counseling to work on social skill improvement. He both bullied and was bullied by peers at school. Scott would often say impulsive and hurtful things to other students in the hallways resulting in frequent physical fights. In talking with Scott, he seemed genuinely confused as to why the other students would become so upset. In Scott's mind, he was "having fun and just joking" and believed that the other students should understand that and not be upset. He desperately wanted friends and felt discouraged that no one "understood" him. At the start of REPC, he had had many meetings in the principal's office and was on the verge of being sent to alternative school. During Scott's first session, he immediately chose a gray Quarter Horse gelding named Snowball who had approached him almost immediately upon entering the pasture. Scott stated that Snowball "liked" him and that he felt good because of Snowball's attention. It became apparent fairly quickly that Scott's pattern of difficulty with people would be similarly experienced with Snowball. During his second session, Scott quickly and abruptly came up to Snowball and was confused when the equine shied away. Later during the session, Scott hid behind a bush to "surprise" Snowball and became upset when Snowball ran away and would not allow Scott to be close for the remainder of the session. During processing, it was clear that Scott could not understand that Snowball would have a different perspective on Scott's actions than Scott himself did. In this case, the treatment team decided to explicitly interpret Snowball's reactions to Scott in order to help Scott develop greater empathy and theory of mind. The next time Scott tried to "surprise" Snowball, the equine specialist immediately reflected Snowball's shying away as fear in response to Scott's actions. When Scott stated that he was "just joking", the equine specialist explained Snowball's worldview as a prey animal. Over time, the treatment team gradually reduced the use of interpretation. Several weeks later when Scott moved quickly to pet Snowball's head and the equine moved away, the treatment team simply reflected Scott's action (moving quickly towards Snowball's head) and Snowball's response (moving away). Scott filled in the interpretation himself that Snowball might have been "scared" by Scott's sudden movement. Eventually, the treatment team was able to refrain from any interpretation and would simply ask "what happened?" when Snowball did not react as Scott expected. By this time, Scott was well-versed in identifying the connection between his behavior, Snowball's response, and Snowball's possible thoughts or feelings in response to Scott's behavior. Scott also learned to self-monitor his own behaviors and was able to plan his actions and anticipate Snowball's possible responses before acting. Scott learned to "ask" Snowball before doing something so that he could observe and evaluate Snowball's response. Throughout this time, Scott's mother began to report small improvements in Scott's behavior at school. He was beginning to identify why the other students often reacted poorly to his actions. Over time, Scott demonstrated less impulsive behaviors and initiated conversations with the other students about their thoughts and feelings on various topics and if they shared the same idea of "fun" as he did. Had the treatment team refrained from all interpretation, Scott and Snowball both would have likely experienced stress, frustration, and confusion. By acting as Snowball's voice when needed and using interpretation intentionally, Scott and Snowball were able to build a healthy relationship in which both felt safe and understood.

Cooperation, Not Domination

Interaction with equines that is based on human dominance over the equine runs counter to the REPC approach. Recent research on equine social structure and human-equine interaction indicates humans cannot physically communicate with equines in the same ways that they communicate with each other given the significant differences in our body structure (Hartmann et al., 2017). Furthermore, I have been unable to find any recent studies supporting the idea that humans can become "dominant" in a way equivalent to a herd member. As researchers have observed that equines will often avoid spending time in close proximity to more dominant equines, attempts to be dominant to the equine may be counterproductive if the client's wish is to be able to physically interact with the equine (Goodwin, 1999). Much of the misunderstandings regarding dominance may be a result of cultural traditions and beliefs about the nature of interaction with and dominion over animals (Goodwin, 1999). McGreevy, Oddie, Burton, and McLean (2009) argued that use of dominance frameworks can lead to increased misunderstanding and conflict between human and equine based on the human's assumption of the equine's understanding of what the human wants. Despite the emphasis on dominance interactions in many training approaches, equines place more weight on affiliative interactions than agonistic ones in the establishment of affiliative relationships (Henshall & McGreevy, 2014). Furthermore, dominance-oriented activities pose a risk of increased equine stress and injury to the client (Fenner, McLean, & McGreevy, 2019). Dominance-focused interactions with equines may compromise both

48 Philosophical Domains

equine welfare and the establishment of a harmonious relationship (International Society for Equitation Science, n.d.).

REPC is conceived as an approach in which the client's experiences can be generalized to the establishment of more satisfying and healthier relationships with other people. Therefore, a client's dominance over the equine would not be conducive to the establishment or strengthening of the client's supportive relationships with other people. In a natural environment with stable herd membership, equines tend to form pair bonds or "friendships" with specific equines. It is likely that some facets of this type of cooperative relationship can likely extend to humans as well. Such relationships are characterized by engagement in affiliative behaviors such as grazing and resting in proximity, mutual grooming, and resting their necks on each other (Goodwin, 1999). These relationships are mutually beneficial for both and provide social support in coping with stressful situations (Goodwin, 1999). Humans can create these types of relationships with equines by being in proximity during grazing and resting, relaxed grooming, and physical contact. Therefore, rather than an interaction characterized by dominance, interaction should be based on safety, clear communication, cooperation, and mutual goal agreement between client and equine(s).

Patterns and Parallels

As has been stated, maintaining respect for the equine's sentience while encouraging the client's development of important relational skills is paramount in the REPC approach. The client's interactions with the equines often reflect a microcosm of the client's unhealthy patterns of thoughts, feelings, and behaviors in their daily life and interpersonal relationships. In REPC, we focus on helping the client to explore and understand these experiences as patterns and parallels. There are other EACP models that promote activities encouraging clients to create metaphors and label the equines' roles within the metaphor. For example, a client struggling with work-life balance may be encouraged when working with various equines to label one equine as "work", one as "family", and one as "self". The client then proceeds to interact with each equine based on what the client has assigned them to represent. I find these types of activities to be antithetical to the development of a healthy, mutually satisfying relationship between client and equine, as this type of activity can dismiss the equine's sentience and reactions. As researchers have shown that equines can perceive and react to people's emotional states (Hama et al., 1996; Smith et al., 2016), it is likely, and even expected, that the equines will perceive and react to the client's emotions associated with the equine's assignment. For example, a client feeling burned out at work may experience more negative feelings, demonstrate negative facial expressions, and respond more negatively towards the equine assigned to be "work." This particular equine will likely experience distress as a result of this treatment. Furthermore, this experience is likely to have a lasting impact on the quality of the relationship between the client and equine (Proops et al., 2018). Knowing this, I wonder what it would feel like for the therapist to take part in such an activity and be labeled "work"? I imagine that most people would feel incongruent at best and hurt, dismissed, or unfairly targeted at worst, despite knowing that the labeling is an exercise and not reflective of the client's true feelings towards the therapist.

Instead, I encourage focus on the identification of parallels and patterns that arise organically and lend themselves to natural metaphors. As the client interacts with the equine, unhealthy belief and behavior patterns are likely to rise to the surface. For example, a client who is struggling with work-life balance is likely to experience this problem in some way, shape, or form in their interactions with the equine. Depending on the particular client, this presenting concern may take many different forms such as perfectionistic behaviors, feelings of guilt, or difficulties with boundary-setting and assertiveness. As unhealthy patterns are revealed through interactions with the equines, the treatment team can help the client to first process and understand what is happening in session and then identify parallels in their daily life and relationships outside of session. This approach allows the client to explore these issues while maintaining respect for the equine's sentience and preserving the integrity of the client-equine relationship. The client can then take the insight and skills gained through this experience and apply them to their daily life and relationships outside of session.

Evidence-Informed

The presence of the equines and facilitation of activities involving the equines is not alone sufficient to provide ethical and effective counseling and psychotherapy services. When describing the REPC approach to others, I like to describe it as "psychotherapy first", meaning that it is rooted in established best practices and evidence-based interventions rather than being conceived as a distinct intervention separate from other established best practices. These interventions are extended to also include the equine. The therapist should strive to integrate established psychotherapy interventions (motivational interviewing, mindfulness, cognitive restructuring, behavioral activation, etc.) based on the client's needs and therapist's clinical judgment. Ultimately, the therapist's approach should be the result of an integration of their theoretical orientation, best practices in psychotherapy, best practices in animal-assisted therapy, and considerations for equine welfare.

Chapter 4

Counseling Environments in Equine-Assisted Counseling and Psychotherapy

Being in an outdoor, natural environment has many benefits for clients in counseling and psychotherapy, even before the equine enters the picture. Dating back to ancient times, shamans used nature to promote healing from physical and psychological ills (Berger & McLeod, 2006). The biophilia hypothesis proposed that people have an innate tendency to be drawn to life and its processes, such as nature and animals, and, as such, interaction with nature plays a role in the development of emotional, cognitive, somatic, and spiritual well-being (Kellert & Wilson, 1993). As people in Western cultures become more disconnected from both nature and each other as a result of technology, interest is growing in ecotherapy. In accordance with this belief, therapists using ecotherapy aim to reconnect clients with nature to improve overall happiness and well-being (Berger & McLeod, 2006). Buzzell and Chalquist (2009) defined ecotherapy as "a new form of psychotherapy that acknowledges the vital role of nature and addresses the human-nature relationship" (p. 18). Given the intrinsic role of nature in most equine-assisted counseling and psychotherapy (EACP) settings and the emphasis on the human-equine relationship, it fits well within the realm of ecotherapy (DeMayo, 2009).

Researchers have documented the numerous benefits of spending time outside or even having a plant in your home. In his seminal work on the healing effects of nature, Ulrich (1984) found that hospital patients who had a window view of nature recovered from surgery faster than patients who had a view of another building. Spending time in nature can increase positive feelings, reduce physiological stress and mental fatigue, and increase attention and engagement (Gidlow et al., 2015; Ulrich et al., 1991). Furthermore, exposure to nature sounds can facilitate recovery from psychological stress (Alvarsson, Wiens, & Nilsson, 2010). Therefore, the experience of being in a natural outdoor environment may help reduce client distress after processing upsetting or traumatic experiences, or working through challenges with the equine. These benefits may be enhanced by physical activity and the act of walking out to or in the pasture, such as in the case of "walk and talk therapy" (Doucette, 2004; McKinney, 2011). Gidlow et al. (2015) and colleagues found walking in nature to be correlated to physiological benefits indicative of reduced stress. Finally, spending time in nature can improve attention, elicit feelings of rejuvenation, and reduce stress (Taylor & Kuo, 2009).

Kaplan (1995) identified components in defining nature as a restorative environment. Based on this work, EACP is likely to provide such an environment to clients. The first component is the experience of fascination, or inherent interest and engagement in the environment. A second component is that the environment elicits a conceptual shift in the client's experience of being in the world. Third, the client must be fully engaged in the environment, almost as if they feel that they are in another world. This particular quality is often reported by my clients, especially during the first few sessions. These clients often cite the impact of the trees, greenery, and open space as helping them to feel transported somewhere far removed from their daily lives. Finally, the intent of EACP to facilitate these experiences is compatible with most clients' need to experience peace and tranquility. When the client is able to be present and immersed in the natural environment, they can experience a reduction in negative thoughts and feelings, such as anger and fear, and an increase in positive thoughts. Clients may also perceive others to be friendlier, resulting in increased trust and engagement with the treatment team (Berto, 2014). The combination of these experiences can facilitate increased client openness and tolerance for distress. Therefore, clients may feel more comfortable processing distressing or traumatic experiences and remain more present and engaged when working through challenging experiences. The benefits of the client's time being spent in nature during the session may carry over to improved emotional regulation and cognitive functioning outside of session as well (Berto, 2014). Exposure to nature over time can lead to improved behavioral outcomes such as increased self-control, decreased anger and violence, and stress management (Berto, 2014).

Benefits of the Natural Environment in EACP

In EACP, I have witnessed numerous benefits to clients participating in sessions outdoors. Berger and McLeod (2006) conceptualized nature as becoming a partner in the therapeutic process. One of the biggest benefits that clients report is feeling an overall sense of peace from being outside. In a study on EACP with clients with substance use disorders, Kern-Godal, Brenna, Kogstad, Arnevik, and Ravndal (2016) found that clients feel more relaxed and experience the EACP environment in a fundamentally different way than a traditional office-based setting. Many clients admit that, other than attending their sessions, they do not spend much time outdoors. Countless clients have expressed the role of nature in promoting feelings of calmness upon first arriving for their session. In my model of EACP for young children, Equine-Partnered Play Therapy (EPPT), the outdoor setting provides ripe opportunities for children to engage with nature. One such client decided to spend a part of several sessions digging out weeds that he believed could "hurt" the horses. Another client found himself mesmerized by a passing butterfly migration, stating that after it had passed he felt reenergized and at peace, like he had just had a massage.

One client in particular found herself spending a lot of time in parks while traveling as a result of the peace she felt during her sessions. After returning from her trip, she vowed to make it more of a priority to carve out time to spend outdoors in her daily life. Another benefit of the outdoor environment of EACP is decreased perceived stigma and increased comfort. I have had many clients state that therapy taking place outside doesn't "feel" like therapy, and others who have reported feeling "claustrophobic" in a typical office environment. Being outside also helps clients be more present and in the moment. Clients often notice things that they may not notice in their daily life, such as the passing butterfly migration mentioned earlier. Oftentimes, we can use the outdoor environment to help clients learn and practice mindfulness and calming skills that they can use outside of session as well. Additionally, as the outdoor environment is much less controlled than an indoor, office-based setting, so the client has the opportunity to practice responding to and coping with unexpected events such as bugs, changes in weather, unexpected sounds, and other unanticipated events. Not only can the therapist witness, in real-time, the client's ability to cope, but they can also help the client practice coping skills in response to real events.

The outdoor environment provides clients with more and different opportunities to express themselves. Engagement in nature lends itself easily to the creation of metaphors, analogies, and use of symbols for clients to find new ways to express themselves or process distressing experiences in ways that feel less threatening (Jordan, 2013). It can also help clients be present and remain in the moment as a result of increased sensory stimuli (Jordan, 2013). For example, one client came into session very angry and distraught over recent events. This particular client requested to go into the pasture and scream loudly to express her frustration, sadness, and anger. Afterward, the client reported feeling as if a weight had been lifted. Had the client been in an office, she likely would have been unable to express herself in this way without disturbing others or with adequate privacy. Another client spent time demolishing a tree stump in order to express her emotions. I have also had clients create new metaphors using the outdoor environment. One client spent time processing her own thoughts and feelings in the context of how she perceived a tree's feelings about losing some of its limbs. A child client once "invited" a fly into his session and spent his time trying to understand and connect with the fly, who chose to stay most of the session. Other clients have sought to nurture the outdoor environment by "rescuing" a caterpillar. Furthermore, the outdoor environment gives clients more space to move. We have had many clients use the increased space available to run, jump, or skip to express themselves nonverbally and also find ways to release excess energy in a healthy way. Finally, the unique challenges (adverse weather conditions, insects, etc.) presented by the outdoor, natural setting can provide opportunities for clients to learn to manage anxiety, develop frustration

Counseling Environments   53

tolerance, and numerous other benefits. Processing and learning skills to cope with these challenges can help clients gain insight into better understanding the challenges that they face outside of session and learn ways to better manage these challenges.

Working Areas in EACP

In the following section, I will review the benefits and pitfalls of holding sessions in some of the most common EACP working areas such the box stall, round pen, arena, paddock, and pasture. Special consideration will also be paid to the positive and negative impacts of each of these areas on the equines. In most cases, the working area will be informed by the facility's structure and design. In all cases, the treatment team should collaborate to identify the best working areas in light of the client's needs, privacy concerns, the equines' welfare, and safety considerations. The equine specialist is responsible for ultimately making decisions regarding the safety of the working area and number of equines who can be safely managed in the working area. This decision should be based on environmental conditions, potential hazards, safety considerations, and the needs of the equines. In all cases, the treatment team should work closely with the facility to establish safeguards to protect client privacy and create policies to minimize risks to client privacy.

Barn and/or Stalls

There are a number of benefits of conducting sessions in a stall when deemed to be in the best interest of both the equine and client. In the case of inclement weather, accessibility to an indoor environment such as the barn can increase comfort for both the client and equine. Additionally, some clients who may feel anxious or exposed by larger, open environments may feel more comfortable in a stall. In addition, outside distractions may be minimized as a result of being in an enclosed space. However, given the small size of the stall, it may be difficult for both members of the treatment team to be in the stall with the client and equine. Furthermore, in most cases, the stall would not be suitable to accommodate groups or families in the same stall. Depending on the stall's design and other facility activities, it may afford more opportunities for privacy than an open environment such as a pasture. Given the considerations that follow for equine stress and welfare, the decision to use the stall should be made deliberately, with consideration for the specific needs of each individual client and equine.

First and foremost, it is important to note that the equine's repertoire of natural behaviors is limited when in a stall (Rivera, Benjamin, Nielsen, Shelle, & Zanella, 2002). When working in a barn where equines are stalled, it is important to consider that the longer the time an equine spends in the stall, the more stress they may experience (Ruet et al., 2019). Oftentimes, equines kept in stalls

54 Counseling Environments

have limited physical or visual access to other equines who can provide a source of comfort and reassurance. Furthermore, the equine's ability to move is significantly limited as well as their ability to provide feedback by using approach or retreat behaviors. The equine's choice for personal space preference and nature of interaction with the client is limited due to the small space. It is important, therefore, to not only consider the impact on the equine's welfare from holding a single session in a stall, but also the cumulative effects of holding multiple sessions in a stall on a daily or even weekly basis. Too much time spent in a stall can result in the equine becoming aggressive or withdrawn in sessions (Ruet et al., 2019). In the context of an EACP session, it is important to attend not only to the added stress of being stalled but also the added stress of physical and/or emotional pressure of participating in the session. Clients who are calmer and engage in more nurturing interactions will put much less stress on equine than a client who is agitated and/or applying pressure to the equine. It is important that, whenever possible, equines are able to move freely and interact with other equines. In working with clients who apply high amounts of physical or emotional pressure, the treatment team should consider holding the session in a more spacious environment.

Round Pen

The round pen has traditionally been used for specific equine training exercises, especially activities which involve free lunging or lunging on a line. The small, enclosed space of the round pen allows for more room than a traditional box stall but not as much as the openness of the pasture. Additionally, activities that involve faster gaits may be better suited for the round pen rather than the paddock due to improved footing and reduced potential safety hazards. The structure of the round pen also lends itself to activities involving leading or lunging the equine. The round pen traditionally accommodates one equine but depending on the size of the round pen and sizes, personalities, and relationships among the equines, it may be able to accommodate more. Depending on its size and the equine(s) involved in the session, the round pen may be able to accommodate a small group of multiple clients or a family.

As much equine training often takes place in a round pen, this experience can impact the session in a number of ways. If the equine participates in frequent training sessions in the pen outside of session, they may respond based on assumed expectations for a training session rather than in response to the client specifically. Other equines who have had negative experiences or training experiences characterized by conflict or punishment may demonstrate withdrawn, aggressive, or agitated behaviors. Additionally, the construction of the round pen and its location in relation to the visibility of other equines can also impact the session. For example, round pens that are enclosed or do not allow a view of other equines may result in the equine in session becoming distracted or agitated due to separation from other equines. To best set the equine up for success in EACP sessions in the round pen, the equine specialist or other facility personnel should acclimate the equine to the round pen independent of specific training exercises.

Arena

The use of a defined, circular-shaped training area dates back to the ancient Roman use of the *gyrus* to prepare horses for battle (Spiedel, 1996). Most commonly, the arena or "riding ring" is used for mounted activities. Depending on the facility's specific disciplines, the arena may also contain certain objects such as barrels, cavaletti, or jumps. The arena offers similar benefits to a round pen, as it is enclosed and usually offers better footing than a paddock or pasture. Arenas can vary in size and will usually be able to accommodate multiple equines in contrast to a round pen. Enclosed or covered arenas can provide a respite from adverse weather conditions. If the arena has lights, it can allow the treatment team to safely provide sessions in the late afternoon or evening after the sun has set.

I have found the arena to be well-suited for activities involving multiple clients such as families or larger groups by making it easier to provide adequate supervision for everyone in the session. Additionally, the treatment team and client can use the different objects that may be readily available such as cones, jumps, or barrels for different types of session activities. The arena may also be beneficial in limiting the equines' access to food which could interfere with certain session activities or be overly frustrating to certain clients (Sheade, 2019c).

However, like the round pen, most equines have previous associations with the arena independent of EACP activities. Therefore, equines' responses may be less naturalistic and limited by the arena's connotation as a training or "work" environment. Furthermore, equines who have negative associations with the arena or riding activities may demonstrate more withdrawn or aggressive behaviors in session. Additionally, depending on the location of the arena on the property and other facility activities, it may be more vulnerable to threats to client privacy.

Paddocks and Pens

In some cases, an outdoor paddock or pen may provide more freedom of movement and response in comparison to an indoor stall or round pen. It is also a more naturalistic environment, as it is outside and does not typically serve as a site for training activities. If the pen is large enough, it may be able to accommodate more than one equine to allow for social interaction among equines. The pen may be a good option for clients who feel overwhelmed by the largeness of the pasture. I have also found the pen to be useful in working with small groups or families in order to monitor all of the equines and counseling participants safely. The inclusion of additional equines can provide benefits to

56 Counseling Environments

both the equines and client. The equine benefits from emotional support from other equines and the client benefits from interaction with the herd and not just a single equine. However, it is important to carefully evaluate the size of the pen in relation to the number of equines in the pen. The number of equines that a pen can safely and comfortably accommodate is largely dependent upon the sizes, personalities, and relationships among the equines. For example, a large, high-energy Warmblood may function best with only one other equine. However, an older, docile pony may be just fine with three or four other ponies or miniature horses. The equine specialist should also evaluate the amount of usable space based on the pen's construction. For example, a large pen interrupted by fences may not allow for as much usable space as a smaller open pen.

Pasture

A large, open space enables the equine to have the most freedom of choice of how and when to interact with the client. Additionally, as the pasture is the most naturalistic environment for the equine, it allows the equine to engage in the most organic and intuitive behaviors in response to the client's emotions, physiological responses, and body language (Sheade, 2019c). In most pastures, the equine will also have access to herd mates. The presence of other herd members can enable not only the client to benefit from the support of the herd, but also the equine. Most of my clients enjoy being in the pasture and choose to have their sessions in the herd. These clients report a greater sense of peace and tranquility and feeling of community among the herd. Some clients report feeling more comfortable in the pasture and feeling less pressure of being observed by the treatment team in comparison to a smaller space (Sheade, 2019c). The client also has the opportunity to observe more naturalistic herd interactions. I often describe the pasture to clients as being the equines' "living room" where we can observe and be a part of the herd going about their daily activities.

Sessions in the pasture enable the equines to respond both as individuals and as a herd. Individual equines can choose to come and go within the session based on direct responses to the client as well as efforts to meet basic bodily needs such as eating, drinking, or defecating. The herd can also engage with the client with the way that they move near the client. In some particularly powerful sessions, the herd has surrounded an especially distressed client resulting in the client feeling a sense of comfort and protection. The open space in the pasture enables the equine to provide adequate space to be self-directed in providing clear feedback.

Amy's session with Oliver is illustrative of this capacity. Amy was a 16-year-old client working on managing high anxiety and panic attacks as a result of being bullied at school. Oliver was a sensitive Arabian gelding who served as the herd's primary leader. After one especially bad day at school, Amy, feeling more anxious than usual, tried to approach Oliver, who immediately moved away as she approached. After a few more unsuccessful attempts, we observed

Oliver approach and deliberately move Romeo, a calm older Quarter Horse gelding over towards Amy. Romeo approached Amy and quietly stood next to her while she stroked his forehead and began to talk about her day. As she spoke, her body began to visibly relax, and Oliver inched closer. Once Amy had calmed down even more, Oliver approached and stood on her other side for the remainder of the session. This case story exemplifies the benefits of the pasture. First, the openness of the pasture allowed Oliver the space to participate in the session at a distance he could tolerate in light of Amy's heightened emotional reactivity. Furthermore, the addition of other herd members enabled Oliver to "delegate" his role to Romeo, an equine who could better tolerate Amy's present state.

I have found that equines can tolerate more stressful sessions much more easily when they have more space to move and have other equines in close proximity. Interestingly, after moving from one location with a large wooded pasture to a new location with a large open pasture, most clients who had been at the wooded location reported that they preferred the open space. These clients perceived that the equines had more room and therefore would feel more comfortable. This preference is supported by research findings indicating that people of Western cultures may have an innate preference for savanna or grassland landscapes characterized by open space with tree clusters, as this environment may have been more conducive to early human survival (Falk & Balling, 2009). However, it is important to keep in mind that clients of non-Western cultures or with different life experiences may show more preference for other types of environments (Hägerhäll et al., 2018).

However, there are also pitfalls to working in the pasture. First, depending on the facility's layout, working in the pasture may provide a direct view of the session to onlookers or visitors. Given that the pasture may include larger groups of equines, it is essential that the equine specialist is extremely competent in understanding, anticipating, and managing herd behavior. Additionally, other facility personnel may need to retrieve other equines from time to time and may interrupt the session. Furthermore, depending on the size of the pasture, the treatment team may have to walk a considerable distance to get to the equines. The treatment team may have a more difficult time providing adequate supervision of groups depending on the size of the pasture and number of equines. From a logistical standpoint, the pasture is also likely much farther from comforts such as the restroom and water. Adverse weather conditions can also have a greater impact on pasture sessions. The treatment team should evaluate the pasture regarding shade and shelter from rain or wind. I have found loafing sheds to be a great help in providing shade from the sun and shelter from rain and wind.

Chapter 5

The Treatment Team in Equine-Assisted Counseling and Psychotherapy

The nature of the client's experience and overall progress in equine-assisted counseling and psychotherapy is directly related to the client's relationship with and overall functioning of the treatment team. As described in Chapter 3, the strength of the therapeutic relationship established between the client and treatment team is a critical variable in predicting the client's outcome in psychotherapy. The treatment team is comprised of both the human and equine participants. The primary human treatment team members include the therapist and equine specialist, and in some cases, specially chosen volunteers. Both the therapist and equine specialist should be knowledgeable in building a therapeutic relationship between the client and equines, self-aware and able to engage in self-examination related to the equine-assisted counseling and psychotherapy (EACP) process and associated countertransference reactions, aware of the ways in which the client's behaviors and presentation may impact the equines, and attentive to the equine's well-being and overall welfare. In this chapter, I will discuss the roles, characteristics, and skills needed for each member of the treatment team to facilitate a safe and effective EACP session.

The Equines

The equine's role in the session falls somewhere between that of a co-facilitator and a group member. As the equine is not participating to receive any sort of therapy, the equine is approaching the session from a fundamentally different perspective than the client. The equine also does not have an "agenda" for the client or personal investment in the client's individual treatment goals and therefore responds to the client naturally and organically. However, through the process of establishing a healthy, mutually satisfying relationship with the client, the equine is likely to benefit as well.

One of the equine's most important roles is to facilitate trust between the human treatment team and the client (Carlsson et al., 2014). Different clinicians may have differing perceptions of the role of the equines as partners, tools, reflections, healers, and/or rewards (Carlsson et al., 2014). In the Relational Equine-Partnered Counseling (REPC) approach of EACP, the equine is viewed as a sentient partner capable of being self-directed in offering valuable feedback and insight through its behavioral responses to the client. In order to enable the equine to contribute freely and openly, it is important for the equine to have freedom and autonomy to respond to the client organically, including the ability to physically and emotionally distance themselves from the session if desired.

All equines should be screened prior to being accepted into an equine-assisted counseling and psychotherapy program (Alden, 2017; PATH Intl., 2018b). Additionally, all equines should be domesticated, as wild species (e.g., zebras) are not recommended for animal-assisted interventions unless a wildlife expert is on staff as a co-facilitator (Chandler, 2017). As the majority of the programs in my practice take place on the ground, we are able to accept a wide variety of equines into our program. However, we do not allow stallions or equines that are aggressive towards humans into our program. It is important to be aware that stallions are more likely to act aggressively. Furthermore, an equine who is gelded after one year of age is likely to retain some stallion behaviors (Hill, 2006).

It is also important to consider an equine's physical health. An equine suffering from pain, whether it be acute or chronic, may experience more stress by participating in sessions and may be more likely to engage in aggressive behaviors towards people. It is important to carefully consider how you will manage this pain in order to create a safe and beneficial environment for both equine and client (Fureix, Menguy, & Hausberger, 2010).

An equine's age and how age will influence the animal's comfort and interaction with the client is also a consideration. In general, younger equines have a more difficult time coping with stressful situations and, therefore, may have more trouble coping with heightened client emotions (Baragli et al., 2014). In my own practice, I have witnessed younger equines appear more reactive to client incongruence. These younger equines will demonstrate behaviors indicative of heightened arousal such as increased pushiness or nipping directed towards the client or overall restlessness. In contrast, older equines may be less likely to demonstrate behaviors indicative of stress even if they are experiencing stress (Baragli et al., 2014). Therefore, it is crucial for the equine specialist to be able to recognize an older equine's subtler stress signals or anticipate situations which may create stress for the equine.

A Note on Working With Injured, Abused, or Neglected Equines in EACP

It is also important to consider not only an equine's physical health but also their emotional health in selecting them for work as a counseling partner. Having personally trained rescued horses who experienced abuse and neglect, I can speak firsthand to the strength of the bond that can form between an equine who has suffered and a person that they have grown to trust. However, I

60 The Treatment Team

encourage anyone interested in (or who is already) partnering with these types of equines (especially equines who are still in physical and/or emotional recovery) to proceed with caution. For example, an equine who is recovering from founder should not be expected to work for an extended period of time on an uncomfortable surface that would exacerbate their pain just because that is where the session is being held. Furthermore, it is important to be aware that equines who are still recovering from emotional trauma (e.g., abuse or mistreatment by people) may be more negatively impacted by clients who apply a lot of "emotional" pressure in the form of expressing strong negative emotions or incongruence. For these equines in particular, it is absolutely crucial to be aware of and recognize the signs of equine stress and take action to minimize the stress so the equine's physical or emotional trauma is not exacerbated. Finally, assuming a strong bond has formed between the client and equine, it is important to consider the potential detrimental impact to the equine when that bond is severed once counseling is terminated. Finally, the client witnessing an equine's physical or emotional distress can create distress for the client by triggering memories of trauma or eliciting strong negative feelings. For this reason, clients should be screened individually for work with these types of equines.

On the flip side, I have also seen these equines experience their own type of "healing" through participation in the EACP. Santiago, a beautiful paint gelding, had suffered from serious hoof problems resulting in almost-constant physical pain. One of Santiago's clients was a Vietnam veteran who could empathize with some of Santiago's pain. During their sessions, the client focused on nurturing Santiago by grooming, stroking, and talking to him to calm not only Santiago but to also help himself self-regulate. During these sessions, Santiago appeared more content and relaxed through this nurturing contact, making their interaction more beneficial than detrimental to Santiago's well-being. Another example of the positive impact of EACP on an equine is Donkey, a miniature donkey who had been neglected for years by a previous owner. When I first began working with Donkey, he would often run from anyone who even moved slightly in his direction. Over the course of several months, Donkey crept closer and closer to certain clients until he began to approach them. I believe that Donkey was reading the body language of all of the clients and, based on these observations, determined who he felt was safe enough to trust. Today, Donkey greets most clients at some point during their session. He invites himself into many sessions and offers some of the clearest and most direct feedback of all of the equines in the herd. However, Donkey does set his own boundaries as well. He often chooses to leave sessions with clients who apply too much physical or "emotional" pressure and are not able to self-regulate.

In summary, I do not have a blanket recommendation as to whether or not to include equines recovering from physical or emotional trauma in EACP. Instead, I encourage everyone to carefully weigh the considerations described and consider each individual equine on a case-by-case basis grounded on their history, current functioning, and how they may be impacted, positively or negatively, by working in your practice.

Animal-Assisted Therapy in Counseling (AATC) Competencies Framework

Stewart et al. (2016) created the Animal-Assisted Therapy in Counseling (AATC) Competencies Framework, which serves as a useful guide for all therapists regardless of specific licensure or discipline. I believe this framework can also serve as a guide in ensuring that the equine specialists co-facilitating with a therapist possesses adequate competency in their role. Although created specifically for therapists who include their own animals in the process, I believe this framework to be useful for all practitioners, even those who do not incorporate their own personal animals. The framework is comprised of three domains: knowledge, skills, and attitudes. In the context of EACP, the *knowledge domain* encompasses formal training in EACP, knowledge of equines, and knowledge of ethical requirements; *the skills domain* includes mastery of basic counseling skills, understanding of the scope of practice, use of intentionality, and development of a specialized skill set in EACP; the *attitudes domain* encompasses equine advocacy, professional development, and personal values. The following sections will use Stewart and colleagues' (2016) AATC Competencies Framework as a guide in identifying the competencies and experiences needed for therapists and equine specialists seeking to practice EACP.

The Therapist

First and foremost, the therapist must hold a license (this may vary in countries outside of the United States) to practice counseling and psychotherapy. Although they may go by different names, individuals holding licensure as mental health counselors, professional counselors, psychiatrists, psychologists, marriage and family therapists, and social workers are the most common mental health providers. As a general rule of thumb, a therapist should only provide EACP to the types of clients that they would be qualified to see in any other setting. For example, a psychologist who is not competent to see young children in an office-based practice should not work with young children in EACP. Alternatively, a licensed chemical dependency counselor would only be competent to provide EACP to clients with concerns that fall within their scope according to the standards of their professional organization and state board. Any therapist wanting to work with a new population in EACP (e.g., military veterans) should ensure that they receive the training and peer supervision—the same as they would to ensure competency if they were to begin serving this population in a traditional office-based setting.

As with any new specialty area of practice, therapists seeking to practice EACP must ensure that they receive the appropriate education, training, consultation, and supervision to practice ethically and competently (American Counseling Association, 2014; American Psychological Association, 2017; National Association of Social Workers, 2017; Stewart et al., 2016; Wycoff, 2019). Therapists who cannot demonstrate competency based on the ethical codes noted here are at risk of disciplinary or legal action by their professional association and/or licensing board. Furthermore, practicing in an area in which one does not have competence can elevate a therapist's risk of a negligence and being sued for malpractice (Welfel, 2010).

Knowledge Domain

Formal Training

Given the unique nature of this work it is essential that therapists complete a formal evaluative course to gain the requisite knowledge needed to practice in this area. It is important that the therapist's training also includes learning how to effectively provide EACP interventions and understanding the human-animal bond. It is also important that therapists first practice EACP under the supervision of a qualified EACP therapist in order to receive feedback and an assessment of skills. The more knowledge that the therapist has, the more effective they will be in facilitating EACP.

I also recommend specialized coursework in related areas. It will be very useful for all therapists to complete coursework in group counseling, not only to work with groups in EACP but also to be able to better manage and attend to group dynamics between the group comprised of the therapist, equine specialist, client, and equine(s), even in individual therapy. Other recommendations include taking the experiential courses often offered as electives such as play therapy, art therapy, dance therapy, music therapy, adventure-based therapy, and/or wilderness therapy to obtain a solid knowledge base in facilitating experiential therapies. Many of the skills learned in these courses will be transferable to an EACP practice. Finally, the therapist should have a basic understanding of clinical supervision in order to better facilitate debriefing sessions with the equine specialist and/or volunteers and to process any distressing content or conflicts that might arise during the EACP session, within the treatment team, or between the client and members of the treatment team or volunteers (PATH Intl., 2017).

Equine Knowledge

It is important that the therapist possesses a working knowledge of equines including ethology, training techniques, and ways to establish and maintain a strong working relationship between the client and equine. Ethological knowledge includes equine physiology, behavior, history, care and husbandry, and limitations of partnering with equines. An understanding of training techniques is important to ensure that the equine is prepared to participate in EACP, and that the therapist can manage equine behavior in session. Understanding the dynamics of the human-equine relationship including potential stressors, signs of stress, and ability to manage equine stress in session is important to helping build a strong working relationship between the client and the equine.

From my personal experience, therapists lacking this basic knowledge are likely to be less effective in facilitating the relationship and may unintentionally and inaccurately conceptualize and process the client's interactions with the equines. However, I should note that there are others who believe that a therapist should be less familiar with equines so as to not project onto the equine for the client. (For a more comprehensive discussion of this issue, see the Considerations of Including the Equine Specialist section that follows.) In any event, should the therapist be considered less than expert in any of these areas, they must partner with a competent equine specialist.

Ethical Knowledge

The therapist should possess a thorough understanding of the ethical requirements of both clinical practice and interaction with equines, with the ability to integrate both. These requirements include understanding and recognition of the specific ethical implications of EACP, understanding any ethical and multicultural implications relevant to EACP, establishing a safe environment for both clients and equines, and using effective risk management strategies. See Chapters 11 and 12 for a detailed review on these topics.

Skills Domain

Basic Counseling Skills

It is essential that therapists seeking to practice EACP possess a solid foundation in basic counseling skills. The therapist should be able to integrate theoretical orientation and best practices into EACP and should possess knowledge of how to integrate EACP with clinical treatment goals and assessments of a client's progress and outcomes.

I also believe in the importance of new therapists having a solid foundation in counseling and psychotherapy skills in an office-based setting before venturing into practicing EACP. I recommend that any new therapist wanting to practice EACP complete their initial practicum (or internship), depending on the field or university, in an office-based setting to establish this foundation. After training many student interns in EACP, I have come to see that the learning curve in moving from traditional office-based therapy to EACP can be quite steep, especially for therapists with no significant amount of past equine

64 The Treatment Team

experience. Learning to practice in an uncontrolled outdoor environment with not only a human co-facilitator (i.e., the equine specialist) but also multiple equine "co-facilitators" can be quite a challenge for a new therapist working to hone their budding psychotherapy skills with all of these additional variables.

Intentionality

The therapist should be able to demonstrate an understanding that EACP requires specialized skills and is more than a love for equines or simply including them in a counseling session. The therapist should be able to clearly describe the role of the equines within their theoretical approach and the client's treatment plan, and assess the validity of the EACP interventions being used. The therapist should be deliberate in choosing specific EACP interventions based on each client's needs and treatment plan, and be able to assess the effectiveness of EACP for a particular client.

Specialized Skill Set

The therapist should possess a specialized skill set in facilitating experiential therapy and responding to spontaneous occurrences. As mentioned previously, if the therapist does not possess the skills needed related to equine behavior and management, an equine specialist possessing these skills should be included as a co-facilitator. The therapist should also be skilled in balancing the needs of the client with the welfare of the equines by being able to assess the impact of the session on everyone involved—clients, equines, and session personnel such as equine specialists and volunteers. The therapist should be capable of assessing, utilizing, and interpreting the equine's feedback in meaningful ways by facilitating the client-equine relationship; by making connections between client-equine interactions and their relationship to the client's presentation, behaviors, treatment plan, and conceptualization; and by modeling appropriate ways of relating and interacting with the equines. Furthermore, the therapist should maintain high standards of equine welfare by structuring sessions to minimize the risk of equine stress and detecting and responding to equine stress when it does arise in the session. The therapist should also be capable of evaluating each equine's suitability for participation in EACP independent of personal emotional bonds towards the animals. Finally, the therapist should maintain compliance with welfare standards and legal requirements for animals participating in EACP. Additionally, I strongly encourage therapists seeking to practice the REPC approach for EACP (see Chapters 3 and 6) to be skilled in equine handling, even if they intend to co-facilitate with an equine specialist. I believe that in the REPC model, the therapist's competency in equine behavior and handling not only enables them to conceptualize the session and process more effectively, but it also creates a safer environment for all involved.

Attitude Domain

Advocacy

The therapist, in conjunction with any other human co-facilitators, should advocate for the equines' welfare, rights, and needs—all of which have a direct impact on a client's positive experience and safety in the session. The therapist can practice this advocacy by enabling the equine to be self-directed in their participation and avoid intentional or unintentional exploitation. If co-facilitating with an equine specialist, both treatment team members can support each other and the equines in this regard.

Professional Development

As with any other type of counseling or psychotherapy practice, the therapist should participate in ongoing professional development through peer consultation and participation in continuing education. In my opinion, and particularly for those that want to practice the REPC model of EACP, the therapist should actively work to further their equine knowledge, enabling them to more effectively understand equines and therefore more effectively facilitate the client-equine relationship and process the interactions. Finally, the therapist should work to stay up to date on emerging EACP research and support the field's development.

Professional Values

It takes a unique type of individual to practice EACP. I encourage any therapist interested in this practice area to take some time to self-reflect. The therapist should demonstrate professional values such as enthusiasm, passion, flexibility, openness, creativity, and empathy. Additionally, the therapist should be able to respond calmly to unexpected events, welcome the experiential nature of EACP, and be responsive to changing situational factors such as weather or unexpected responses by the equines. Working in an outdoor environment among the equines can be very rewarding but also very challenging. A therapist doing this work should be prepared to work in all kinds of weather—hot, cold, rainy, snowy, and stormy. It is important to consider your level of tolerance for spending time standing, walking, or working in more strenuous terrain or adverse weather conditions. In addition, it is important to consider your comfort level in potential encounters with bugs such as bees, wasps, mosquitos, ants, flies, spiders, snakes, etc., and with other wildlife. If the thought of this makes you squeamish, you'll want to spend some time thinking about how you'll overcome this discomfort in session. Therefore, it is highly recommended that therapists self-assess in evaluating their levels of patience, empathy, humor, flexibility, and openness to change and other unexpected events.

66 The Treatment Team

The Equine Specialist

Knowledge Domain

Formal EACP Training

First and foremost, the equine specialist should complete a formal training course—such as the Professional Association for Therapeutic Horsemanship International's (PATH Intl.) Equine Specialist in Mental Health and Learning (ESMHL) Workshop—to gain knowledge of the EACP process and their role in that process. Following the workshop, the equine specialist can elect to take the horsemanship skills test and complete requirements to acquire the renewable PATH Intl. ESMHL credential. This credential provides a verification of the equine specialist's equine handling skills and completion of training requirements endorsed by PATH Intl. For any mounted work, the equine specialist should receive additional training and certification such as a Certified Therapeutic Riding Instructor (CTRI) through PATH Intl. or as a certified Instructor of Riders with Disabilities (IRD) through the Certified Horsemanship Association (CHA).

I believe that it is important for the equine specialist to have a working knowledge of different mental health concerns to better understand a client's basic history, symptoms, and goals in order to co-facilitate more effectively in session. Although the session goals are created by the therapist and client, the equine specialist can collaborate with the therapist to identify appropriate session activities and interventions to work towards the client's goals. Additionally, it is helpful for the equine specialist to have a working understanding of the therapist's theoretical orientation to understand the session process and clinical rationale (Sheade & Box, 2017). Finally, the equine specialist should possess an understanding of the role of the equine in the EACP session and how to effectively co-facilitate with both the therapist and equines (PATH Intl., 2017), as well as an understanding of the human-equine relationship and how equines are impacted both positively and negatively by interaction with people.

Equine Knowledge

It is essential that the equine specialist have an expert-level understanding of equine behavior, physiology, and husbandry practices. This training can be obtained through a number of different avenues such as becoming a working student under an established equine expert or participating in formal learning experiences such as equine behavior or training clinics. The equine specialist should possess understanding of the role of husbandry practices on the human-equine relationship and create practices that strengthen those relationships (Hausberger et al., 2008).

The equine specialist should also be knowledgeable of equine learning theory and positive training techniques to prepare the equine for participation in sessions, appropriately manage equine behavior during sessions, and address behavioral issues during training sessions outside of EACP sessions. It is critical that the equine specialist possess a deep understanding of the equine's identity as a prey animal and how this identity influences equine stress in order to prevent and respond to equine stress in session. The equine specialist should also understand the role of the equine's environment outside of session in impacting the animal's ability to manage stressful situations during sessions. The equine specialist should possess knowledge of the equine's identity as a herd animal and the importance of relationships with other equines in the herd to experience a sense of safety and security. The equine specialist should be aware of the different relationships among the different equine herd members. (This knowledge can help the equine specialist maintain a safe environment by being able to anticipate how different equines may behave when in close proximity to one another.)

Ethical Knowledge

The equine specialist should be knowledgeable of best practices related to equine welfare and be able to identify and manage threats to equine welfare both during session and outside of session. Such knowledge includes identifying and addressing potential safety issues, modeling and maintaining respect for all involved in the session (both human and equine), and understanding the role of the equine specialist's own personal beliefs or biases about equines on their interactions with the client, equines, and the session overall.

The equine specialist should receive training to gain a working knowledge in a number of areas of the psychotherapy process in order to act as an ethical and effective co-facilitator. These areas include, but are not limited to: multicultural and diversity sensitivity; responding to a client in crisis (suicidality, report of abuse, etc.); concepts of transference and countertransference and the ability to recognize the presence of these dynamics in the session; a basic understanding of confidentiality, the consequences of a confidentiality breach, and safeguards to protect client privacy and confidentiality; identifying threats to a client's welfare, such as violation of therapeutic boundaries; and other multiple relationship issues (Sheade & Box, 2017). Additionally, the equine specialist should be knowledgeable in safety procedures and minimizing the risk of zoonosis transmission.

The equine specialist should also be knowledgeable of risk management strategies specific to interaction with equines, including liability and legal issues. The equine specialist should also be capable of verifying a potential therapist partner's competency prior to partnering. If approached by a therapist seeking a partnership to practice EACP, the equine specialist should verify that the therapist is appropriately licensed to practice psychotherapy independently in their state. If a therapist holds a provisional license or is a student intern, the equine specialist should verify the therapist's qualifications and competency to practice with the therapist's supervisor (Sheade & Box, 2017).

68 The Treatment Team

Skills Domain

Facilitative Skills

The equine specialist should develop the facilitative skills necessary to be an effective co-facilitator such as observational skills, attending skills, nonverbal communication, verbal communication, and limit-setting. Some of these skills can be gained through formal training; others should be taught by the therapist with whom the equine specialist seeks to co-facilitate sessions in EACP. These skills are essential in helping the client to feel both emotionally and physically safe during the session. The equine specialist should be able to use these skills intentionally and effectively without crossing psychotherapeutic boundaries (see Chapter 6 for a detailed review). The equine specialist should also be skilled in identifying and co-facilitating activities designed to meet the client's treatment goals (Sheade & Box, 2017).

Intentionality

The equine specialist should act deliberately and intentionally in co-facilitating EACP. The equine specialist should interact with the client and structure activities that are consistent with the client's clinical goals. Furthermore, the equine specialist should be capable of identifying the difference between facilitating a client-equine relationship versus facilitating the relationship in a riding or horsemanship lesson.

Specialized Skill Set

As the equine specialist's most important job is to assist in facilitating a safe and healthy relationship between the client and equine(s), it is critical that the equine specialist possesses the skill to accomplish this goal in a way that benefits both the client and equines. The equine specialist should be highly skilled in working with equines on the ground. I have known many equestrians who have successfully competed at high levels of specialized disciplines such as show jumping or barrel racing. However, these individuals often lacked experience in relating to equines on the ground, especially in a herd. As much of EACP takes place in the herd (particularly in the REPC model), it is essential that the equine specialist has experience working with equines in a herd and managing the herd as a whole, not just the individual equines. They should be highly skilled in reading both the overt and subtle body language signals of the equines, and should be competent in using this information to interpret the equine's emotional state and anticipate future behaviors. The equine specialist should also be familiar with equine movement and gaits. Being able to anticipate when an equine is going to move and with which hoof can help keep the client safe and avoid getting stepped on. Finally, the equine specialist should also be able to recognize when the equine has become distracted and is no longer attentive

The Treatment Team 69

to the client, which can pose a safety risk and may contribute to problematic behaviors.

The equine specialist should be skilled in recognizing and responding to inappropriate or dangerous equine behavior using established best practices in equine training (McGreevy, Christensen, von Borstel, & McLean, 2018). Most equines provide several cues or indicators prior to engaging in an aggressive behavior towards a person or another equine. The equine specialist should be skilled in reading these subtle cues, such as an increase in muscle tension or a weight shift. The equine specialist should also be knowledgeable of appropriate ways to manage problem behaviors such as nipping or using pressure to move the equine when needed. Furthermore, the equine specialist should assess and evaluate the factors that may have influenced the equine's display of inappropriate behavior to understand the behavior and avoid escalating the situation (Mills, 1998). It is essential that the equine specialist discuss potential discipline strategies with the therapist in advance to ensure that these methods will not negatively impact or unintentionally re-traumatize the client.

One of the most important skills needed by the equine specialist is the ability to anticipate and recognize signs of equine stress in response to specific aspects of the session, such as the client's presentation, behaviors, and session activities. If the equine specialist notices signs of emotional stress in the equine, they should not only address it in the session but also take time to "debrief" with the equine after session by providing calming and reassuring interaction.

Should the equine specialist recognize an imminent physical or emotional threat to any equine's or person's safety, the equine specialist should take action to intervene. If there is no immediate threat but the interaction may develop into a possible safety or stress-related concern, the equine specialist should collaborate with the therapist prior to interrupting the activity in order to agree upon the best way to go about intervening (PATH Intl., 2017). Finally, the equine specialist should survey the environment for potential hazards to the equine, such as holes in the ground or dangerous plants, and be able to respond to equine emergencies as well as provide basic equine first aid.

Attitude Domain

Equine Advocacy

One of the equine specialist's most important responsibilities is to advocate for the equine's welfare and well-being both in and out of session. The equine specialist should collaborate with the therapist to create sessions that are conducive to positive equine welfare and respond to indications of poor welfare or stress within session. Additionally, the equine specialist should advocate for appropriate husbandry and welfare outside of session as well. Poor welfare will not just impact the equine outside of session but is likely to negatively both the client's and equine's experience and safety in session.

Professional Development

The equine specialist should participate in ongoing professional development related to both equine behavior and husbandry and mental health. PATH Intl. requires continuing education in order to maintain the ESMHL credential. Equine specialists can gain this education by attending conferences, clinics, or mental health continuing education sponsored by local mental health agencies.

Personal Values

The equine specialist should embody personal characteristics conducive to the practice of EACP such as openness to change, authenticity, warmth, self-awareness, accepting, empathic, humility, flexibility, patience, and professionalism (Sheade & Box, 2017; Stewart et al., 2016). The equine specialist should be open, patient, and flexible while facilitating the client's process of discovery-based learning, even if it runs counter to the ways that they may teach certain skills in riding or horsemanship lessons, provided there are no physical or emotional risks to the clients or equines by doing so. The equine specialist should model a collaborative, empathic relationship with the equines.

Considerations for Including the Equine Specialist

There are varying opinions on the benefits of having a separate equine specialist in addition to the therapist in EACP sessions (Schlote, 2009). Above all else, the decision as to whether or not to include a separate individual as an equine specialist should hinge on the ability to maintain physical safety for all involved. Whereas some models, such as the Equine Assisted Growth and Learning Association (2018), require the inclusion of an individual separate from the therapist as an equine specialist, others, such as the Professional Association of Therapeutic Horsemanship (PATH Intl., 2018b), suggest but do not require the inclusion of a separate individual to act as equine specialist if the therapist is dually credentialed in both roles. In my practice, we always require therapists who are not fully and independently licensed and/or do not possess expert-level equine experience to co-facilitate with a separate equine specialist. In my opinion, to qualify as an equine expert, one must meet the criteria described as well as rigorous standards for equine experience, such as those outlined by the Equine Assisted Growth and Learning Association (2018). These standards include the approximate equivalent of three years of full-time work with equines and at least one hundred hours of continuing education or completion of professional training under expert-level equine professionals with a focus on groundwork and equine psychology and body language. In special cases, therapists who are fully independently licensed, hold certification as an equine specialist, and possess expert-level equine experience may be allowed to facilitate individual

EACP sessions without a separate individual. However, group sessions involving more than one client should always be co-facilitated by a therapist in combination with an equine specialist and/or qualified volunteers.

Individuals and organizations in favor of inclusion of a separate individual as equine specialist maintain that the primary benefit is enhanced safety, as the equine specialist can maintain a sole focus on safety and equine welfare without having to also attend in depth to the client and facilitate psychotherapeutic processing. Although many therapists pursue a career in EACP because of a love for equines, the vast majority do not possess expert-level equine experience. In addition, some therapists may struggle to maintain a dual focus on attending to both the client's needs and equine's needs, and risk compromising welfare for one or both. Furthermore, therapists acting in both roles may have more difficulty maintaining objectivity in accurately reading the equine's cues and may have an enhanced risk of countertransference, especially if the therapist is working with their own personal equines.

However, other practitioners maintain that the inclusion of an additional person in the role of equine specialist can create potential ethical issues influencing the session. Schlote (2009) described how the presence of a separate equine specialist may add additional pressure for the therapist to also take responsibility for the behaviors, feelings, and reactions of the equine specialist and how this may impact the client and session overall. As most equine specialists are not trained therapists, some may not possess skills related to self-awareness and self-regulation to act therapeutically towards the client and in managing their own countertransference reactions in session, thus impacting the session in negative or unproductive ways (Gilbert, 2013). The distinction in roles and boundaries can often feel disjointed and uncomfortable to some clients, as the treatment team may not be viewed or perceived as a unified whole. As many clients feel significant pressure simply by participating in counseling or psychotherapy, the addition of a second person in the role of equine specialist can exacerbate this feeling. For some clients, the presence of two people may feel overly intimidating and result in less client openness and increased anxiety during the session, thus impeding the client from achieving maximum benefit from EACP.

The Treatment Team Relationship

First and foremost, it is crucial that both human members of the treatment team have a highly developed, respectful working relationship with each equine and should take time to get to know each equine outside of counseling sessions. Even if the therapist does not possess the equine skills to be competent to act in the role of an equine specialist, they should seek to establish their own relationship with each equine. The importance of this relationship is supported by findings from Stewart, Chang, and Rice (2013). Evidence of a strong working relationship between the human treatment team member and the equine is characterized by the ability to read each other's body language and anticipate each other's actions (Birke & Hockenhull, 2015). In many of the herds that I work with, the equines and I have learned to communicate with subtle cues during a session. For example, over time, most of the equines recognize that if I straighten my posture and hold up a single finger (of course provided that the finger is in their line of sight), I am indicating to them to stop their approach. In most cases, they respond willingly until I relax my posture and lower my finger, allowing them to approach at that time if they still desire to do so. This response is not the result of structured training, but learning to read and understand each other in the pasture over the course of many hours of sessions spent together instead.

Both human members of the treatment team can follow the five interconnected principles identified by Fredrickson and Stewart (2003) to strengthen their partnership and build trust with the equines. First and foremost, the treatment team must respect that the equines have lives outside of session, including friendships and social bonds with other equines. The treatment team should also strive to understand the equines' perceptual world by observation and applying knowledge of the nature of equines (see Chapter 2). The treatment team members should develop emotional awareness of their own impacts on the equines and work to understand the equine's behaviors and responses in the context of emotional transmission from not only the client(s) but also the treatment team. The treatment team should work to facilitate mutually beneficial interactions between the equines and all counseling participants. The treatment team members should be sensitive to the equine's cues and work to understand their experiences. Finally, the treatment team members should respect the equine's communication of their related to desired level of engagement and self-direction in the session.

It is the critical that each member of the treatment team has a defined role and associated responsibilities that both members agree on. Development of a strong relationship between the therapist and equine specialist can take time and treatment team members often experience a steep learning curve in finding their footing as co-facilitators (Gilbert, 2013). Additionally, treatment team members should discuss safety rules, client precautions and contraindications, documentation responsibilities, crisis procedures, and volunteer training requirements (PATH Intl., 2017).

The relationship between the therapist and equine specialist is unique in that although the equine specialist may meet the technical definition of a paraprofessional, they have a defined and important role distinct from the therapist. However, it is important to guard against resentment and conflict as a result of the equine specialist feeling dismissed due to a lack of psychotherapy knowledge or the therapist feeling left out of equine-related activities (Gilbert, 2013). Both have a mutual reliance on each other's respective roles to ensure that the session runs smoothly and safely for all involved (Gilbert, 2013). One way to conceptualize the relationship is to view the therapist and equine specialist as

The Treatment Team   73

assistants to each other within their respective roles. For example, the therapist is responsible for all psychotherapeutic content in the session, and the equine specialist assists but does not lead these interactions. Along the same lines, the therapist may assist the equine specialist in maintaining physical safety and equine welfare, but the equine specialist is ultimately responsible for these factors. As the relationship between the therapist and equine specialist grows, the treatment team members will learn to understand and trust each's thoughts and intent, including recognition of nonverbal cues to communicate without disrupting the client's process. The treatment team should also have agreed upon protocols to handle differences of opinion that can occur during the session, including deferring to each other's judgment based on the nature of the concern (clinical versus equine-related) during the session (Sokolof & Stuart, 2000).

The formation of the treatment team and selection of its specific members should be deliberate and intentional, taking into consideration each member's personality and level of experience. For example, in many cases pairing a therapist new to EACP with an equine specialist experienced in providing EACP can be very beneficial in supporting the new therapist. However, if the equine specialist has a strong or dominant personality, the therapist may find themselves feeling walked over and excluded from the session. It is also important to note that it can be very difficult for some equine specialists experienced in providing EACP to work with a new therapist, especially one who is also new to the field of EACP and is still learning the ropes and honing their skills. In particular, conflict may arise from the therapist's fear of equines or fundamental lack of understanding of equine psychology and behavior resulting in the equine specialist feeling frustrated by the therapist's ineffective facilitation or negative interference in the relationship between the client and equine (Gilbert, 2013). Unfortunately, I have also witnessed conflict in treatment teams arising between a new therapist and a seasoned equine specialist resulting from the therapist's insecurity and desire to prove themselves and the equine specialist's feelings of confusion or hurt by the therapist's actions in session or dismissal of the equine specialist's contributions.

The client can benefit from a team approach through observation of the team as a model for healthy relationships. How, for example, the therapist and equine specialist work through disagreements, misunderstandings, and miscommunications in a healthy relationship. The client, who may be struggling to form their own healthy relationships with family, friends, and coworkers, can learn new ways to communicate, compromise, and manage conflict. Therefore, it is crucial that the team members themselves have a healthy relationship and engage in frequent debriefing to not only discuss the client's needs but also how they are functioning as a team. Treatment teams who struggle to establish cohesion should enlist peer supervision from another therapist at the agency or another therapist in the community to strengthen their working relationship and ensure that any conflict does not impact client needs and progress.

A Note on Volunteers

In some cases, it may be useful to include volunteers in EACP sessions. The most common reason for including volunteers is to maintain a safe environment beyond what the therapist and equine specialist can manage alone. Typically, volunteers are most often utilized in either mounted sessions or sessions involving multiple clients and equines, such as groups. To safeguard the client's emotional safety and privacy, I always recommend including the minimum number of volunteers needed to ensure a safe environment and I do not permit observation of any EACP sessions by visitors. It is crucial that the facility creates and maintains policies and procedures related to volunteer training and management (PATH Intl., 2018b). The treatment team should screen potential volunteers for experience in working with clients with mental health concerns, personal characteristics conducive to supporting EACP clients, and equine-related competencies. The treatment team should thoroughly discuss volunteer roles and responsibilities, expectations (including attendance requirements), and dismissal policies (PATH Intl., 2018b). It is important to train volunteers on specific topics such as the nature and purpose of EACP, client privacy, appropriate therapeutic boundaries, considerations for working with specific mental health concerns, strategies for interacting with the clients, safety rules, equine handling guidelines, and emergency procedures. The treatment team should be available and closely monitor volunteers' interactions with clients to ensure a positive experience for all involved. Following each session, it is important for the therapist to lead the debriefing to discuss the session's content and client's behaviors, especially in the case of distressing occurrences such as client-related crisis or injuries.

Chapter 6

Facilitating Relational Equine-Partnered Counseling

Human-Animal Relational Theory

The foundation of the Relational Equine-Partnered Counseling (REPC) approach of equine-assisted counseling and psychotherapy (EACP) is supported by Chandler's (2017) Human-Animal Relational Theory (HART), which presents a guiding theory of human-animal interaction in counseling and psychotherapy. (See Chapter 3 for a detailed discussion on the philosophical domains of the REPC model.) Chandler's (2017) theory emphasizes the role of interspecies neurobiology in understanding and facilitating EACP sessions. Additionally, both HART and REPC emphasize the importance of the relationship between client and equine and the importance of Relational Moments (RM).

Chandler described a special type of RM called a Significant Human-Animal Relational Moment (SHARM), which represents "impactful events between a person and animal, an animal with which that person feels connection or desires to feel a connection" (p. 140). A SHARM can take many different forms in an REPC session. For example, Jenny, a survivor of military sexual trauma, was highly anxious during her first REPC session. Jenny reported that she not only felt fearful among the equines but also felt fearful almost constantly, whether she was at home or out in public. As she spoke about her fear, Captain slowly began to approach her from across the pasture. As Captain got closer, Jenny reported her anxiety rising. Captain abruptly stopped a few feet away. A few moments later, he extended his neck to sniff Jenny's hand without moving his feet and thus remaining a "safe" distance from Jenny. Jenny immediately breathed a sigh of relief and stated, "he gets it!" Jenny stroked Captain's nose and explained that she felt he understood her fear and respected her space by not moving his feet too close. Jenny then moved towards Captain and hugged his neck. This SHARM illustrated a connection between Jenny and Captain that ultimately resulted in Jenny's feelings of being understood and accepted. Scott's experience with Snowball (see Chapter 3) illustrated a different type of SHARM. Scott, a teenage boy who struggled to form peer relationships, also struggled in relating to Snowball. During his second session with Snowball, Scott stated that he wanted to be "friends" with Snowball and

76   Facilitating Relational Equine-Partnered Counseling

proceeded to "surprise" Snowball by jumping out from behind a bush. Unsurprisingly, Snowball shied away. Scott felt confused and discouraged that his attempt to "have fun" with Snowball had not worked the way he had expected. In this type of SHARM, Scott's desire for connection is evident; Snowball's response provided valuable feedback to Scott that helped in his development of social skills, empathy, and self-control.

Chandler identified seven different categories of SHARMs: Greeting, Acknowledgment, Speculation, Interpretation, Comfort, Assurance, and Checking In. During a Greeting SHARM, the treatment team facilitates the initial interaction between the client and an equine, such as an equine who approaches the client from across the pasture. During an Acknowledgment SHARM, the treatment team reflects the equine's communication to the client. For example, the equine specialist may reflect the equine's licking and chewing behavior to signify a potential shift in the equine's emotional state.

The treatment team may utilize a Speculation SHARM to help the client to gain insight or self-awareness. For example, the treatment team may comment on an equine moving closer to a client and wonder aloud what may have shifted to cause the equine to decide to move closer. I have found these types of SHARMS to be especially profound in many sessions. During one of my sessions with Daniel, a teenage boy suffering from depression, he talked about his sadness over his parents' divorce while stroking his horse, Gerry. Suddenly, Gerry abruptly began stomping his foot and swatting his tail. As we could see no external annoyance (e.g., insects or other approaching equines), we asked Daniel what he thought was happening. Daniel looked down at the ground and quietly said, "I feel angry but don't think that I'm allowed to be angry. And I think Gerry knows." Gerry immediately relaxed and went to sleep. Gerry's response to Daniel's behavior provided a valuable opportunity to enable Daniel to express feelings that may have otherwise gone unacknowledged and contributed to Daniel's distress.

An Interpretation SHARM is used by the treatment team to help the client understand what the animal is communicating or experiencing. For example, as yawning in equines may be reflective of changes in emotional arousal (Górecka-Bruzda, Fureix, Ouvrard, Bourjade, & Hausberger, 2016), the treatment team may consider reflecting this behavior as a possible indication of the equine's response to a client's emotional state. For clients who tend to avoid negative or uncomfortable emotions, it may help draw out feelings by enabling the client to check in with themselves and express their feelings. A Comfort SHARM is characterized by the treatment team's reflection of an equine engaging in spontaneous physical contact. An equine resting their head or wrapping their neck around a client who is processing their trauma would be an example of a Comfort SHARM. An Assurance SHARM is a relational moment in which the client experiences a sense of assurance or self-assurance as a result of the client's interpretation of the equine's behavior. For example, one child I worked with in play therapy, Sophie, spent much of her session trying to brush Bravo's legs. Bravo had always demonstrated discomfort in having

Facilitating Relational Equine-Partnered Counseling   77

his legs brushed and his movement away was not a result of anything specifically related to Sophie. As the treatment team explained this, Sophie decided
that she wanted to help Bravo overcome his fear. She then proceeded to give
him a "pep talk" and told him that she was not going to hurt him. Much to
my surprise, Bravo then allowed Sophie to brush his legs without any signs of
discomfort. As Sophie often struggled in peer interactions, Bravo's trust in her
greatly elevated her confidence. Finally, the Checking-In SHARM refers to the
treatment team reflecting the equine's attempts to check in with the client or
to check in with the equine. Checking in with the animal serves as a healthy
model for care and relationship development. I observe Checking-In SHARMs
on a regular basis during my sessions. Most of the time, this SHARM takes the
form of equines in the pasture approaching clients, especially during moments
of client distress. In one herd, the boss mare, Raven, tended to act aloof and
disinterested in most clients. However, whenever a client appeared to be in a
heightened state of distress, Raven would almost always approach and make
a point of staying within a few feet of the client until the client's distress had
abated. Even though most clients did not interact with her on a regular basis,
almost all the clients reported her presence and care for them to be a source of
comfort. For me, her check-ins alerted me to the significance of what the client
may be experiencing even when it was not initially apparent to me.

The processing of these SHARMs is referred to as Human-Animal Relational Processing, or HARP. This type of processing can take two forms:
internal (I-HARP) and external (E-HARP). During I-HARP, the client processes their own private dialogue internally. During E-HARP, the client and
treatment team process together externally (Chandler, 2018). To use HARP
effectively, the therapist must draw on their clinical skills for psychotherapy.
Chandler (2017) also cautioned against over-utilizing or under-utilizing the
client-equine interaction. An example of over-utilizing the client-equine interaction can occur if the treatment team becomes overly focused on a specific
task or activity during the session. For example, imagine that the treatment
team is facilitating a backing up activity to help the client develop boundaries
or assertiveness. If the treatment team becomes too focused on coaching or
directing the client on how to back the equine up, they may miss the equine's
efforts to communicate during the activity and thus miss a significant relational moment. In contrast, when processing the client's experience of the
activity, if they are not also attending to the equine during the process, there
is a risk of under-utilizing the interaction by missing or ignoring the equine's
response.

Together, the SHARM and the HARP give rise to the Human-Animal Relational Therapeutic Impact (HARTI). The HARTI can take place over time and
further develop as time progresses (as in Scott's story) or can be a single "a-ha"
moment. It is important to keep the importance of the quality, not quantity of
the SHARM and subsequent HART in mind. Even one SHARM, when processed effectively, can lead to lasting and impactful change in the client.

Equine Communication in Session

From the moment we step into the pasture, we become a part of the equine's environment and possibly even recognized as a part of the herd (Wilsie & Vogel, 2016). Equines use a variety of ways to communicate with both people and other equines. They observe us closely, especially our breath and body language, to understand us and anticipate what we might do. Equines do not show affection towards people in the same way as predators (e.g., dogs and cats). In the initial stages of relationship formation, they communicate their comfort and interest by first allowing us to be in their space or by attempting to enter into our space (Wilsie & Vogel, 2016). It is important that the equine specialist is highly skilled in understanding equine psychology and in noticing and understanding even the subtlest cues. Much of the time, the equine will communicate the message in a more subtle than overt manner. If this communication is not acknowledged or responded to, it may be followed by a much more overt behavior. For example, if a client reaches out to stroke an equine's face too quickly, the equine may slightly turn to the side. A seasoned equine specialist will immediately recognize this as an indication of the equine's discomfort. However, if this cue is missed or ignored, and the client continues to behave in a way that the equine finds unsuitable, the equine may escalate to threatening to bite or simply walk away from the client. Likewise, an equine will usually provide several warnings before they go to kick another equine or a person. One of the first signs is typically an increase in physical tension in the equine's body followed by other warning signs, such as ear pinning or raising a leg to threaten to kick.

There are several behaviors that I believe are essential for the equine specialist to be capable of recognizing and responding to. First and foremost, it is important that the equine specialist can recognize any behavior in the context of the environment and entirety of body language. For example, is a cocked hoof an indication that the equine is threatening to kick? Or is the equine simply resting? What does the rest of the equine's body language reveal? What or who else is in the equine's immediate environment? Observing both the environment and the equine's behavior in the context of the entirety of their body language from nose to tail will be most reflective of the equine's emotional state and intent.

In evaluating the equine's level of calmness or agitation, it is important to attend to a variety of cues such as physical tension, ear positioning, head and neck positioning, tail movement, and facial cues. The equine's ears can be one of the most obvious signs of the animal's feelings and intent. The ear positioning can not only indicate what or who the equine is paying attention to, but it can also indicate interest, relaxation, or anger. Additionally, the equine specialist can anticipate the equine's feelings, intent, and subsequent behaviors based on an observation of shifts in body position and directional movement. For example, it is crucial to me that equine specialists can observe subtle weight shifts and movement patterns to anticipate what direction an equine is likely to move next and with which hoof. From a safety standpoint, accurate anticipation can prevent injuries like a client getting stepped on.

Other behaviors can reveal the equine's level of comfort and interest in the session itself. Approach, retreat, and avoidance behaviors can indicate any number of things and may even differ depending on the equine. While some equines may respond to client's distress by moving away, others may respond by moving closer. Additionally, the equine's posture indicates whether they are alert, withdrawn, or relaxed. Given that both a withdrawn and a relaxed equine display a lowered head, it can be difficult for a less experienced equine specialist to detect the difference. A withdrawn equine will demonstrate a similar height between neck and back, open eyes, and a stretched neck. In contrast, a relaxed equine will stand with one foot cocked and a lower and rounder neck position. There will also be decreased muscle tension throughout the equine's body that may be especially evident in the ears turned sideways, dropping lower lip, and eyes partially or fully closed (Fureix, Jego, Henry, Lansade, & Hausberger, 2012). Finally, the equine's amount of locomotion (i.e., stillness or high movement) can be indicative of the equine's level of comfort and relaxation or excitement, agitation, or restlessness.

Equines have several behaviors that can provide useful information not only about the equine's experience in the session, but also information about the client. For example, equine yawning and stretching behaviors may be indications that the equine is feeling increased emotional arousal. However, yawning can also be reflective of transitioning to a lower state of arousal such as going to sleep. Yawning in equines has been demonstrated in response to an excitatory state associated with heightened emotions, such as anticipation of food. Especially when combined with stretching, yawning can be indicative of heightened arousal and may function to lower arousal (Górecka-Bruzda et al., 2016). Although it is difficult to comment on the relation of yawning to specific emotional states, depending on context, it may also be associated with negative feelings such as stress or frustration (Fureix, Gorecka-Bruzda, Gautier, & Hausberger, 2011). Yawning may also have a social context based on displays of yawning behavior when equines interact with other equines both affiliative and aggressive (Górecka-Bruzda et al., 2016). I have experienced countless sessions during which multiple equines would yawn and stretch when a highly anxious client became more tense and fearful while processing something upsetting. Upon pointing out the equines' behavior, the client's anxiety would often be disrupted and result in the client's deliberate efforts to downregulate in response to the equines' feedback. We often utilize the equine feedback to help the client recognize when their anxiety has become unmanageable and a calming skill is needed to de-escalate. Over time, the client learns to recognize these cues within themselves and implements calming skills without needing the equines' feedback.

The equine's level of playful or pushy behavior may also be reflective of the equine's level of comfort with and interpretation of the client's body language and emotional state. I have noticed in many sessions that some equines have a stronger outward reaction to client incongruence and often respond by becoming overly pushy or "nippy" towards the client. In some cases, the demonstration of increased play behavior in adult, domesticated horses may be an indicator of stress and serve as an effort to cope with or reduce stress (Bloius-Heulin et al., 2015; Hausberger, Fureix, Bourjade, Wessel-Robert, & Richard-Yris, 2012). It is possible that this behavior may be reflective of equine stress or may be an effort to disrupt perceived tension in the client.

Another significant equine behavior is licking and chewing. In my opinion, this is one of the most important behaviors to attend to in an EACP session. There continues to be a lack of agreement about the meaning of this commonly demonstrated behavior. Many horse trainers believe this behavior to be an indication of submission. However, some researchers believe this behavior may function as a comfort behavior to reduce anxiety (Goodwin, 1999) or an indication of a physiological change in arousal (Henshall & McGreevy, 2014). The most promising theory indicates licking and chewing behavior may occur in response to relaxation following a state of stress or heightened emotional arousal (Kydd, Padalino, Henshall, & McGreevy, 2017; McDonnell, 2005). Oftentimes, I observe equines demonstrate this behavior in response to the client coming to a "a-ha" moment during processing. Other times, I observe this behavior when the client has an emotional release such as crying or a feeling of relief during trauma processing. In this way, the equine appears to be attuned to the client's state of heightened stress or arousal and experiences a release of tension as the client does. Schlote (2018b) described a similar interpretation of this phenomenon of equines co-regulating with clients in the context of the Polyvagal Theory.

Finally, I have observed equines actively work to move or "manage" the people in the session including client(s) and treatment team members. In some cases, the equine moves the client without touching them, but simply moves towards them until the client steps away. Other times, the equine will physically apply pressure with their nose, shoulder, or hindquarters to move a client. I have observed equines "herding" clients away from other equines. I have also witnessed the herd leader move (and keep) a pushier equine away from the session. I have experienced equines herding me and the equine specialist away from a client while the client interacted with another equine. I have also experienced equines herding me closer to a client who appeared to be in distress. During one couple's session, Billy, an older bay gelding, was very active in managing each member of the couple and their position in relation to each other. During moments of heightened negative emotion, Billy would very deliberately split the couple with one member on each side. When the couple became calmer, he would allow them to be close again. During my sessions with Suzy, a high-functioning anxious client, Frosty would often "split" me and Suzy whenever Suzy began to avoid talking about her feelings and became overly focused on rationalizing her behaviors. Frosty seemed to sense a change in Suzy during these moments and disrupted my continued interaction with Suzy. Over time, Suzy got used to Frosty's pattern during her sessions and admitted to her avoidance, knowing that Frosty would continue to split us until Suzy became congruent. Once Suzy became more present and began to acknowledge what she was feeling and experiencing, Frosty would step back and allow our discussion to continue. To my knowledge, there is no published research documenting this phenomenon or its cause or function. I would hypothesize that the equines in these sessions are noticing and responding to different states of arousal in the human participants. When the equines detect a state that seems unsatisfactory, they take action to disrupt the process until congruence or harmony is restored. Therefore, it is crucial that the treatment team not only notices but actively responds to this behavior. Ignoring this behavior or simply moving back around the equine can result in the loss of valuable feedback and information.

The Team Approach

Many EACP approaches promote the benefits of a team approach consisting of a therapist and equine specialist who maintain separate but equally important roles in co-facilitating the session. The therapist is responsible for the psychotherapeutic content and the equine specialist is responsible for maintaining client safety with regard to the equines. However, approaches may differ regarding which treatment team member takes the lead in interacting with the client and facilitating activities.

In the Relational Equine-Partnered Counseling (REPC) and Equine-Partnered Play Therapy (EPPT) approaches, the therapist takes the lead. The equine specialist serves the crucial role of maintaining safety and facilitating a positive relationship between the client and equines, but acts more as a paraprofessional than a lead facilitator for psychotherapeutic content (Gilbert, 2013). However, it is worth noting that in situations where the equine specialist determines that the client is in danger, the safety of the client becomes paramount and the equine specialist takes the lead until a safe environment is established.

By contrast, in some other EACP approaches, the equine specialist is expected to take the lead in not only maintaining client safety, but also in developing and leading activities while the therapist observes and processes at designated times but does not have a hands-on role during the session. In these models, communication between the therapist and equine specialist in advance of the client session becomes essential, not only to define roles but also to anticipate potential scenarios in which therapist intervention becomes necessary. The failure of such communication can lead to potential ethical and perhaps legal issues. A similar situation arises when the equine specialist is dual-credentialed as a therapist. Ethical and legal issues may arise regarding which professional is actually acting as the therapist and is responsible for the client's psychological welfare. Once again, communication in advance of the client session is critical.

Client Presentations

When conducting an EACP session, clients in REPC tend to fall into three loosely defined types of presentations: the "talking-focused" client, the "activity-focused" client, and the "self-directed" client. Some clients maintain a consistent presentation from week to week; others can change from week to week or even within the same session. It is important to be flexible and responsive in facilitating EACP with each type of client presentation.

Talk-Focused

There are many different reasons why a client may choose to focus on talking during an EACP session. In many cases, allowing the client to talk rather than redirecting them to the equine can result in a transformative session by meeting the client's immediate needs. Some clients just process better through verbal dialogue. There is a reason that psychotherapy has been referred to as the "talking cure." By verbally processing in a safe, accepting environment, the client can find ways to express and articulate thoughts, feelings, and experiences and reconstruct the narrative of their experiences (Cozolino, 2016). However, in other cases, the client may use talking to avoid interaction with the equine. In this case, it is important for the treatment team to explore the potential avoidance while still working to meet the client where they are. The equines' presence during a talk-focused session can help the client to feel safe, accepted, and understood. Furthermore, stroking or being in close proximity to the equines can help clients to self-soothe and remain grounded during moments of heightened distress. The equines' responses to the client can elicit unexpressed thoughts and feelings, as well as create spontaneous opportunities for observational learning and psychoeducation. For example, a client discussing difficulty setting boundaries with a friend may notice an interaction occurring between two equines in the pasture. The client and treatment team can use their observation of this interaction to indirectly process the client's thoughts and feelings while identifying potential communication and problem-solving strategies.

Activity-Focused

Activity-focused clients prefer to spend time in active engagement with the equine. Many of these clients may feel uncomfortable "revealing" themselves by talking directly about their concerns or expressing thoughts and feelings. In collaboration with the client, the treatment team may set up different activities for the client to try with the equine. Though processing for some clients may be limited to the client's immediate experience with the equine, the client is likely making connections consciously or subconsciously that can impact their daily life in a positive way. This can be especially true with older children and young teenage clients who are uncomfortable talking. Even with minimal verbal processing, if at all, these clients will often take the learnings from their session and begin applying them to daily life and relationships. For example, Joey often approached his horse, Sienna, abruptly and failed to attend to Sienna's reactions to him. Over time, Joey began to observe Sienna as he approached and notice Sienna's nonverbal behaviors. Joey used this information to make decisions on how to approach Sienna and modify his behavior when needed. Even though Joey rarely processed verbally during session, his mother reported that he had begun to note that when she appeared preoccupied or busy Joey would wait until she was finished before launching into a story or requesting assistance.

Self-Directed

Finally, the self-directed client is one who can identify and take action to meet their own needs during the session. Jason, a Navy veteran, became very self-directed early in the EACP process. During the first two sessions, Jason discussed his current concerns and goals for EACP and later practiced calming skills with his chosen horse, Bella. By the third session, Jake became self-directed. At the start of each session, Jason would check in with the treatment team on his needs and goals for the session. Jason would then proceed to walk out to Bella and spend the session in different activities with Bella ranging from practicing calming skills, to grooming, to haltering and leading. He would check in with the treatment team periodically during the session. At the end of each session, Jason would process his experience based on needs and goals identified at the start of the session. For Jason, the session served as an opportunity for him to experience quiet and calmness so he could connect with Bella and subsequently reconnect with himself. In these types of sessions, one may wonder if the therapist is really "needed" and the therapist may wonder if they are "doing enough." To both questions, my answer is absolutely yes. Clients who participate in EACP do so because they have significant mental health concerns or trauma. The presence of the therapist creates an inherently safer environment as they are qualified to detect and respond to increasing or unmanageable client distress. Small adjustments in the session structure based on the therapist's assessment and clinical judgment can greatly impact the client's progress. Even in sessions with minimal processing, the therapist's training and clinical experience enables them to understand the client and the client's needs on a deeper level in order to lead meaningful processing and facilitate the client's creation of meaning in their experiences with the equine.

Session Themes

During each session, various themes will emerge based on the client's presenting concern, current functioning, and session content. The treatment team may choose to facilitate or initiate activities based on these themes to promote movement towards the client's goals. These themes include relationship-building, nurturing, mastery/challenge, self-regulation, and creativity and free expression (Sheade, 2019c). The same type of activity may be reflective of different themes and produce different client outcomes in different sessions and for different clients based on client presentation and the therapist's clinical orientation. Table 6.1 provides a summary of the different themes and potential session activities associated with each theme. Although many of the activities are the same as those taught in a traditional horsemanship or equestrian lesson program, the focus of an EACP session is not to teach horsemanship. Instead, the treatment team uses the activities to facilitate discovery-based learning and insight. Furthermore, the therapist should integrate clinical best practices and evidence-based practice into each activity or interaction. For example, imagine that a client is struggling to lead the equine and the becomes discouraged. The therapist may choose to integrate different clinical interventions such as mindfulness, motivational interviewing, identification of automatic thought patterns, body psychotherapy, or cognitive restructuring to facilitate meaningful processing of this experience (Ferruolo, 2015). Furthermore, the therapist may follow this processing by helping the client learn and implement specific coping skills such as communication, problem-solving, relaxation, or decision-making. As the client participates in the activities, thoughts, feelings, and behaviors will arise that can reveal information about the client's overall functional and presenting concerns. The treatment can use these activities to help the client gain insight and self-awareness, practice new coping skills, and create a safe place for the client to express themselves. More details on specific strategies to facilitate activities based on these themes with suggested clinical observations and processing prompts can be found in Sheade (2019c).

Facilitation Skills in REPC

In order to effectively facilitate REPC sessions, the therapist and equine specialist work together to co-facilitate sessions ethically and effectively. The therapist must learn how to adapt counseling and psychotherapy skills for use in REPC. The equine specialist must learn how to read equine behavior in a therapeutic setting. Both the therapist and the equine specialist must learn basic co-facilitation skills to build relationships and respond to the client. The skills described in this section are modified from Ivey and Ivey's (2007) basic counseling skills (Sheade, 2019c). These skills fall into three general categories: observation skills, attending skills, and verbal skills (Sheade, 2019c).

Observation Skills

These skills are vital to establishing the therapeutic relationship and facilitating the relationship between client and equine(s). These skills are comprised of observation of nonverbal behavior, verbal behavior, discrepancies and conflict, and style of expression. As the majority of communication among both

Facilitating Relational Equine-Partnered Counseling 85

Table 6.1 Session Themes in REPC

Theme	Description	Client Outcomes	Sample Activities
Relationship-building	Client works to establish and strengthen safe relationships by practicing relational and communication skills, building trust, and developing empathy in relationship with the equine.	Trust (self and others); assertiveness; communication; empathy; congruence; autonomy	Pasture introductions; grooming; haltering and leading; liberty work; ground tie; backing; obstacle course; art-related activities; herd observation; breathing exercises
Nurturing	Client can provide and receive nurturing through care-taking activities and physical touch.	Self-nurturing; comfort; self-soothing; relaxation; confidence; self-efficacy; autonomy; empathy	Grooming; barn chores; breathing exercises
Mastery/ Challenge	Client gains insight into connections between own thoughts, feelings, and behaviors. Client identifies impact of past experiences or unhealthy thought patterns. Client learns new skills to respond to challenging circumstances and manage negative thoughts and feelings.	Decision-making; problem-solving; coping skills; insight; self-awareness; compromise; empathy; confidence; autonomy; self-efficacy; communication; assertiveness; boundaries	Halter and leading; liberty work; grooming; ground tie; backing; obstacle course
Self-Regulation	Client development of sensory awareness of internal emotional and physiological states. Client practices self-regulation and gains insight based on equine feedback.	Calming skills; self-awareness; insight; empathy; relaxation; mindfulness	Grooming; leading; herd observation; breathing exercises
Creativity and Free Expression	Client experiences freedom to explore innate creativity and move towards growth.	Expression of feelings; creativity; self-trust; congruence; authenticity	Obstacle course; grooming; art-related activities; herd observation

Source: *Relational Equine-Partnered Counseling: Practice Manual* (Sheade, 2019c).

86 Facilitating Relational Equine-Partnered Counseling

humans (Ivey and Ivey, 2007) and equines (Hamilton, 2011) is nonverbal, an ability to interpret non-verbal behavior is critical in any EACP session. Both the therapist and equine specialist should attend to changes in posture, eye contact or gaze, movement or tension, vocal qualities, and facial expressions in both the client and equines as well as within themselves. It is also important to notice verbal qualities such as speech patterns, keywords, and patterns of attention during verbal processing. Finally, the therapist and equine specialist should attend to indicators of potential discrepancy or incongruence in both the client and in the equines' reactions to the client. For example, if the client states that he feels relaxed and content but the equine appears agitated, the equine's behavior may be indicative of a discrepancy within the client.

Attending Skills

Attending skills are crucial in creating an environment where the client feels safe and accepted. Effective use of these skills can encourage a client to be more open in talking and in trying new things with the equines. Use of attending skills should be intentional and flexible based on the client's needs and cultural identity. Attending skills can include the use of eye contact, vocal qualities, and body language. As the equines in the session are going to be most responsive to the treatment team's use of attending skills, it is important to be present and intentional in your use of these skills. The equines will be quick to detect any incongruence or distractedness on the part of anyone present in the session, including the therapist and equine specialist.

Silence

Although arguably one of the most difficult therapeutic skills to master, silence is also one of the most powerful ones, especially in an EACP session. For many novice therapists and equine specialists unfamiliar with the psychotherapy process, silence can, at first, feel uncomfortable. The equine specialist should always follow the therapist's lead in the use of silence in session. Silence provides ripe opportunities for the client to process or gain insight into understanding what is happening in the session and its meaning. Furthermore, it can be difficult to remain silent should a client be in distress. However, silence can allow you to focus better on what is occurring between the client and equines and leave space for the equines to fill. Many of the most powerful moments that I have witnessed in an EACP session occurred during moments of silence that created space for a significant moment to occur between client and equine.

Verbal Skills

Verbal skills also convey the treatment team's interest in and understanding of the client and what is occurring in the session. The specific use of these skills will depend on the therapist's theoretical orientation. These skills include active listening, reflective listening, immediacy, enlarging the meaning, questions, and therapeutic confrontation. Active listening is comprised of several skills such as paraphrasing and summarizing. The equine specialist may use these skills during discussions about the equine with the client. The therapist will use these skills to process throughout all aspects of the session. Reflective listening is one of the hallmarks of counseling and psychotherapy and includes reflections of feeling, content, and meaning. These skills will primarily be used by the therapist. The equine specialist's use of these skills should be limited to reflections of feeling for the equines and some reflection of content for interactions involving the equines.

Immediacy

In my opinion, immediacy is the cornerstone of effective EACP processing. Immediacy refers to reflection of what is presently occurring in the session or within the client. As equines are naturally present and immediate, they are continuously "using" immediacy based on their moment-to-moment behaviors and responses to the client. For novice or inexperienced therapists, immediacy can initially feel uncomfortable and intimidating. However, avoidance of immediacy or overreliance on only processing the client's verbal responses can not only limit the client's progress but can make the session feel disjointed and incongruent by minimizing not only the equines' contributions, but ignoring the client's feelings and behaviors that likely elicited the equines' feedback in the first place.

Enlargement of the Meaning

Enlargement of the meaning can be a critical skill in expanding the therapeutic impact outside of the session itself. The therapist can assist the client in identifying parallels and patterns in interactions with the equines that are relevant to the client's life and relationships outside of session. This process can help facilitate client self-awareness and insight. Furthermore, the therapist can assist the client in translating gains in generalized skills practiced in session to daily life, and in making positive changes as a result of increased self-awareness and insight.

Therapeutic Questions and Confrontation

The use of therapeutic questions and confrontation can help the client to gain greater self-awareness and insight into the connection between thoughts, feelings, and behaviors. Oftentimes, confrontation will accompany immediacy if a possible discrepancy or incongruence is detected. It is essential that the equine specialist follows the therapist's lead during these times and does not apply

88 Facilitating Relational Equine-Partnered Counseling

additional pressure to the client. For example, imagine that a client is processing, and the equine suddenly begins to yawn in succession. Assuming other variables unrelated to the client seem unlikely, the equine specialist may reflect "Jade has suddenly started yawning. It seems something might be happening in our session". If the client does not immediately respond, the therapist may choose to continue probing with the use of therapeutic questions. However, depending on the therapist's assessment of the client in the moment, they may also choose not to pursue this line of processing. These types of interactions can be very powerful and act as a catalyst for the client going into increased depth and processing thoughts, feelings, or experiences that had been previously avoided or outside of conscious awareness. Questions of any type should always be deliberate and intentional.

The Use of Child-Centered Play Therapy Skills

I have found many of Landreth's (2012) child-centered play therapy skills to be extremely useful in facilitating REPC sessions. These skills include tracking, returning responsibility, encouragement, and limit-setting strategies. Tracking is a verbal response in which the therapist or equine specialist verbally states what they are observing in the session. The equine specialist tracks the equine's behaviors and client behaviors that impact the equine's behavior directly. An example of an equine specialist tracking response is: "I noticed that when you started to look outside of the arena, the equine started to slow down". The therapist tracks the client's behaviors. An example of therapist tracking is: "You are brushing the equine very slowly and carefully". By returning responsibility to the client, the treatment team provides help when needed but encourages the client to figure things out independently and does not do for clients what clients can do themselves. Use of this skill can help to promote client autonomy, decision-making, and confidence. By focusing on encouragement (i.e., client's process and effort) rather than praise (i.e., positive judgment on client's "accomplishment"), the treatment team fosters a greater internal locus of control for the client. Statements such as "you're really figuring that out!" can go a long way in building confidence and self-efficacy.

In order to protect human or equine welfare, it is often necessary to set limits within the session. When modified based on client's age or developmental stage, I have found the A-C-T model to be very effective in limit-setting for EACP sessions for clients of all ages. The "A" refers to acknowledgment of the client's feeling or intent, "C" refers to communication of the limit, and "T" refers to targeting alternatives. An example with a teenage client may be: "I see that you want to stand close to the horse. However, it's not safe to stand right behind the horse. You can choose to stand near his head or next to his shoulder". For more information on limit-setting, see Chapter 11.

Chapter 7

Integration of Counseling Theory in Equine-Assisted Counseling and Psychotherapy

In this chapter, I review some of the most common theoretical orientations integrated with equine-assisted counseling and psychotherapy (EACP) and their utility within the form of EACP that I developed and use in my practice for older children and adults called Relational Equine-Partnered Counseling (REPC). It is important to keep in mind that this chapter does not represent all the different theories that may be integrated with EACP or the REPC approach. The REPC approach is trans-theoretical and intended to be usable by therapists of diverse clinical orientations. A therapist's clinical orientation will inform what aspects of the session are deemed most meaningful, how they choose to process with the client, and their overall conceptualization of the client's presenting concerns and progress. The most important part in implementing the REPC model is maintaining the importance of the client-equine relationship.

Few researchers have attended to a theoretical basis for the practice of equine-assisted counseling and psychotherapy (EACP) (Bachi, 2012). Bachi (2013) highlighted the need for counselors to fill the gap between the theory and practice of EACP through integration with counseling theories to provide guidelines for practice. Chandler, Potrie-Bethke, Barrio Minto, Fernando, & O'Callaghan (2010) highlighted strategies to implement specific animal-assisted therapy techniques with different theoretical orientations. Counseling theories most commonly integrated with equine-assisted counseling and psychotherapy include Cognitive-Behavioral Therapies, Gestalt, Person-Centered, and Behavioral (Gergley, 2012; Schlote, 2009). This chapter is intended to provide a snapshot of each of the major theories often integrated into EACP. In truth, each theory, and its integration in EACP, could warrant a chapter of its own. By strengthening your foundation in your understanding and practice of your identified theory, it will be easier to integrate it with REPC as well as other EACP approaches.

Psychoanalytic Therapy

The primary focus of psychoanalytic therapy is to bring the client's unconscious into conscious awareness. As people, we often avoid things that make

90 Integration of Counseling Theory

us feel threatened, uncomfortable, or vulnerable (Shedler, 2006). People often experience internal conflict and unconsciously prevent themselves from reaching their goals. For example, a person may desire a close, intimate relationship with their partner, but take actions to keep the partner from coming too close. Other times, a client may disavow specific emotions such as anger. The hallmarks of psychoanalytic therapy are described by Shedler (2010): a focus on the client's affect and emotional expression; exploration of the client's avoidances of upsetting thoughts and feelings; identification of the client's recurring themes and patterns that cause distress; exploration of past experiences in understanding present distress; an emphasis on processing the client's relationships with others, including with the therapist; and exploration of the client's wishes and fantasies.

In EACP, the therapist can facilitate the client's identification and expression of emotions occurring while interacting with the equine. Oftentimes, processing emotions related to the client's experience with the equine can feel less threatening than to process emotions related to experiences outside of session. Clients who may otherwise avoid processing distressing emotions may be more engaged and more relaxed as a result of the equine's presence in the session. The therapist can help the client identify parallels between the client's feelings, thoughts, and behaviors while interacting with the equine and client's experiences outside of session. These parallels may be indicative of self-defeating patterns. The therapist can help the client enlarge the meaning of these experiences to understand the influence and role of the client's past experiences and how they may contribute to present distress. The therapist can also facilitate processing of the interspecies relationship occurring between the client and the equine. By processing the client's feelings and thoughts while in relationship with the equine (i.e., transference), the therapist can help the client uncover unconscious patterns and create healthier ones in the present relationship with the equine. For a more detailed reviewed of the integration of depth-oriented, psychoanalytic EACP, see Filippides (2016).

An example of this transference is illustrated in my work with an adolescent named James who was brought to EACP to treat anxiety and oppositional defiant behaviors. He experienced excessive worrying and often teased and verbally lashed out at others. One day, he decided that he wanted to walk his horse, Dandy, on the lead line. James hooked the lead line to the halter and immediately walked off without attending to Dandy. As soon as the rope became taut, James immediately stopped. When the equine did not move to follow him, he became angry. He then proceeded to call Dandy "stupid" and "lazy". As James had not cued Dandy using the rope, it was clear to the treatment team that Dandy did not know what the client wanted him to do. James stated that he should not have to apply pressure on the rope to direct Dandy and instead the horse should "just know" what he is supposed to do. Through continued processing, James later revealed a fear of Dandy becoming angry if he were to assert himself. In later sessions, James related this fear to childhood experiences of being yelled at or hit when he would ask his father for something that he needed, such as a glass of water. He also reported that his father would often call him "lazy" and "stupid" during these exchanges. Over time, James began to practice communicating his wishes to Dandy. As feelings of fear arose during these sessions, James was able to identify and express these fears. By bringing his feelings to his conscious awareness, he was able to then evaluate them against Dandy's calm response to him in the moment. Over time, James became comfortable in expressing his wishes to Dandy. He later began to do the same with his friends and foster parents.

Adlerian Therapy

Adlerian therapists view human behavior as the result of an interaction of inherited traits with the environment. Functioning is influenced by two innate motives: striving for superiority and social interest. People strive for superiority in order to continually grow and better themselves by seeking competency, belonging, and significance, not necessarily to be superior over others. As we grow from infancy, we evaluate and develop strategies to strive towards superiority. These strategies become our "lifestyle". Adlerian therapists seek to understand a client's early life and family experiences to better understand the individual's lifestyle and uncover the client's private logic. The client's behavior is viewed as purposeful and goal-directed in continued striving for superiority (Dinkmeyer & Sperry, 2000). Social interest and community feeling are crucial to positive mental health. Although social interest is innate, it must be fostered by relationships in early life. An individual with a strong sense of social interest seeks to experience belonging and usefulness in interaction with others. The emotional aspect of belonging and an overall feeling of social connectedness is referred to as community feeling. People who are isolated or disconnected from others experience poorer mental health. Adlerian therapists focus on four main tasks in therapy: development of a trusting, egalitarian therapeutic relationship; assessment of the client's lifestyle; facilitation of client self-understanding of and insight into lifestyle and conclusions about self, others, and the world; and reorientation by taking effective action to make positive changes (Dinkmeyer & Sperry, 2000).

Equines are highly motivated by social connection with others. As a herd animal, an equine perceives social connectedness to be necessity for survival. Equines who are not able to engage in regular, physical contact with other equines or who struggle to get along with other herd members often demonstrate signs of stress. Interaction with the equines can enable clients to experience social connectedness not only with their chosen equine but also with the entire herd. In EACP, clients can work towards the formation of a safe, trusting relationship with their chosen equine(s). From there, clients can explore their own family histories through observation of the herd dynamics and their experience of being a part of the herd. The client's interpretations of the herd

92 Integration of Counseling Theory

dynamics and the meaning of their experience in the herd can provide valuable information to the therapist in assessing the client's lifestyle and associated private logic. As therapy continues, the client examines his or her private logic and the attributes of the interactions with the equine(s) and identifies connections to significant early life and family experiences. The Adlerian therapist can present tentative interpretations of what the client may be experiencing through the interaction with the equine. Through this process, the client's private logic and mistaken beliefs will be uncovered. The client can then engage in reorientation by taking action to try new ways of being and interacting with the equines. These experiences can then be generalized to the client's life outside of session. The therapist can also help the client to enlarge the meaning of experiences with the equine to gain insight and self-awareness in creating a healthier lifestyle. The treatment team can facilitate the client's development of social interest through the formation of relationships with the equines. Through their interactions with the equines, clients can explore problem-solving skills to meet their own needs while balancing the needs of the equine. Furthermore, clients can engage in activities to contribute meaningfully to the equine's well-being through grooming and other care-taking activities.

Person-Centered Therapy

Person-centered therapy is a humanistic, insight-oriented, nondirective approach pioneered by Carl Rogers. A cornerstone of person-centered therapy was Rogers' inherent trust in the client to move towards growth and healing or self-actualization (Rogers, 1964). Dysfunction arises from a disconnect between an individual's self-concept and their experience interacting in the world (i.e., reality). This disconnect is referred to as incongruence. Incongruence leads to internal tension within the client as a result of this disconnect (Fall, Holden, & Marquis, 2010). Rogers identified the three therapist attributes of congruence, empathy, and unconditional positive regard as required to create a growth-promoting environment (Rogers, 1992). The therapist must be present and immediate with the client in the moment. The goal of person-centered therapy is not for the client to solve a specific problem, but instead for the client to move forward in their growth process so that they are better equipped to cope with problems. Through this process, the client will become more congruent and therefore more open to experience, have greater self-trust, a stronger internal sense of evaluation, and move towards continued growth (Corey, 2009).

As the therapeutic relationship is considered to be the primary change agent in Person-Centered Counseling, REPC's emphasis on the inclusion of the equine(s) in the therapeutic relationship in a natural environment where they are free in an organic manner is a good fit for a person-centered therapist. Equines are active participants in building this relationship, as they naturally embody Rogers' core conditions (Chardonnens, 2009). It is likely that clients will perceive these conditions of empathy, acceptance, and authenticity in the equines (Jenkins et al., 2014). The client's experience of relating to the equines can be nondirective, as the equines will approach the client without a specific agenda or directing the client towards a specific clinical outcome. Based on the equine's feedback towards the client, the client will necessarily become more congruent in their interactions with the equine in the formation of a healthy, mutually satisfying relationship (Chardonnens, 2009). Furthermore, the treatment team and the equines approach the client in the same way and are both consistent in being nondirective, present, and immediate. The person-centered therapist's clinical intentions of establishing rapport, trust, and safety are compatible with the REPC approach (Chandler et al., 2010). In a person-centered EACP session, the therapist can take a nondirective approach in allowing the client and equine(s) to establish their own relationship. All members of the treatment team, both human and equine, reflect the client's feelings, enabling the client to gain awareness and insight towards becoming congruent. The therapist can use reflective techniques to process the client's experience of the relationship and spontaneous interactions that arise (Chandler et al., 2010). In my experience, equines are very sensitive to client incongruence in session. For example, I once had a client named Amy. She was a military veteran suffering from posttraumatic stress as a result of a military sexual assault. She appeared tense at the start of the session, but repeatedly stated that she was fine. Suddenly, Captain, the herd leader, abruptly drove the other horses away from Amy. When I turned back to Amy, I asked her what she believed had happened. She stated that she had been trying to push aside an intrusive memory and tell herself that she was fine. However, the memory kept coming back and she believed that Captain could feel what was happening. From there, Amy spent the rest of the session processing the memory while Captain stood at her side. Other equines that I've interacted with over the years have had varied responses to client incongruence. Some equines will walk in-between me and the client to split us. I've witnessed others become pushy or even nippy with clients. In all these cases, the equines' feedback has been a crucial component in encouraging clients to become aware of and acknowledge their actual experiences. As the client begins to process their actual experience, I typically see the equines demonstrate behaviors that may be indicative of relaxation or stress release such as stretching, licking and chewing, or lowering their and closing their eyes. The equines' responses to these clients creates an environment of empathy, acceptance, and authenticity, helping them to feel safe.

Behavioral Therapy

Behavioral therapy is a present-focused, action-oriented approach in which the client's presenting concerns are viewed in the context of the role of their environment as an influence on an individual's behaviors. The goal of this form of therapy is to change specific, unhealthy behaviors. It is based on the belief that clients will demonstrate consistent patterns of behavior across similar types

94 Integration of Counseling Theory

of environments (Fall et al., 2010). The therapist is responsible for conducting a functional assessment to identify the environmental conditions maintaining the problem behavior. From this assessment, the therapist and client establish clear, concrete behavioral goals and assess the effectiveness of the interventions on an ongoing basis. Minimal attention is paid to past experience or gaining insight. Instead, the focus is on current functioning. Clients are expected to engage actively in session by engaging in self-monitoring in and out of session, learning and practicing coping skills, and role-playing new behaviors (Corey, 2009).

Behavioral therapists affirm the importance of the creation of an empathic, accepting therapeutic relationship. As the therapist provides positive reinforcement for the client's progress towards behavioral goals, the equine also provides reinforcement in response to the client. When the client approaches and interacts with the equine in a manner that makes the equine feels safe and comfortable, the equine is likely to respond positively towards the client by attending to the client and staying in proximity to the client. When the client approaches the equine in a manner unsuitable to the equine, the animal is likely to move away or display a behavior to indicate their discontent. Assuming the client is motivated to interact with the equine, the equine's responses will influence the client's continued use of healthy, relationship-building behaviors or the discontinuation of unhealthy behaviors. The treatment team can also use modeling to demonstrate specific skills or behaviors with the equine so the client can learn assertiveness skills. The equines can also serve as a model to the clients. I have had many clients observe the herd and identify strategies for themselves to use. For example, I once had a client observe that an equine had become stuck in a fence and could not get himself free. As I approached the equine to assist, he became calm and remained calm while I removed him from the fence. The client used him as a model for remaining calm and using problem-solving skills during anxiety-provoking situations in her own life.

Due to the experiential nature of EACP, clients are often more engaged and motivated to learn and practice different skills. This increased interest and motivation may result in a higher success rate in generalizing use of these new skills to experiences outside of session. The therapist may choose specific interventions such as relaxation training, systematic desensitization, exposure therapies, Eye Movement Rapid Desensitization (EMDR), social skills training, and mindfulness. When practicing mindfulness or relaxation skills, an equine will often respond to any changes in the client's body language or physical tension. This feedback can assist the client in evaluating the effectiveness of their use of the particular skill that they are practicing. For example, if a client is practicing a mindfulness exercise but the equine remains agitated, the client may then become aware of a distracting thought interfering with their ability to be fully present. The client can then address the distraction and proceed with the activity. When using exposure therapies such as EMDR, the presence of the equine can feel comforting and help the client stay grounded during the session. Clients can practice different types of social skills and mindfulness skills through interaction with the equine. For example, a young child struggling to get along with peers might be taught to recognize the different equine body language cues and what they mean. This intervention can be very helpful in facilitating the client's development of social skills and self-monitoring skills to notice similar cues in people and understand how his or her behavior impacts someone else's behavior or response. A client can also practice identifying and setting boundaries with an equine and generalize these skills and experiences to real-life situations with other people. Clients can also learn to practice self-monitoring strategies by identifying different activity goals with the equine and observing both their responses and the equine's behavioral responses during the activity. These self-monitoring skills can then be generalized and used to meet other behavioral goals outside of session. In the REPC model, it is important that the behavioral therapist does not become overly task-focused to the point that the equine's reactions to the client are missed and the equine becomes more of a tool to practice with than a sentient, self-directed participant in the relationship.

Cognitive-Behavioral Therapies

Cognitive-behavioral therapy is a directive, present-centered approach. There are several different approaches that I will review under the umbrella term "cognitive-behavioral therapy". The most prominent ones are Albert Ellis' Rational Emotive Behavior Therapy (REBT), Aaron Beck's Cognitive Therapy, and Donald Meichenbaum's Cognitive-Behavioral Therapy. All these approaches share a common belief that the root of dysfunction is the result of disturbances in the client's cognitive processes (i.e., faulty thinking) and that clients are best helped by changing their cognitions to create changes in affect and behavior. Additionally, these approaches all utilize a structured approach to reality testing and exploring a client's faulty thought patterns. These approaches differ in the value placed on the therapeutic relationship, the therapist's specific approach to changing faulty thinking, and the therapist's overall view of faulty thinking (Corey, 2009).

Different cognitive-behavioral therapists have differing views of the importance of the therapeutic relationship. Most, like Aaron Beck, emphasize the importance of the relationship and partnership with the client in providing more effective therapy. However, Albert Ellis minimized the importance of the therapeutic relationship in REBT, instead viewing the therapist like a teacher (Corey, 2009). This belief runs counter to the REPC model, especially because the equines approach clients to establish a mutual relationship and cannot perceive themselves to be a "teacher" to the client. Due to this basic philosophical discrepancy, therapists may find it harder to integrate REBT with REPC. It is expected that the client is likely to use the same maladaptive beliefs and negative thought patterns in understanding and interpreting interactions with the equine. Therefore, the therapist can explore and challenge these thought

96 Integration of Counseling Theory

patterns as they are occurring in the present moment between the client and equine. Therapists of different cognitive-behavioral theories will use different ways of identifying, processing, and challenging these beliefs in session. A cognitive therapist may choose to help the client identify the core beliefs and associated automatic thoughts and cognitive distortions. Next, the therapist can assist the client to explore and modify negative schemas in the context of the client's experience with the equine (Beck & Dozois, 2011). An REBT therapist may dispute the client's irrational beliefs or teach the client to change his or her language about the equine's intent in responding to the client in a way that the client perceives to be rejection. In addition, the therapist can enlarge the meaning of the client's experience in session with the equine to the client's present problems occurring outside of session. In using a role-play intervention, the client may find it easier to practice role-playing a new skill or behavior with the equine rather than another person (Chandler et al., 2010). The example of the cocked hoof described in Chapter 3 is a good example of how cognitive-behavioral therapy approaches may be used in identifying and changing faulty thinking.

Gestalt Therapy

Gestalt therapy is an existential, process-based approach in which the therapist focuses on the client's relationship to the environment. This approach is inherently relational and therefore allows for natural integration with REPC (Yontef, 2002). The phenomenological focus of therapy facilitates an understanding and awareness of the client's experience in the here and now, including what they are presently experiencing and how they are experiencing it. Change is expected to occur as a result of increasing self-awareness. Experimentation is a crucial part of Gestalt therapy in order to increase a client's awareness of what they are doing and how they are doing it. An understanding of the client's present-moment experience is viewed as much more important than understanding why they are having the experience in the first place. Gestalt therapists also focus on illuminating the client's "unfinished business" or unexpressed feelings that affect the client in the present moment. By gaining increased self-awareness, Gestalt therapists help clients assume responsibility and ownership over their experiences and develop skills to meet their needs in a healthy way. In order to accomplish these goals, a Gestalt therapist will help a client gain awareness of their sensory experiences and nonverbal body language. The Gestalt therapist can also focus on aspects of the client's language in processing their experiences interacting with the equines in the here and now (Corey, 2009). Finally, a relational approach to Gestalt therapy enables the therapist to view the client's relationship with both the equine(s) and human treatment team as a microcosm or "hologram" reflecting client's life outside of session (Yontef, 2002, p. 32).

As equines are highly attuned to nonverbal body language, they can naturally and organically open the door to processing the client's body language and

Integration of Counseling Theory 97

associated feelings and sensory experiences. The equine's response to the client's body language can help the client gain awareness of their feelings. The therapist might ask the client to interpret how the equine may perceive the client's body language. The therapist can also draw the client's attention to incongruencies in the client's language and experience based on the equine's response to the client. This type of processing can facilitate the client's increasing awareness of their feelings and experiences in the present moment. The Gestalt therapist can also facilitate the client's experimentation in interactions with the equines. Kirby (2010) emphasized the importance of not only the client's relationship with the treatment and equines, but also the treatment team's relationship with the equines. The client's experience of a safe, trusting relationship with the treatment team and equine can enable the client to feel safer when engaging in these experiments. The presence of the equine can be grounding during experiments in which the client may imagine a threatening encounter. Alternatively, the client can use experiments with the equine to uncover feelings and experiences in the here and now. More details on integrating Gestalt therapy with EACP can be found in Kirby (2010).

My session with Dana illustrates the use of experimentation in EACP. On this particular day, Dana was processing her social anxiety and difficulty expressing her needs to others. I asked Dana if she would be willing to try an experiment in which she would try to move the herd of horses from one of the pastures to the other using only her body language. As the experiment progressed, Dana began to identify feelings of anxiety and insecurity. She reported feeling "silly" while using exaggerated movements to herd the equines across the pasture. Dana later discussed feelings of inhibition in the present and associated sensory indicators of anxiety such as a tightness in her chest. As Dana continued to process her present-moment experiences, she gained increasing self-awareness.

Existential Therapy

An existential approach to psychotherapy endorses the notion that people are free and responsible for our own choices and actions (Corey, 2009). Clients are encouraged to reflect on life, recognize their choices, and make decisions in order to live a meaningful existence (Corey, 2009). An existential therapist focuses on the alleviation of feelings of emptiness and the creation of personal meaning through the development of increased self-awareness of the inner self (Bugental & Bracke, 1992). Although specific approaches to existential therapy may differ, all share a focus on the ambiguity and uncertainty of existence (Correia, Cooper, & Berdondini, 2015). The therapist focuses on understanding the client's subjective experience and client's process in the session (rather than specific content or interpretations). As clients develop greater self-awareness, they experience increased feelings of control, responsibility, and choice in living authentic, meaningful lives. Through this process, clients can clarify their own personal values and decide what purpose and meaning they want for their lives. Clients work towards the creation and acceptance of their own personal identity and learn how to form healthy relationships with others. Finally, clients work towards an acceptance of normal anxiety as a part of facing life's events and an acceptance of death and nonbeing (Corey, 2009). Corey (2009) summarized Bugental's (1990) three main tasks of existential therapy: becoming more present and aware of limiting patterns, confronting anxieties that have been avoided, and redefining identity and meaning in their lives.

Interaction with equines can facilitate the client's increased awareness of becoming present and identifying patterns that interfere with their ability to be present. Additionally, the presence of the equines can be grounding and soothing as clients work to identify and confront their anxieties. As clients process their interactions with the equine, they gain more self-awareness of their experiences in the present moment (Chandler et al., 2010). Through the formation of the relationship with the equines, the client can explore and gain self-awareness in the creation of their self-identity. Oftentimes, I will ask clients a simple question: who do you want this equine to see you as? This question can help clients in the process of clarifying self-identity and values. As one of the most crucial tasks of an existential therapist is to model authenticity and presence, equines are natural models for these ways of being (Fall et al., 2010). Engaging in different activities with the equines can help clients become more aware of the freedom that they have in making choices and taking responsibility. Furthermore, clients can observe and process the concepts of freedom and choice in their observation of the equines' behaviors and responses to the client in session.

Choice Theory and Reality Therapy

Therapists practicing the Choice Theory approach believe that all people have choice in how they act, think, and live their lives (Bradley, 2014). All people have five basic needs: survival, love and belonging, power, freedom, and fun. In addition, all behavior is comprised of four parts: acting, thinking, feeling, and physiology (Bradley, 2014). Our behavior is goal-directed in trying to meet all our needs and wants.

In Reality Therapy, the therapist takes a present-focused approach and helps clients take more responsibility for their lives. These therapists operate from the belief that people experience the most unhappiness when they experience dissatisfaction or disconnectedness in their relationships. The client's quality world is comprised of everything that the client believes leads to happiness and satisfaction (Bradley, 2014). Through reality therapy, clients learn to regain control to cope with these experiences and make choices to change our lives.

The REPC approach is a good fit with Choice Theory and Reality Therapy given the shared emphasis on the importance of satisfying relationships. Therapists practicing EACP from a Choice Theory perspective can facilitate clients' exploration of ways to meet their five basic needs. As survival is a universal physiological need among all beings, both human and equine, clients can process the ways that equines work to meet this need and the choices that they make as prey animals to survive. Clients can also explore feelings of love and belonging in processing their interactions and relationships with members of the herd. Oftentimes, clients who feel disconnected have experienced newfound feelings of belonging with the equines. The relationship formed with the equines can serve as part of the client's quality world in helping them learn to establish satisfying relationships. The equines' empathy and lack of judgment enables clients to process and evaluate their own behaviors and how they are being received by the equines in the present moment. These experiences also enable the client to identify their choices and take responsibility for their contributions in their relationship with the equine. Clients can learn lessons through the interactions with the equines that they can then generalize to resolving day-to-day problems (Bradley, 2014). As EACP progresses, the therapist can use the WDEP (wants, doing, evaluation, and planning) system to help the client create meaningful change outside of session. For a more detailed review of the implementation of Choice Theory and Reality Therapy with EACP, see Cameron and Robey (2013) and Minatrea and Wesley (2008).

I once worked with a Vietnam veteran named Bill who had struggled with feelings of loneliness, isolation, and depression for years. Based on his experiences in Vietnam, Bill had developed major depression and posttraumatic stress. He felt mistrustful of most people and had few people connections. He chose a quiet, calm equine named Sammy. Bill spent much of his time brushing and providing nurturing to Sammy. As their relationship grew, Bill said in one particularly meaningful session that he believed the "connecting part" of his brain had turned back on and he wanted to start trying to connect with people again. He stated that he felt love towards Sammy and that his self-imposed isolation served to allow him to survive in what he perceived to be a hostile world. Through the course of Bill's time with Sammy, he began to try new activities such as leading Sammy or getting Sammy to follow him. Bill experienced a sense of power in feeling respected by Sammy and successful in accomplishing these new activities. Bill also experienced freedom and fun in deciding what types of activities he wanted to try with Sammy and in observing Sammy's sometimes comical responses or playfulness in response to Bill's requests.

Constructivist Therapies

There are several different theoretical approaches that fall under the category of constructivism such as Solution-Focused Therapy, Narrative Therapy, and Mahoney's Constructivist Psychotherapy (Fall et al., 2010). Although these approaches diverge in certain areas, especially the actual practice of therapy itself, they share similar philosophical underpinnings. People create worldviews based on their unique perception of the world around them. Clients seek therapy in order to reduce pain and suffering. From a constructivist approach,

100   Integration of Counseling Theory

positive mental health is comprised of feelings of hope, use of problem-solving, well-defined flexible creation of meaning, balance and active engagement in life, and support of freedom and well-being for both self and others (Fall et al., 2010). Change occurs as clients acquire and organize information about self, others, and the world. The therapist focuses on helping the client identify who they are and where they want to go. From there, clients identify their own strengths and how they can be used to power change. All constructivist therapists work towards creating a safe environment, working to understand the client's views and strengths, encouraging change, and promoting client self-determination (Fall et al., 2010).

By integrating constructivist therapy with EACP, clients can work towards greater self-identity and associated strengths in interaction with the equines. The therapist will work to understand the client's unique perceptions and worldview in interacting with the equines and in processing the client's life outside of session. The client's interactions with equines and the processing of those interactions can help reveal the client's unique perceptions and worldview. Through interaction and different activities with the equines, clients are presented with opportunities to experiment with new ways of doing things. The nature of equine behavior presents opportunities for discussion related to power dynamics in helping the client to gain more insight, and therefore more choice, in how they live their lives (Fall et al., 2010).

Family Systems Therapy

Family systems theory is conceptual framework (rather than a set of techniques) in which a client's interactions, relationships, and context in their environment is primary to understanding the client (Coyne & Liddle, 1992). There are several specific types of family therapy. I will review general themes across different types of family therapy. Individual clients are best understood in the context of their experiences and interactions in their family system (Corey, 2009). The client's behaviors and symptoms are influenced by the family system and the functioning of the family system is influenced by the client (Corey, 2009). Family systems can take many different forms but are a universal human experience. All family systems function to help its members survive and stay healthy (Fall et al., 2010). Healthy families promote the mutual welfare of the system and its individual members. The system also works to maintain equilibrium based on subconscious family "rules". When this equilibrium is threatened, the system works to "correct" and reroute back to homeostasis. Systems therapy does not require the participation of all family members in each session.

An equine herd offers a similar function to a human family. The purpose of the herd is to keep its members safe and healthy. Additionally, one can easily observe differences between a healthy herd, in which the equines appear relaxed and harmonious, and an unhealthy herd marked by excessive conflict and aggression. Equines also work to maintain homeostasis in the herd. The establishment of herd "rules" helps the herd maintain equilibrium through the establishment of a herd system, which dictates the nature of interactions among herd members. Even groups of stallions have been found to establish a stable system in order to minimize conflict and aggression and increase cohesion among the herd members. The introduction of a new herd member or the injury or illness of existing herd member often threatens the herd's equilibrium, which often results in increased conflict or aggressive behaviors. Observation of or interaction with the equines can elicit memories, thoughts, and feelings related to a client's experiences in their current family or family of origin. The interconnectedness of human families is illustrated in the functioning of the equine herd. The client can observe the herd members' roles, boundaries, rules, and communication styles to process and gain insight into their own family functioning and experience within the family. Additionally, the client's experience in the herd can help the client to process thoughts and feelings arising in the present moment as part of the equines' herd "family".

Chapter 8

Practice of Equine-Assisted Counseling and Psychotherapy Across the Lifespan

Mental Health Needs of Children and Adolescents

It is estimated that between 13–20% of U.S. children are diagnosed with a mental, emotional, or behavioral disorder each year (Ghandour et al., 2019). According to the Center for Disease Control (2019), common youth diagnoses for children and adolescents in the United States include attention-deficit hyperactivity disorder, anxiety and depression (which have increased steadily over the last several years), oppositional defiant disorder, conduct disorder, Tourette syndrome, obsessive-compulsive disorder, and posttraumatic stress disorder. It should be noted that it is likely much of the data collected primarily focused on youth ages 12 to 17.

Whereas anxiety and depression are more common in adolescents, behavioral problems are more common in young children. In young children (ages two to eight), one in six has a diagnosed mental, behavioral, or developmental disorder. The most common presenting concerns in young children that may indicate a need for mental health care include frequent tantrums, irritability, excessive fear or worry, somatic complaints (e.g., stomachaches or headaches), inability to sit quietly, sleep problems, nightmares, peer difficulties, school problems, or compulsive behaviors (National Institute of Mental Health, 2019a). Warning signs that may indicate the presence of mental health problems in adolescents include loss of interest, low energy, sleep problems, isolation, weight-related concern, excessive diet or exercise, self-harm behaviors, substance use or abuse, risky behaviors, suicidality, highly elevated energy, or delusions (National Institute of Mental Health, 2019a). Additionally, more than two thirds of children in the United States experience a traumatic event by age 16 (Substance Abuse and Mental Health Services Administration, 2017b). Evidence of trauma or neglect can manifest as acute stress disorder, adjustment disorders, reactive attachment disorder, or posttraumatic stress disorder.

Children and Animals

All over the world, children demonstrate an innate curiosity and interest in animals (Melson & Fine, 2010). In some cases, children prefer caring for pets more

Practice Across the Lifespan 103

than other human family members (Bekoff, 2007). Children, especially children who have experienced trauma, may perceive greater support from animals than from people (Bekoff, 2007). Regular interaction with animals increases a child's self-confidence, empathy, and social development. These interactions can also help children develop an understanding that others can experience different thoughts and feelings than they do (Bekoff, 2007). These valuable social skills, learned through interactions with animals, can later be generalized in forming relationships with other children.

In equine-assisted counseling and psychotherapy (EACP), all children are likely to perceive Rogers' core conditions of empathy, acceptance, and authenticity from the equines during the session (Jenkins et al., 2014). Therefore, the addition of a therapy animal in child psychotherapy sessions can help the child feel supported and create a bridge in building the relationship between the child and the treatment team. The equines can also provide certain things that the therapist likely cannot offer, such as physical affection (Chardonnens, 2009). As interaction with therapy animals has been demonstrated to produce positive feelings and reduce anxiety, the presence of the equines may also help children to feel more at ease and relaxed during sessions (Halm, 2008; Kaminski et al., 2002; Sobo et al., 2006). The presence of a therapy animal can help children express their feelings. Children may be more inclined to speak to or in the presence of therapy animals (Chardonnens, 2009). Additionally, children may feel more comfortable expressing feelings by projecting them onto the equines. Other times, children may feel more comfortable expressing thoughts, feelings, and experiences to the equines rather than directly to the treatment team (Reichert, 1998).

An EACP approach may be particularly beneficial for children who have experienced trauma or neglect and may therefore suffer from posttraumatic stress or reactive attachment disorder. These children often experience impaired brain functioning as a result of experiences that interfered with or inhibited the developmental processes. Because the most critical developmental periods occur during childhood, trauma sustained during this time is more likely to have a stronger negative impact (Perry, 2009). A child deprived of needed relational experiences critical to early life development many go on to develop reactive attachment disorder or experience other forms of lasting impairment in relating to others or overall functioning. Healthy relationships are critical in preventing and healing from the adverse effects of trauma. These children may struggle to process trauma in talking-oriented treatment approaches (Kemp, Signal, Botros, Taylor, & Prentice, 2014). Therefore, EACP is a good alternative for these children. EACP has been suggested to be helpful for children with PTSD who struggle to self-regulate (Yorke, 2010). The goals for these children are no different than those in talking-oriented treatment—sequential focus on developing self-regulation, followed by improvement and strengthening of healthy relationships, and then learning behavioral and cognitive skills (Perry, 2009). The establishment of a safe relationship with equines, followed by appropriate activities and interactions, merely helps facilitate meeting all of

104 Practice Across the Lifespan

the afore-mentioned goals for the child that struggles to process trauma in a talk-oriented treatment approach.

After conducting a comprehensive literature review, Lentini and Knox (2015) and Kendall and colleagues (2015) concluded that equine interventions are beneficial for child and adolescent clients with mental health concerns, especially in the case of at-risk youth and others with histories of neglect, abuse, and eating disorders. Other researchers have suggested EACP benefits include providing opportunities for care-taking activities, socialization, self-esteem development, and companionship and affection (Rothe, Vega, Torres, Soler, & Pazos, 2005). Researchers and clinicians practicing diverse models of EACP have found it to be beneficial in improving behavioral and emotional problems in children and adolescents (Schultz, Remick-Barlow, & Robbins, 2007; Trotter, Chandler, Goodwin-Bond, & Casey, 2008). Regarding trauma, EACP interventions have been beneficial for children and adolescents who have experienced trauma and suffer from posttraumatic stress in reducing symptoms of depression, anxiety, and trauma-related distress (Kemp et al., 2014; Signal, Taylor, Botros, Prentice, & Lazarus2013; McCullough et al., 2015; Naste et al., 2018). For young children, including equines in play-based approaches can provide the benefits of EACP while meeting the child's developmental needs (Sheade, 2019a, 2019b; Sheade & Box, 2014; VanFleet & Thompson, 2010).

Equine-Partnered Play Therapy: EACP for Young Children

There is significant evidence demonstrating the effectiveness of play therapy in addressing a wide range of mental health concerns for young children (Ray & McCullough, 2016). Play is the natural language of children and a way to communicate their experiences, feelings, self-concept, wishes, wants, reactions, and needs (Landreth, 2012). Axline (1969) developed the first nondirective play therapy approach based on the work of Carl Rogers. Building on Axline's work, Landreth (2012) developed an approach called Child-Centered Play Therapy (CCPT). A hallmark of the CCPT approach is the belief in the child's innate ability to move towards growth and healing, therefore the child is allowed to lead during the session. Rather than simply a set of techniques, CCPT is a philosophy for relating to young children.

Grounded in the philosophy of CCPT, Equine-Partnered Play Therapy (EPPT) is a model of EACP that endorses the belief that play is universal among children worldwide (Axline, 1969). In EPPT, the CCPT model has been adapted to move the playroom setting outdoors and invite equines into the play session. Like, CCPT, the EPPT model is based on Piaget's (1951) conclusion that young children experience the world in concrete ways and that talking alone is insufficient for them to process and express themselves in the world. Including equines in play therapy can enable children to not only express themselves through play, it also allows the children to project their feelings onto

Practice Across the Lifespan   105

the equine. Children in EPPT often experience benefits such as improved emotional regulation, development of coping and social skills, enhanced empathy, improved self-control, increased confidence, and opportunities to provide and receive nurturing (Levinson & Mallon, 1997; Sheade, 2019a, 2019b; Sheade & Box, 2014).

A trusting relationship with a therapist who embodies the characteristics of warmth, genuineness, and empathy is crucial to the creation of an emotionally safe environment where the child can feel free to explore and express him/herself openly (Landreth, 2012). In EPPT, this relationship is extended to also include the equine specialist and the equines. Like the therapist, the equine specialist is trained in basic facilitative responses to relate to the child in positive a way. Equines respond to a child in much the same way as the treatment team should strive to, by focusing on the child in the present moment as opposed to focusing on the child's "problem".

The presence of the equines can help the child remain grounded in the present moment (Landreth, 2012; Levinson & Mallon, 1997). With the equines, the child has the opportunity to communicate and form a relationship in ways other than talking. The inclusion of the equines in a session provides opportunities for social interaction and expression beyond that which is possible with toys alone (Levinson, 1962; Nielsen & Delude, 1989). For example, the child can engage in activities with the equine that may be uncomfortable or inappropriate for the human members of the treatment team to engage in, such as a providing and receiving physical affection (Karol, 2007). Interactions with the equines enable the child to develop social skills, empathy, and increased self-awareness without feeling judged or criticized. A child who struggles with impulsive behavior may initially run up to the equines out of excitement. In most cases, a well-trained equine will simply move (or run) away. This response provides valuable, immediate feedback to the child regarding their behavior and its impact on someone else (i.e., the equine). As most children are highly motivated to interact and form relationships with the equines, the child will gradually develop enhanced self-awareness and empathy (Sheade, 2019a, 2019b). Over time, the child will understand that the equine has an emotional response to the child's behavior and the child will learn valuable self-monitoring skills to reduce impulsive behavior. After "practicing" new behaviors with the equine, the child is then likely to generalize these experiences and begin relating in healthier ways to others outside of session. I have heard many reports from parents who first witnessed this change occur between the child and a family pet who had previously avoided the child, followed by improvements with siblings and peers.

The inclusion of equines in the session also provides opportunities for the treatment team to gain information about the child and build a relationship with the child. By observing the child's interactions with the equines, the treatment team can better understand the child's thoughts and feelings about self, others, and the world, and better understand the content of the child's symbolic play (Parish-Plass, 2013). Additionally, the child can play out specific themes with the equine to explore relational dynamics and express themselves before inviting the human treatment team to participate. In this way, the equines' presence can serve as a bridge to connect the child and human treatment team. These relationships, once established between the child and all members of the treatment team, then become a vehicle to facilitate positive change in the child.

There are a number of considerations in providing an emotionally and physically safe environment for all involved, both human and equine. First and foremost, it is essential for the treatment team to establish clear and consistent limits for the child's interaction with the equine (Levinson, 1962; Sheade, 2019a). I have found limit-setting methods traditionally employed in CCPT to be very useful in EPPT for fostering a healthy relationship between the child and the equines (Sheade, 2019a). Facilitative responses used in CCPT are adapted to include the equines and observations of the child's relationship with the equines. (For more information on facilitative responses, see Chapter 6.) There are a number of considerations in the creation of the physical play area to be used in the EPPT model of EACP such as privacy, materials and construction, inclusion of additional toys, and physical comfort for all involved (Sheade, 2019a).

Finally, there are also a number of considerations with respect to the equines participating in EPPT. *Equines should be carefully selected based on size and temperament.* Given the smaller size of most children in play therapy, I prefer to include miniature horses rather than ponies or full-size equines. Miniature equines pose less of a physical safety risk to a small child and will likely be perceived as less intimidating by the child. All equines participating in the EPPT should be thoroughly desensitized to the toys (and the ways in which the toys may be played with) prior to participating in EPPT. Given the high energy and intensity of some play sessions, I recommend inclusion of a pair of equines, rather than a single equine. In this way, the equines can communicate with each other and provide and receive social support. It is critical that the equines have a strong trusting relationship with the treatment team, especially the equine specialist. In my work in EPPT, I have often experienced that the equines will stand close to a member of the treatment team when they are uncertain of a child's behavior (i.e., throwing a ball) rather than choosing to leave the session. In this way, the equine was able to stay engaged in the session while receiving the needed reassurance from the human team member. In this same vein, it is essential that the equines have adequate space to move away from the child's play and have an "escape route" to get there in order to provide for the safety needs of all involved.

EACP for Adolescents

Adolescents may seek EACP for a number of reasons such as bullying, low self-esteem, or depression (Ecken, 2012). Participation in EACP can lead to positive changes such as improvements in self-image, self-control, trust, and life satisfaction (Bachi, Terkel, & Teichman, 2011). The biggest barriers in providing psychotherapy to adolescents include developmental immaturity, perceived stigma of psychotherapy, and feeling forced into participation (Oetzel & Scherer, 2003). An initial challenge in working with many adolescents is the establishment of a strong, trusting therapeutic relationship. Adolescents are unlikely to participate willingly in continued psychotherapy if they do not perceive a positive relationship with the therapist (Fernández, Krause, & Pérez, 2016). Therefore, EACP is well-situated to provide a low-stigma environment where the adolescent can first form a relationship with the equines that can then be used as a bridge to formation of a relationship with the human treatment team members. The equine's inherent qualities of empathy and genuineness can have a significant impact on helping adolescents feel safe and engaged. Many adolescents struggle with feelings of loneliness and insecurity. The relationship with the equine can provide a sense of acceptance and comfort. In my experience, some of the adolescents who present as the angriest and most disengaged at the start of EACP turn out to be the ones who demonstrate the highest levels of physical affection with their chosen equine and report the strongest emotional bonds with the equine. Adolescents are likely to feel more comfortable and have more trust in the therapist in the presence of a therapy animal (Chandler, 2017). Witnessing the treatment team interact with the equines enables the adolescent to have a window into seeing who they are as people, not just as a treatment team (Oetzel & Scherer, 2003).

Many adolescents are unaware of their own problematic behaviors and oftentimes disagree about the need for psychotherapy. The presence of the equines can serve as a motivator to encourage participation in the counseling process (Karol, 2007). Furthermore, many adolescents may find EACP more appealing as it does not require them to talk or process verbally (Waite & Bourke, 2013). Much can be gained through interaction with the equines, processing of equines' feedback, and subsequent integration of feedback into changing behaviors. Therefore, it is important that the treatment team does not pressure the adolescent client to talk and instead trusts the therapeutic process. Allowing the adolescent to choose their own experience and activities for the session can promote increased autonomy and increase engagement (Oetzel & Scherer, 2003). More often than not, providing this choice enables the adolescent to have positive experiences that can become internalized and improve the adolescent's overall way of functioning and creation of meaning.

Adolescents cognitively straddle between the concreteness of childhood and increasing abstractness of adulthood (Oetzel & Scherer, 2003). For this reason, they often fall between the cracks when therapists apply approaches that do not match their developmental level. Interaction with the equines enables the adolescent client to process and express themselves in both concrete and abstract ways based on their developmental level. Furthermore, the adolescent's interaction and processing of interactions with the equines can reveal their current

108 Practice Across the Lifespan

level of functioning and associated indications of potential maladjustment. From there, the treatment team can identify ways to tailor activities and processing with the adolescent to best meet their needs. In my experience, adolescents, especially younger adolescents, tend to require more structure and opportunities to actively engage in specific types of exercises and activities than older adolescents or adults.

My sessions with Zach are illustrative of the power of EACP in working with adolescents. Zach was a 16-year-old who was on the verge of being placed in long-term residential care. He did well in school and with peers, but frequently got into intense verbal conflict with his mother that often ended in Zach punching holes in the wall. When Zach arrived for his first session, he informed me that he did not like horses. He stated that they were ugly and smelly and that he wanted nothing to do with them. He continued to state that he did not need therapy and that his mother was "crazy". He begrudgingly accompanied me to the pasture to meet the equines. Once in the pasture, Zach appeared nervous and kept his back against the barn. Throughout the session, one of the miniature equines, Cuddlebug, had been observing Zach. As the hour progressed, she gradually made her way closer and closer until she was only a foot away. Zach appeared suspicious and asked if she was going to bite him. Cuddlebug moved in closer to me and I began to stroke her neck. She slowly closed her eyes and lowered her head. Zach began to move away from the wall and asked if he could pet her. As he reached his hand towards Cuddlebug, she took a step towards him. Zach smiled broadly and exclaimed "she likes me!" By the end of the session, Zach's affect had completely changed. As we went to leave the pasture, he said he was willing to come back the following week stating that if that "little horse" liked me, he was willing to give me a chance, too.

Adolescents have unique mental health concerns that often arise in EACP. As suicide is the second leading cause of death among individuals ages 10–24 years old in the United States (National Institute of Mental Health, 2019b) and among individuals 15–24 years old worldwide (World Health Organization, 2019), it is crucial to assess past and current suicidal ideation in adolescent clients. In my work with adolescents with suicidal ideation, the presence of the equines can be comforting and soothing. Many adolescent clients report that it is easier to discuss upsetting thoughts or feelings in the presence of the equine. Furthermore, interaction with the equines can help clients learn and practice new calming skills to manage negative feelings. Bauducco's (2012) study supported EACP as a beneficial intervention for adolescent girls with suicidal ideation.

Another prominent mental health concern in adolescence is non-suicidal self-injury (NSSI), which is defined as "the intentional, self-inflicted damage to the surface of the body without suicidal intent, which is not socially sanctioned" (Brown & Plener, 2017, p. 19). Recent studies estimate the prevalence of NSSI to range between 17% and 60% for adolescents (Brown & Plener, 2017) worldwide and equally among both sexes (Swannell, Martin, Page, Hasking, &

St John, 2014). Many clients who engage in self-harm experienced childhoods characterized by physical abuse, emotional abuse, or neglect by their primary caregivers. The behavior may be triggered by intrusive memories of attachment injuries and criticism. This behavior can also reflect the client's attempt to self-regulate by gaining attention or raising oxytocin levels (Cozolino, 2016). These clients can gain this attention (and possible oxytocin increases) in healthy ways through interaction with the equines including positive physical touch. This interaction may raise both oxytocin and endorphins, resulting in feelings of safety and warmth. Furthermore, as self-harm behaviors are believed to release endorphins, which decrease anxiety and increase sense of calm, interaction with equines can help clients find healthy ways to elicit these feelings by replacing self-destructive behaviors with more adaptive ones (Cozolino, 2016). Connection with equines can also to reduce distress by creating a safe place to name and share these feelings (Cozolino, 2016).

Adolescents, especially younger adolescents, experience much difficulty with emotional regulation. This difficulty is exacerbated in adolescents with a high fear of rejection from others (Silvers et al., 2012). The nonjudgmental and accepting nature of equines can enable adolescents to feel safer and to build trust not only with the equines but also with the treatment team. The clear and objective feedback from the equine in response to the adolescent can help him or her evaluate their own current level of self-regulation. Furthermore, the desire to maintain and deepen the relationship with the equine can serve as a strong motivating factor for the adolescent in learning to regulate their emotions. The treatment team can facilitate activities between the adolescent and equine, such as mindfulness exercises, specifically designed to help the adolescent to become more self-aware and learn strategies to self-regulate.

EACP for Adults

There is well-established research on psychotherapy approaches and best practices in working with adult clients. However, for many of the adults seeking EACP, these approaches are insufficient or ineffective. Many of the adults I have seen in my practice initiate services due to discomfort with traditional office-based approaches or dissatisfaction with the results of traditional therapy. Others state that they initiated EACP because they "love" horses and believe EACP will be a better fit for them. Adult clients have much to gain from EACP not only in treating mental health concerns but also in improving life and coping skills, increasing self-awareness, developing of healthier thought patterns, forming more satisfying personal relationships, experiencing professional enrichment, and improving self-esteem and self-concept (Torbett, 2017).

It has been my experience that many adults seeking therapy are experiencing the continued effects of adverse childhood experiences. For these adults, EACP can be particularly powerful, as they can process and relate to the equine in ways other than talking to resolve childhood trauma (Karol, 2007).

I have worked with several adult clients who experienced emotional abuse or neglect as children. Many of these clients form strong attachments to their chosen equine. As their sessions progress, these clients often assign characteristics of protectiveness, nurturing, or mothering to their equine. As a result of the establishment of an emotionally safe, trusting relationship with the equine, these clients can also experience a healing, reparative relationship, much like the one that can form in office-based psychotherapy between client and therapist (Badenoch, 2008; Cozolino, 2016).

For other clients, the relationship with the equine can provide a valuable source of social support and acceptance. Older adults can be particularly susceptible feelings of isolation and loneliness as a result of changing levels of socialization and overall activity due to retirement or increasing physical and cognitive limitations. Even brief, weekly interactions with a therapy animal can reduce loneliness in older adults (Banks & Banks, 2002). As many military veteran clients feel isolated and detached from others as a result of posttraumatic stress, depression, or moral injury, interaction with equines can help them experience a sense of reconnection, reconstruct sense of self-identity, and feel a sense of social support, acceptance, and comfort. For both types of clients, interaction with equines can elicit positive feelings that the client may struggle to experience elsewhere and provide motivation to engage in more activities.

Finally, adults can benefit from the potential for more abstract processing in EACP sessions. As the client interacts with the equines, the treatment team can help facilitate the identification of patterns and parallels between the client's interactions with the equine and struggles in both their intra- and interpersonal relationships. I have witnessed some of the most powerful "a-ha" moments with high-functioning adult clients. I began my work with Kate, a principal at a large school district, after Kate realized that her accumulating work stress was creating unmanageable anxiety and intermittent anxiety attacks. During her first session, Kate selected a gentle paint gelding named Henry. Kate identified Henry's calm demeanor as a welcome contrast to the chaos and stress among the students and staff at her school. During Kate's third session, she decided to try haltering Henry. Not knowing how to put the halter on, Kate froze. As the halter balanced precariously on one ear, Henry shook his head and the halter came tumbling off. Kate was frustrated and stated that she could feel the familiar signs of an anxiety attack coming on. Henry then stepped over the halter and proceeded to urinate right on top of it. Kate burst out laughing and exclaimed "That's it! Henry just took away all the pressure because I'm certainly not going to put the halter on him now!" As her processing continued, Kate realized that she did in fact feel too much pressure to be perfect and to be in control of everything and everyone. Her need to be perfect caused her to freeze in trying to halter Henry and in her panic attacks when she felt overwhelmed at school. She also realized that her need for "perfection" was likely impacting her staff and resulting in low morale. From that point forward, Kate made a point of exploring her perfectionism in both her interactions with

Henry and in analyzing her anxiety at school. She slowly began to implement changes not only in herself but also in her responses to the staff and students at her school. At the conclusion of EACP, Kate discussed her belief in its benefits of coming to her "a-ha" moments more quickly. She said that EACP helped her put "two and two together" in a way that she might never have achieved in an office setting. She reported that she had spent years in previous therapy to change her thought patterns, but until Henry helped her connect her thoughts to her emotions and somatic sensations, she never realized the negative impact of her perfectionism and the role it had on her overall well-being and that of those around her.

Chapter 9

Counseling and Psychotherapy Formats in Equine-Assisted Counseling and Psychotherapy

There are several different formats that can be used to provide equine-assisted counseling and psychotherapy (EACP) such as individual, group, couple/marriage, or family. Each approach has unique benefits and challenges. Researchers and clinicians have implemented EACP in different formats with a variety of presenting client concerns. The decision of which format to use should be based on the nature of the client's presenting concerns, treatment goals, and the therapist's clinical judgment or theoretical orientation. For some clients, a combination of approaches may be appropriate based on setting, client's needs, and availability of different treatment team facilitators to maintain the approach's therapeutic boundaries. In sessions that involve more than a single client, it is important to maintain the equine's role as a valuable, sentient participant interacting in the relationship, just as in individual counseling. The equine should never be "used" as a tool to simply create a "metaphor" or become an obstacle or challenge for the couple, family, or group to overcome. As the human-equine relationship is not the primary relationship in these formats, as in individual counseling, it can be tricky to strike the balance between maintaining the focus on the relationship among the human clients without minimizing the equine's contribution to the relationship. When facilitated successfully, the equine's contributions enable the clients to gain deeper understanding of each other and learn practical relational skills to use in their daily lives. I encourage couples, families, and groups to invite the equine to participate as an honorary member of the family or group in which all are working towards accomplishing the same shared goal.

Individual EACP

Just as in individual psychotherapy, the focus is on providing EACP to a single client during the psychotherapy hour. In individual EACP, the main focus becomes the relationships that the client establishes with the equines and treatment team. However, even individual EACP sessions share many inherent qualities with group psychotherapy, such as the creation of a microcosm of the client's social world in interaction with the equines, reenactment of familial experiences, and learning through interspecies relationships (Ish-Lev & Amit,

2013). Through these relationships, the client works towards achievement of individual goals.

For many clients, it is helpful to participate in individual EACP to resolve intrapersonal issues and develop coping skills before participating in couple or family therapy in order to clarify their own needs and goals. In comparison to couple, family, or family EACP, clients participating in individual EACP may experience reduced fear of judgment, increased privacy for personal details, and more opportunities to focus on the client's unique needs as they arise in the session. Individual EACP enables the pace and content of the session to be dictated by the client's unique needs to gain insight and skills into managing thoughts, feelings, and behaviors that may be interfering in client's satisfaction in daily life and relationships. Finally, certain presenting concerns, such as depression, may respond better to individual EACP than group EACP (McRoberts, Burlingame, & Hoag, 1998).

There are several challenges and limitations in providing individual EACP. One of the greatest challenges in providing individual EACP is cost. As most EACP sessions involve both a therapist and equine specialist, the combined fees paid to the treatment team may average much higher than payment to a single therapist. Furthermore, as the cost of providing EACP is higher once the equine/facility fees and additional insurance coverage are included in comparison to office-based psychotherapy. In many cases, providing individual EACP can become cost-prohibitive for both the client and therapist. Another challenge for some clients in individual EACP is overcoming the uncomfortable feeling they may have of being in the spotlight or "watched" by the treatment team when participating in activities with the equines. Finally, clients's inability to observe and learn coping and relational skills from other clients struggling with similar concerns may present a limitation for some clients.

Couple and Family EACP

Goldenberg and Goldenberg (2008) described how a couple or family approach to therapy assumes the notion that people exist in the context of their network of relationships comprised of interactive patterns and belief systems. The focus, therefore, of couple and family therapy is to understand the process of these interactions. Individual clients are understood in the context of the functioning of the couple or family system. The system and its associated relational patterns and interactions become the focus of psychotherapy rather than the individual client. Problems in an individual (i.e., the "identified patient") are indicative of problems in the system. Additionally, couple and family therapy can help to reveal mechanisms (e.g., unspoken rules) that maintain dysfunctional family patterns. For more specific information on the theory of the systems approach, see Chapter 7.

Witnessing the different family members' interactions with the equines can help family members see each other in a new light, thereby increasing empathy

114 Counseling and Psychotherapy Formats

and understanding of each other's thoughts, feelings, and strengths. Additionally, the family's or couple's observations of equine herd behavior can provide valuable opportunities for communication, processing, and problem-solving. Observation of conflict in the herd can prompt discussion of similar conflict experienced at home. By processing observations of the equines, family members or couples may feel safer and less defensive in discussing problems, expressing feelings, and identifying possible solutions for problems they face. A relational approach with the equines, characterized by building compassion and empathy with the equines in EACP, can help the clients to also enhance those qualities within the couple or family system (DeMala-Moran, 2019; Green, Rolleston, & Schroeder, 2019). In particular, families with high conflict between parents and adolescents may benefit from family EACP. In these cases, family EACP (rather than individual EACP) may result in benefits such as improvements in relational skills, communication, empathy, and perspective-taking (Guo & Slesnick, 2013). The inclusion of equines may serve as a motivating factor to engage the adolescent in family psychotherapy (Chandler, 2017). Furthermore, as many adolescents struggle to trust adults, the inclusion of the equines may provide enhanced emotionally safety, as the adolescent is likely to perceive the equine as unbiased and nonjudgmental in responding to all family members involved in the session (Jenkins et al., 2014; Oetzel & Scherer, 2003).

Researchers have suggested EACP for couples may be especially helpful in resolving issues related to relational adjustment, communication, conflict, parenting differences, trust, and vulnerability (Ham, 2013; Russell-Martin, 2006). Holloway (2009) proposed the utility of the integration of EACP with Gottman Method Couples Therapy. Research on effectiveness of EACP with couples or families is limited. However, Romaniuk, Evans, and Kidd (2018) found EACP to be beneficial with military servicemembers with PTSD and spouses.

Ultimately, the therapeutic goal for couples or families with conflict is to move towards a healthier way of functioning in which the addition of the treatment team and equines become a part of the system and act as a disturbance to the system's functioning (Fall et al., 2010). The equines in EACP can be very helpful in accomplishing this goal. Animals are highly attuned to human emotion, especially highly charged emotions, and will respond to these emotions (Walsh, 2009). As equines naturally strive to create stability and harmony in the herd (Goodwin, 1999), they are likely to respond to conflict in the family or couple. In this way, the equine's presence can help to moderate conflict (Walsh, 2009). Billy, a calm bay gelding, often chose to participate in couples' sessions. During moments of agitation in the couple, Billy would sometimes split the couple by putting himself in the middle. His intent seemed to be to disrupt the tension. He would often nudge one member of the couple while pressing into the other member of the couple. Both would become momentarily distracted by Billy's behavior and start to stroke him. As they stroked him, both would become calmer and more able to engage in continued discussion. Another couple that I worked with chose Zorro as their "couples horse". Zorro had the opposite reaction to the Billy when the couple became agitated. He would simply leave the session. Zorro's leaving became a signal to the couple that emotions had become too high to be productive. Both members of the couple would then consciously work to calm themselves down. Once both were able to approach Zorro we resumed verbal processing.

Given the impact of this type of emotionally charged environment, it is crucial for the equine to be able to have the freedom to respond organically and have the choice to leave. I was told about another therapist's experience in which the equine felt confined to the session. In this particular instance, two members of the couple were participating in individual counseling with separate therapists at the same agency. One day, the couple and therapists decided to conduct a joint couple's session with each member of the couple's chosen equine partners. The session was held in a smaller pen without much room for the equines to move. (Both equines knew each other and lived in the same herd.) During a particularly emotionally charged moment, the wife's chosen equine kicked out at her. In talking to the therapist later, she hypothesized that the equine had probably felt overwhelmed by the high emotion within the couple but had no way to leave to escape the tension. Finally, it is important to note that, in some cases, the nature of the relationship between the couple or family members may create risks to emotional or physical safety that may not be manageable in the context of EACP. Such cases may include couples or families with histories of domestic violence, physical or emotional abuse, or intimate partner violence. In these cases, the appropriateness of couple or family EACP should be carefully evaluated and only provided by a therapist with who specializes in working with these types of couples or families.

The primary challenges in implementing couple or family EACP include potential for increased equine stress and financial cost. One of the challenges to be managed by the treatment team in couple or family EACP is the potential for increased risk of stress to the equine. More people participating in the session may add pressure to the equine(s) as well the risk of confusion if the equines do not know which client to respond to if they are receiving mixed messages from different clients. Furthermore, any conflict or negative emotions experienced among the clients may be felt by the equines resulting in heightened stress (Hama et al., 1996; Lanata et al., 2018; Smith et al., 2016). Equines participating in couple or family therapy sessions may remember and respond more negatively to the client who they perceive to experience more negative emotions than other clients in the session (Proops et al., 2018). It is also important to be aware of indications of triangulation of the equines participating in the session in which the couple or family members draw the equines into the conflict in unhealthy ways during moments of heightened tension or arousal (Walsh, 2009). Finally, it should be noted that family or couple EACP may be more expensive than individual EACP if the sessions require a longer duration or if additional equines or personnel are needed to meet goals and maintain safety.

Group EACP

Group psychotherapy is a well-established psychotherapeutic approach to treating a variety of mental health concerns (Gladding, 2008; Yalom & Leszcz, 2005). A group should be created deliberately on the basis of similar presenting concerns or psychotherapeutic goals across group members. Just as the client's interactions with the equines in individual EACP serve as a microcosm of the client's daily life and relationships outside of session, the presence of the human group members further enhances this experience. In addition, clients have the opportunity to not only practice new skills with the equines but also with the other group members and receive immediate feedback from both (Fuhriman & Burlingame, 1990; Yalom & Leszcz, 2005). Clients can experience feelings of universality in that they are not alone in their struggles and experience a sense of shared community with other group members (Dunlop & Tsantefski, 2018; Fuhriman & Burlingame, 1990; Yalom & Leszcz, 2005). Clients who may benefit from a group approach, but who avoid office-based groups, may be more inclined to participate in a setting with equines (Perry, Rubinstein, & Austin, 2012). Group EACP has been shown to benefit children with behavioral and emotional problems (Trotter et al., 2008; Vidrine et al., 2002), female survivors of intimate partner violence (Schroeder & Stroud, 2015), clients at a residential treatment facility (Klontz, Bivens, Leinart, & Klontz, 2007), children exposed to problematic parental substance use (Dunlop & Tsantefski, 2018), and clients with substance use disorder (Kern-Godal, Arnevik, Walderhaug, & Ravndal, 2015).

There are two primary approaches to group work in EACP. The first approach focuses on the relationships between the individual group members and incorporates the equines to help the group develop cohesion and strengthen existing relationships. In this approach, the group members may participate in various activities as a group designed to promote development of group cohesion and specific skills such as communication, conflict resolution, and problem-solving. In these types of groups, the treatment team must be careful to protect the equines from becoming mere tools for the group to project onto or use to develop skills. The way in which the treatment team presents activities and processes with the group can have a large impact on the nature of the equines' participation and in maintaining respect for their sentience. By presenting the equines as a "co-facilitators", the treatment team can help group members to adopt the mindset of the equines as valuable contributors rather than "challenges" to be overcome.

The second approach focuses on the group members' individual relationships with their chosen equine and parallel participation in individual equine activities. These types of groups work especially well with clients struggling with similar mental health concerns such as grief, substance abuse, trauma, and eating disorders. Group members have the opportunity to benefit from vicarious learning and gain support within the group by observing each other's interactions and processing individual experiences as a group. These clients can gain both peer social support and equine support through the formation of a safe, trusting relationships with all involved (Fuhriman & Burlingame, 1990; Yalom & Leszcz, 2005). In these groups, it will be particularly important for the treatment team to deliberately attend to building group cohesion in light of each group member's focus on their relationship with their equine (Yalom & Leszcz, 2005).

While some researchers have found group psychotherapy to be as effective as individual psychotherapy (McRoberts et al., 1998), certain clients may not benefit from group psychotherapy alone as much as individual psychotherapy (Baehr, 1954). Given the importance of group cohesion in traditional office-based approaches, it is important to note that it may be more difficult to build cohesion among human group members depending on how the group is structured and facilitated (Yalom & Leszcz, 2005). There are also additional safety considerations for both human and equine participants. Depending on the size of the group, it can often be a challenge to acquire adequate personnel beyond the treatment team (e.g., volunteers) in order to maintain a safe environment. Furthermore, if space or access to equines is limited, the treatment team will need to carefully consider how to balance the needs of the group and its members with available resources and safety considerations. Finally, just as in couple and family EACP, the presence of more clients can add more pressure and stress to the equines, especially clients who experience strong negative emotions during session.

Chapter 10

Implementing Equine-Assisted Counseling and Psychotherapy With Different Client Populations

There are many different clients that you are likely to encounter who are seeking services for equine-assisted counseling and psychotherapy (EACP). In my experience, many of the clients seeking EACP have refused to try office-based approaches or have been dissatisfied with the results of other approaches. As a result, these clients have often struggled for quite some time and may present with more severe concerns than other clients with similar experiences or diagnoses. Frequently, the relationship with the equine and excitement about seeing the equine motivates clients to attend therapy sessions—a motivator not present in office-based therapy. As many clients with diverse mental health concerns may initiate treatment, the therapist should be prepared to decide which types of client concerns they believe they are competent to treat. In this chapter, I will describe the symptoms of and treatment goals for common mental health conditions and the benefits of using EACP approaches. In addition, I include a section devoted to discussing the needs of military clients and their family members.

Grief

Clients who are experiencing grief or unresolved loss may experience ongoing difficulties characterized by sadness, confusion about the future, disengagement, disruption of daily activities, feelings of guilt, or avoidance. These effects may be compounded in the case of traumatic grief or unexpected loss. Movement through the grief process is marked by completion of loss-focused (e.g., looking at photos or talking about the deceased) and restoration-focused (e.g., establishing new goals and routines) tasks (Jordan & Litz, 2014). Some clients may also experience complicated grief (i.e., prolonged grief) more than six months after the loss characterized by intense yearning; preoccupation of memories, thoughts, and feelings related to the deceased person; strong negative emotions; avoidance; and difficulty experiencing positive feelings or finding meaning. This type of grief can be debilitating and last for decades (Shear, 2010). Treatment for this type of grief should focus on helping the client establish or strengthen supportive relationships with others, providing psychoeducation,

Different Client Populations | 119

and facilitating client work through loss-focused and restoration-focused tasks (Shear, Frank, Houck, & Reynolds, 2005). Loss-focused tasks may include imagining the deceased, telling stories about the deceased, or "talking to" the deceased. Restoration-focused tasks can help the client to establish new goals, create new routines, and engage in meaning-making regarding the loss.

Researchers and clinicians have found interaction with equines to be beneficial for grieving clients (Schlough, 2019; Strom & Wilson, 2009; Symington, 2012). The presence of the equines during counseling can be comforting and grounding to the client, enabling them to feel safer and more in control when thinking or talking about the loss as they work through the loss-focused tasks. In this way, the relationship with the equine can serve as a supportive relationship in which they can feel accepted and understood. Clients who experience obsessive thoughts or strong negative emotions can learn and practice coping skills with the equines. Oftentimes, the equines' feedback can help the client gain more awareness into somatic reactions and find ways to self-soothe and self-regulate. Some clients feel paralyzed or unable to move forward in their daily lives. Oftentimes, these clients struggle with decision-making and problem-solving, even in the EACP session. Through interaction with the equines, clients have the opportunity to relearn and practice these skills through different activities that can then be generalized to restoration-focused tasks in their daily lives. Processing interactions and experiences with the equines can help the client identify parallels and patterns in their daily lives and gain insight into their own needs while finding meaning in the loss and future ahead.

Jay's experience in Equine-Partnered Play Therapy (EPPT) is a powerful account of the impact of EACP on promoting healing from grief. Jay came for EPPT following the sudden and unexpected death of his father in a factory accident. Upon entering the play area during the first session, Jay immediately chose one of the "grown-up" chairs and promptly sat down, leaned back, and put on his oversized sunglasses. As he glanced at the toys, he stated, "I don't play—I have more important things to do" and further slouched in his chair. As the horses moved around the play area, he would often peek from over his sunglasses, but remained silent with his arms crossed. As the hour progressed, Jay began to list all of his responsibilities such as going to his job (i.e., school), taking care of his baby sister, and making the grocery list every week for his mom. His formal speech and nonverbal gestures made him almost appear as a "mini adult". The following week, Jay returned and adopted the same posture once again, sliding his sunglasses down over his eyes. This time, Sunshine, one of the miniature equines in the session, moved closer to Jay in the play area. She observed Jay from a distance and periodically turned to look directly at him. At one point, she started to move towards him, but stopped after a few steps. The equine specialist reflected that it seemed that Sunshine wanted to approach Jay but wasn't sure if Jay would be okay with it. Jay peeked out from under the sunglasses and mumbled, "it's okay". Sunshine immediately walked right over the Jay and put her nose in his lap. Jay began to stroke her face

120 Different Client Populations

in silence for the next several minutes. Afterward, he removed his sunglasses stating that he didn't "need" them. In later sessions, Jay would reveal that the sunglasses had belonged to his father. Over time, Jay began to "teach" playful games to Sunshine that he used to play with his dad. Through his continued interactions with Sunshine in session, Jay allowed himself to play again as his family worked towards a new way of life.

Eating Disorders

According to the National Institute of Mental Health (2019c), eating disorders are characterized by problematic eating behaviors accompanied by related thoughts and feelings. For some clients, these disorders can also include preoccupation with food or body weight or image concerns. There are three primary types of eating disorders: anorexia, bulimia, and binge-eating disorder. Clients with anorexia tend to see themselves as overweight, even if they are underweight, and have a distorted body image. They may engage in food restriction, excessive exercise, or purging after eating. These clients are the most at-risk of serious physical health concerns including death. Clients with bulimia experience frequent episodes of eating excessive amounts of food followed by compensation behaviors such as forced vomiting, taking laxatives, fasting, or excessive exercise. Clients with binge-eating disorder may consume excessive amounts of food but do not follow the episodes with efforts to compensate. Both clients with bulimia and binge-eating disorders report feeling a loss of control during the episodes. Treatment for eating disorders should focus on providing psychoeducation, identifying and challenging unhealthy thought patterns, and addressing any underlying trauma contributing to the eating disorder. As many clients with eating disorders are disconnected from their bodies and bodily sensations, it is important to process somatic experiences and help clients increase somatic awareness (Lac, 2019; Sharpe, 2013).

Researchers and clinicians have found EACP can be beneficial in treating mental health concerns related to eating disorders (Cumella, Lutter, Lutter, & Lutter, 2014; Lac, 2019; Lac, Marble, & Boie, 2013; Lutter, 2008; Marx & Cumella, 2003; Sharpe, 2013). EACP can be helpful in both empowering clients and helping them to gain somatic awareness. As interpersonal difficulties are common in many clients with eating disorders, relationship-focused EACP approaches, such as Relational Equine-Partnered Counseling, can facilitate the creation of a safe, trusting relationship with the equine. From this experience, the clients can learn valuable relational skills to establish and maintain healthy interpersonal relationships and improve overall treatment outcomes for the eating disorder (Ung et al., 2017). Additionally, gaining the cooperation of a large animal can help clients feel a sense of self-efficacy and empowerment (Cumella et al., 2014). Furthermore, learning to communicate and set boundaries with an equine can promote an increased sense of control while also learning valuable skills to improve satisfaction in interpersonal relationships. The increased physical activity inherent in EACP (in comparison to office-based therapy) can provide additional benefits in helping clients gain increased somatic awareness and attunement (Sharpe, 2013). For example, even brushing an equine requires physical activity and coordination. Clients may gain this awareness and insight through these types of activities and by engaging in physical touch with the equines. As equines are highly attuned to body language, including physical tension, posture (Goodwin, 1999), and facial expressions (Smith et al., 2016), their feedback can help clients connect with their bodies and increase somatic awareness. For example, Jodi, a client in treatment for anorexia, was once working with a large draft horse named Dante. Jodi reported that she felt "safe" and "protected" with Dante. However, Dante seemed disinterested, distracted, and moved away from Jodi when she began to brush him. Jodi was unaware of her own posture and physical tension and its impact on Dante's response to her. As the treatment team led Jodi in an exercise to notice her posture and physical tension, she identified tension in her shoulders. She also noted that although her shoulders were leaning in towards Dante, her torso was tilted away from him. Once she brought her body into alignment and relaxed the tension, she began to feel a stronger connection to her body and to Dante. Dante lowered his head and let out a big sigh followed by licking and chewing. Jodi reported feeling that a weight had been lifted and began to draw connections between her somatic experiences and associated thoughts that co-occurred with her eating disorder.

Autism Spectrum Disorder (ASD)

Clients with autism spectrum disorder (ASD) can differ widely in their presentation and level of impairment. Most notably, these clients all share varying degrees of difficulty with communication and social interactions, restricted interests and repetitive behaviors, and trouble functioning at home, work, and/ or school. It is most often diagnosed in young children but can be diagnosed later in life, including adulthood. The most effective therapies for treatment of clients with ASD focus on teaching life skills, reducing problem behaviors, identifying and utilizing strengths, and learning social, communication, and language skills (National Institute of Mental Health, 2018b).

Interaction with equines in EACP can impart unique benefits to clients with ASD in comparison to other treatment approaches. As oxytocin may be linked with enhanced social learning, positive physical touch between the client and the equine may release oxytocin and help the client to better learn and generalize social skills and empathy through interaction with the equines Hollander et al., 2007; Odendaal & Meintjes, 2003). Faa-Thompson (2019) suggested that certain activities, such as bathing the equine, can promote benefits such as sensory opportunities, development of frustration tolerance, empathy-building, and learning boundaries. Ecker and Byrnes (2019) described other benefits of participation in EACP for individuals with ASD such as improvements in

122 Different Client Populations

emotional regulation, social-emotional reciprocity, communication, mood, and thinking patterns.

Steve's sessions with Penny are illustrative of the benefits of EACP for clients with ASD. When Steve first arrived for EACP, his father identified goals related to reducing angry and aggressive behavior, improving communication, and helping Steve make friends. During Steve's first session, he drew a line in dirt and stated that none of the horses could cross it. Only a few minutes after drawing the line, Penny, a quiet chestnut mare, walked over the line to get some hay. Steve became enraged and started yelling at Penny for "breaking the rules". He tried to chase her away, stating that he had learned that you have "tell the horse who's boss". When he tried to approach Penny later, she wouldn't let him come near her. The following week, Steve decided that he wanted to try to build a relationship with Penny. Before the treatment team could stop him, he began to walk towards Penny waving his arms, again stating that she needed to know he was "the boss" to trust him and that he'd watched many YouTube videos on how to do it. At this point, the treatment team initiated processing with Steve. The equine specialist used psychoeducation to discuss the horse's mentality as a prey animal. Steve, proud that he had learned about prey animals earlier in the school year, immediately said that Penny ran from him because she thought he was an "alligator" about to attack. As he processed with the treatment team, he reflected on why Penny had run from him and what he needed to do to "gain her trust". During the third session, he told the treatment team that he had decided that he would rather be Penny's friend than her boss. He said that he had realized that if she wanted to be his friend, he would like it if she did "nice things" for him. Steve then proceeded to gather hay and approached Penny to begin feeding her so he could do "nice things" for her. As his sessions progressed, Steve continued to learn new ways to communicate and manage his frustration when Penny did not respond as he had hoped. He later generalized these experiences to family and peers and was able to develop stronger connections and more satisfying relationships.

Attention-Deficit/Hyperactivity Disorder (ADHD)

Attention-deficit/hyperactivity disorder (ADHD) is one of the most commonly diagnosed childhood disorders. However, ADHD is not limited to children; it can also be present in adolescents and through adulthood. The rate of children diagnosed with ADHD continues to increase each year. This disorder is characterized by difficulty maintaining attention and self-control, impulsive behavior, and hyperactivity. Medication continues to be the primary form of treatment for ADHD (National Institute of Mental Health, 2019c). However, many clients prefer to avoid medication or report dissatisfaction with medication side effects (Taylor & Kuo, 2011). Recommendations for counseling and psychotherapy treatment of ADHD include focus on teaching self-monitoring and self-control, increasing awareness of thoughts

Different Client Populations 123

and feelings, and learning coping skills to manage stress (National Institute of Mental Health, 2019c).

Clinicians and researchers have advocated for the benefits of EACP in treating clients with ADHD (Jang et al., 2015; Taylor, 2019). Independent of the effect of the equines, children with ADHD who have regular exposure to outdoor green spaces may experience reduction in the severity of ADHD symptoms. The open space associated with being in a pasture may impart additional benefits beyond just being outside (Taylor & Kuo, 2011). The restorative environment in EACP can be greatly beneficial in improving attention and reducing mental fatigue (Kaplan, 1995).

The presence of the equines and the experiential quality of EACP may be more engaging and impactful for clients with ADHD than office-based approaches (Devon, 2011). For example, imagine an 8-year-old who is excited to see their horse and impulsively runs to the horse. The most likely result is that the horse will move or run away, thus providing immediate feedback on the negative impact of the client's behavior. This feedback, combined with the motivation to connect with the horse, can help the client learn to connect internal feelings with behaviors resulting in improved self-monitoring and self-awareness, ultimately leading to increased self-control and reduction in impulsive behavior. Furthermore, the horse's feedback can also help the client to identify emotions associated with impulsive or inattentive behavior. In other cases, the treatment team can facilitate the client's practice in mindfulness-based skills using activities such as mindful grooming to develop skills related to task completion and focus (Taylor, 2019) or improve self-regulation.

Participation in activities with the horse can also help the client practice pre-planning, problem-solving, and communication skills. In working with clients with ADHD, one of the greatest indicators of progress that I look for is the client's success in walking the equine on a lead line. Although it sounds relatively simple, I have observed this activity to be extremely difficult for some clients with ADHD due to the high amount of incoming stimuli and the focus required to safely and successfully complete the activity. It can be challenging for these clients to maintain a safe hold on the rope, hold the rope an appropriate length, pay attention to where they are going, and attend to the equine's behaviors all at the same time. These clients often feel quite proud when they can accomplish all of these tasks at once and successfully walk the equine from point A to point B. As individuals with ADHD often struggle with low self-esteem and low self-confidence, interaction with an authentic, nonjudgmental equine can help clients feel safe to take risks in trying new things and experience success in accomplishing tasks that they previously struggled to achieve.

Depression

Depression is one of the most commonly cited mental health concerns, affecting more than 300 million people worldwide. For some people, depression

124 Different Client Populations

can lead to suicide, with almost 800,000 people dying by suicide every year. Depression is also the leading cause of disability worldwide and usually affects a person's functioning in all areas of life, including family, friends, work, and school. Unfortunately, less than half of people needing treatment for depression receive it. Symptoms of depression can include depressed mood, sadness, low energy, poor sleep and appetite, decreased interest or positive feelings, lack of motivation, difficulty concentrating, and feelings of guilt or low self-worth. Depression can present as mild, moderate, or severe, and can be a single episode or recurrent episodes (World Health Organization, 2018). Treatment goals for depression may include alleviation of symptoms; return to previous level of functioning; recognition, acceptance, and coping with depression symptoms; development of healthy thinking patterns; establishment of healthy interpersonal relationships; and grieving of losses (Jongsma, Peterson, & Bruce, 2014).

Researchers and clinicians have found animal-assisted activities and therapies to be beneficial in treating depression (Berget & Braastad, 2011; Souter & Miller, 2007). Researchers and clinicians of different EACP approaches have found it to be beneficial in several ways such as reducing depression-like symptoms in adolescents by improving social relationships and reducing isolation, increasing positive feelings, self-esteem, and self-efficacy (DePrekel & Runge, 2019; Ecken, 2012; Frederick, 2019; Frame, 2006). Even without the inclusion of equines, Korpela Stengård, and Jusilla (2016) found nature walks to be associated with significant decreases in depression.

In clients with depression, higher levels of emotional involvement (i.e., experiencing) can be predictive of decreased symptoms of depression (Castonguay et al., 1996). In other words, the more that a client focuses on their inner thoughts, feelings, and experiences in session, the more relief they may experience. For these clients, interacting with equines can be beneficial in not only creating a safe place to identify and process these experiences, but also in eliciting affective experiences that can be processed during the session. In particular, the client may experience an increase in positive feelings as a result of feeling accepted by and connected with the equine. The strength of the relationship between the client, treatment team, and equines can reduce the client's avoidance of negative thoughts and feelings, and enable the client to feel safe to process these experiences in a healthy way.

In the treatment of depression, behavioral activation (e.g., physical activity and movement) that leads to positive feelings is considered a crucial part of treatment. Clients who struggle with low motivation and loss of interest in daily activities may be more inclined to participate in EACP than in other office-based therapies. Furthermore, through physical contact with the equine, a client can experience positive physiological benefits and positive feelings, further enhancing interest and motivation. The physical nature of EACP (walking to the pasture, stroking the equine, leading the equine, etc.) can engage the client in higher levels of physical movement. In addition, the client also has the opportunity to develop and practice a number of skills that can help in the

Different Client Populations 125

alleviation of depression such as problem-solving, decision-making (Jongsma et al., 2014), and mindfulness techniques.

Through the relationships established with the equines, clients can also learn ways to identify and maintain healthy relationships with both themselves and others through opportunities to engage in reality-testing and practice relational skills. In this way, clients learn to identify unhealthy negative thought patterns or beliefs maintaining the depression and challenge and replace these thoughts with healthier ones. The therapist can facilitate the client's development of self-monitoring skills for thoughts, feelings, and actions by observing and processing them as they occur in session. The client can also practice relationship-based skills such as communication, assertiveness, boundary-setting, and conflict resolution to strengthen connections with others (Jongsma et al., 2014).

Bart was a teenager coming to EACP to address concerns related to severe depression. He had missed more days of school than he had attended and was at risk of having to repeat seventh grade. Bart felt tired all the time and often said that he was "worthless" and that no one liked him. During Bart's first session, he was immediately approached by a large mule named Rosie. As she pushed her nose under Bart's hand, she began to lick to him. Bart burst out laughing, exclaiming "that tickles!" He spent the remainder of the session stroking Rosie's forehead. When it was time to leave, he said that he hadn't felt "happy" like he did with Rosie in a long time. Over the next several weeks, Bart's unhealthy thought patterns began to play out in his interactions with Rosie. On one such occasion, Rosie abruptly left the session to get a drink of water while Bart had been petting her. Bart immediately stated that he must have done something wrong and that Rosie didn't like him anymore. However, in encouraging Bart to observe Rosie, he noted that she had gone to get a drink of water and then returned directly to him. In processing this experience, Bart identified that he is used to assuming the worst and expects to be rejected by others. Over time, Bart began to identify and challenge these unhealthy beliefs as they arose in session. He reported that he liked being "active" with Rosie by walking her around the pasture and began to take walks around his neighborhood when he felt sad. Over time, Bart was able to apply more and more from his sessions with Rosie to his daily life and found ways to better manage his depression.

Anxiety

Anxiety is another commonly cited mental health concern, affecting 19% of adults in the United States each year. There are several different types of anxiety such as generalized anxiety disorder, separation anxiety, social anxiety, panic disorder, specific phobias, agoraphobia, and selective mutism. Symptoms of anxiety can include feeling restless or on edge, fatigue, difficulty with concentration, feelings of irritability, muscle tension, difficulty controlling worry, sleep problems, and mutism (National Institute of Mental Health, 2018a). Clients

126 Different Client Populations

with anxiety often perceive somatic symptoms such as rapid heartrate, sweating, tension, difficulty breathing, or chest tightness indicative of activation of the nervous system. Clients with panic disorder are likely to be more sensitive to and anxious about somatic sensations and have a higher autonomic arousal level (Biedel, Christ, & Long, 1991; Hoehn-Saric, McLeod, Funderburk, & Kowalski, 2004). Treatment for anxiety can vary depending on the type of anxiety, but general treatment goals may include reduction in the frequency, intensity, and duration of anxiety; stabilization of anxiety and an increase in daily functioning; resolution of the core conflict of anxiety; and implementation of coping skills to manage anxiety (Jongsma et al., 2014).

Clinicians of diverse approaches have documented the benefits of EACP for clients with anxiety (Bailey & Bailey, 2019; Shultz-Jobe, McFarland, & Jobe, 2019; Willerson, 2019). Even in a nontherapeutic context, interaction with equines can be beneficial in reducing anxiety symptoms (Donovan, 2017). For many clients, simply discussing the anxiety itself can be anxiety-provoking. The calm presence of equines can help comfort and ground the client while discussing anxiety, core conflicts, and topics that elicit anxiety. Interestingly, clients with anxiety can often relate to an equine's instincts as a prey animal. Observation of how equines cope with anxiety-producing elements in their environment can help a client feel understood and identify ways to cope with their own anxiety. Researchers have found interaction with animals, including equines, to decrease present moment (i.e., state) anxiety (Shiloh et al., 2003). Furthermore, as the release of oxytocin and vasopressin may reduce anxiety, stress, and fear (Carter, 1998), oxytocin released while stroking an animal (Odendaal, 2000; Odendaal & Meintjes, 2003), when combined with perceived social support from the others like the equines (Heinrichs et al., 2003), may lower the client's anxiety in session.

Anxiety can often present with different somatic sensations such as chest tightness, abdominal discomfort, or rapid heartbeat. I believe that equines are sensitive enough to be able to perceive changes in client physiology associated with heightened anxiety and that many equines respond to such changes. I have often used the equine's feedback or sudden changes in behavior as an opportunity to check in with the client on what they are feeling. More times than not, the client identified a specific somatic change related to their anxiety concurrent to the equine's feedback or behavior change. For clients who are experiencing heightened somatic symptoms, the therapist can also facilitate calming or mindfulness-based interventions with the equine to help the client learn to decrease somatic arousal.

For other clients, learning to manage their fear of equines' large size enables them to learn that they can generalize the same skills to manage anxiety with things that they may encounter outside of session as well. In fact, one client of mine stated that she had a "eureka moment" upon realizing that she had overcome her fear of large horses and therefore felt renewed hope that she

Different Client Populations 127

could apply that experience in managing her anxiety in other settings. Clients with anxiety can also learn problem-solving skills to address specific problems and worries through interaction and activities with the equines. Additionally, clients have the opportunity, in their interactions with the equine, to learn positive interpersonal skills to establish healthier and more satisfying relationships with others.

Janice's experience with Flicka illustrates the power of EACP in resolving anxiety. Janice was a 14-year-old adolescent presenting with extreme social anxiety resulting in depression and thoughts of suicide. She described significant worries about being judged by others that prevented her from making friends, resulted in poor grades in group projects, and made it difficult for her to even order a meal in a restaurant. Initially, Janice worked on building a relationship with Flicka by engaging in nurturing and self-soothing activities. During the activities, Janice observed Flicka's response to her to identify and quantify Janice's own anxiety. With my guidance, Janice practiced different calming skills and observed the change in Flicka's behaviors towards her as she began to feel calmer. Janice felt comforted in knowing that Flicka "saw" and understood Janice's anxiety, but never left her side. Over time, Janice began to try walking Flicka around the pen. At first, Janice felt scared to direct Flicka where to go, resulting in Flicka leading Janice. During one particularly meaningful session, Janice stated that she had had enough of Flicka leading her places that she did not want to go in the pen. Although she was anxious, Janice attempted to provide direction to Flicka and found that the equine immediately responded to her cue. Through this process, Janice began to identify and challenge maladaptive beliefs that were contributing to her anxiety. She began to test out what it was like to speak her mind with close friends and reported that her friendships had become stronger.

Trauma, Posttraumatic Stress (PTS) and Posttraumatic Stress Disorder (PTSD)

Trauma

The Substance Abuse and Mental Health Services Administration (2014) defined trauma as resulting from "an event, series of events, or a set of circumstances experienced by an individual as physically or emotionally harmful or life-threatening with lasting adverse effects on the individual's functioning and mental, physical, social, emotional, or spiritual well-being." Trauma can occur not only in response to events that an individual directly experiences but also in response to events that the individual observes or learns about happening to others. Trauma can result from a single event such as an accident, natural disaster, assault, abuse, neglect, or combat, or as result from a series of traumatic events such as ongoing childhood abuse, warzone exposure, or a combination

128 Different Client Populations

of unrelated traumatic events. Trauma can manifest in child welfare problems, legal or criminal issues, or educational problems (Substance Abuse and Mental Health Services Administration, 2014).

Early-life trauma is particularly impactful, as it occurs during the most critical periods of brain development after birth. A landmark study on Adverse Childhood Experiences (ACEs) identified ten different types of childhood trauma that can cause in lasting effects (Felitti et al., 1998). It is estimated that more than 80% of people experience at least one ACE during childhood. The more ACEs that an individual experiences, the more at risk they are of negative effects such as injury, mood health issues (e.g., suicidality, depression, anxiety, or PTSD), pregnancy-related issues, infectious diseases, chronic diseases, engagement in risky behaviors, and loss of educational or vocational opportunities.

Researchers have found EACP can be beneficial in treating trauma for many different types of clients such as military servicemembers (Romaniuk, Evans, & Kidd, 2018; Sheade, 2015; Wharton, Whitworth, Macauley, & Malone, 2019), youth (Dziegelewski, 2014; McCullough et al., 2015; Naste et al., 2018), survivors of interpersonal violence (Schroeder & Stroud, 2015), individuals with childhood trauma (Johansen, Arfwedson, & Biner, 2016), child sexual abuse survivors (Kemp et al., 2014), and others with varied trauma experiences (Earles, Vernon, & Yetz, 2015; Staudt & Cherry, 2017; Trotter & Baggerly, 2019a). Other programs have been proposed to use EACP to help other types of clients recover from trauma such as Australian Aboriginal peoples (Bennett & Woodman, 2019) and survivors of domestic violence (Froeschle, 2009).

All treatment approaches should be trauma-informed and characterized by inclusion of the "4 Rs" including **realization** of the widespread impact of trauma and recovery paths, **recognition** of the signs of trauma, **responses** that integrate knowledge about trauma, and efforts to **resist re-traumatization** (Substance Abuse and Mental Health Services Administration, 2014). Van der Kolk (2014) offered several recommendations for treating trauma by focusing on six areas: management of hyperarousal, mindfulness, relationships with others, rhythms and synchrony, touch, and taking action. The Relational Equine-Partnered Counseling approach is well-equipped to address all of these areas (Sheade, 2015). Interaction with equines can enable clients to have a safe place to practice bottom-up regulation strategies to *manage hyperarousal*, such as breathing exercises. Furthermore, the presence of the equine may decrease anxiety and help clients maintain a state of physical relaxation while confronting traumatic stimuli. As a result of oxytocin that may be released when interacting with animals (Odendaal, 2000; Odendaal & Meintjes, 2003), clients with physiological reactivity associated with trauma may feel calmer in session and better able to remain grounded when engaging in trauma processing or in response to trauma reminders (Heinrichs & Gaab, 2007). Clients can practice *mindfulness* activities with the equine, using the equine's feedback to increase self and somatic awareness. Healing *relationships* are critical to prevent and heal from the adverse effects of trauma by positively impacting the stress response and social bonding systems (Perry, 2009). Equines can offer a relationship through which clients can experience the contact and attunement necessary to increase self-regulation (Van der Kolk, 2014). The treatment team can promote trauma-informed relationships by establishing a physically and emotionally safe environment and by establishing trust. The presence of the equines in the session can help build trust between the client and treatment team. The equine's authenticity in interacting with both the client and treatment team strengthens this trust. The treatment team should work to not only create a collaborative relationship with the client, but also between the client and equines. Clients can work on *rhythms and synchrony* by both observing the movement of equines or engaging directly with the equines through movement-focused activity, helping the client become more attuned to both themselves, others, and the environment (Van der Kolk, 2014). Clients can also reconnect with their own bodies through *touch*-based activities, such as stroking or brushing, enabling them to feel safe to relax and release tension (Hama et al., 1996; Odendaal, 2000). The client has the opportunity to *"take action"* by initiating movement-related activities in partnership with the equine. By being able to realize certain physical impulses through movement with such a large animal, the client can internalize feelings of strength rather than vulnerability (Sheade, 2015).

Posttraumatic Stress (PTS) and Posttraumatic Stress Disorder (PTSD)

In the immediate aftermath of a trauma, an individual can develop acute stress disorder (ASD) within 30 days of the event. Individuals suffering from ASD benefit from approaches that are trauma-focused, strengths-based, and psychoeducational (U.S. Department of Veterans Affairs, n.d.). However, symptoms lasting longer than 30 days may indicate the presence of posttraumatic stress disorder (PTSD). It is important to note that some prefer use of the term posttraumatic stress (PTS) rather than including the word "disorder" to avoid pathologizing an individual's response to a traumatic experience and/or to describe individuals who do not meet diagnostic criteria for PTSD.

Posttraumatic stress is triggered by the body's response to a traumatic event resulting in an experience of "fight-or-flight" intended to reduce the risk of future danger and impair normal functioning until the danger passes. A diagnosis of PTSD is characterized by experiencing symptoms in four clusters: re-experiencing, avoidance, cognition and mood, and arousal and reactivity. An individual must experience a certain number of symptoms in each cluster to meet the criteria needed for a diagnosis of PTSD (National Institute of Mental Health, n.d.). However, some individuals experience PTS or subthreshold PTSD, a condition in which they do not meet the criteria for all symptom clusters, but nevertheless experience heightened emotional distress or impaired functioning equivalent to someone with symptoms that do meet criteria for

130 Different Client Populations

PTSD (Bergman, Kline, Feeny, & Zoellner, 2015). It is important to be aware that trauma resulting in PTS or PTSD is often missed in clients presenting with other significant mental health concerns such as anxiety, depression, or child behavior problems.

There are a number of different types of treatments for PTS and PTSD including some that target symptoms directly and others that focus on improving social, family, or vocational functioning. The most effective therapies include a focus on providing psychoeducation, learning to identify triggers, and implementing skills to manage symptoms. Oftentimes, clients who initiate EACP have tried therapies such as prolonged exposure, Eye Movement Rapid Desensitization (EMDR), or cognitive processing therapy, with little success.

The Relational Equine-Partnered Counseling (REPC) approach to EACP can be especially helpful in identifying PTS-related triggers, thoughts, feelings, and somatic sensations and implementing skills to manage symptoms using feedback from the equine. The presence of the equines can often help clients feel safer to express and process deeply distressing emotions and suffering (Walsh, 2009). Interactions with the equine allow the client to have opportunities to make choices and experience empowerment (Substance Abuse and Mental Health Services Administration, 2014). For re-experiencing symptoms, the client can learn to manage these symptoms by practicing different types of calming skills with the equine. These clients frequently report the presence of the equine to be both comforting and grounding. For avoidance symptoms, I have found that many clients feel much safer telling the story of their trauma in the presence of the equines than in an office-based setting. The physical presence of the equines seems to provide a stronger version of a safe place for these clients. This may be because many clients with PTS can relate to the equine's mentality as a prey animal and feel accepted and understood while processing. Participation in EACP can also help with symptoms related to mood and cognition. I have witnessed tremendous improvement in clients who feel detached, disinterested, and/or have trouble experiencing positive feelings. The formation of the relationship with their chosen equine can provide clients with a renewed sense of connection, motivation, and trust. One such client told me that after spending several sessions with his horse, Sammy, that the "connecting part" of his brain had been "turned on" once again. Other clients who struggle with feelings of shame, guilt, or unworthiness may experience acceptance and empathy from the equines that can lead to lasting changes in how they see themselves. Finally, REPC can also help clients manage symptoms related to arousal and reactivity. One client who struggled with hypervigilance reported that he could let his guard down around the horses because they "protected" him. He later began to identify other areas in his life where he could do the same. Other clients have experienced significant benefits including reduced concentration difficulties or anger issues when practicing activities with the equines focused on being present and mindful.

Substance Abuse Disorder

More than 20 million adults and more than one million adolescents between the ages of 12–18 struggle with substance use dependence or abuse each year. Substance use disorder (SUD) includes both alcohol and illicit drug use, and abuse that results in health problems or impairment at work, school, or home (Substance Abuse and Mental Health Services Administration, 2017a). Furthermore, the U.S. Department of Health and Human Services (2019) has declared the opioid epidemic to be a public health emergency. Most clients in need of treatment for SUD receive inadequate treatment or none at all (Substance Abuse and Mental Health Services Administration, 2017a). The primary goal in SUD treatment is to help the client develop the stability and skills needed to maintain sobriety. This goal is accomplished through interventions designed to strengthen and repair relationships; identify triggers for relapse; increase life satisfaction; develop communication, problem-solving, decision-making, and coping skills; reduce negative thought patterns; and resolve any underlying trauma (Jongsma et al., 2014). Researchers and clinicians have explored the use of different approaches to EACP in treating SUD (Buzel, 2019; Filippides, 2019; Green, Schroeder, Penalva, Rolleston, & Judd, 2019). Use of EACP can serve as a component of a larger treatment plan or as a form of aftercare to prevent relapse.

It can be difficult to engage clients with substance use problems in counseling and psychotherapy, especially young people. The inclusion of equines and establishment of the client-equine relationship in SUD treatment can result in increased client motivation, retention in treatment, and improved treatment outcomes (Kern-Godal et al., 2015; Waite & Bourke, 2013). The presence of a therapy animal can help strengthen the therapeutic relationship between the therapist and the client presenting for SUD treatment (Wesley, 2012). The strength of this relationship can also serve as a motivating factor to encourage the client's continued participation in treatment (Kern-Godal et al., 2015).

As many clients with SUD struggle with interpersonal relationships, the client's experience of establishing and maintaining a relationship with the equine can help them identify unhealthy patterns, try ways of relating in healthier ways, and develop empathy (Buzel, 2019). As SUD has been linked to attachment-related issues, the client-equine relationship can serve as a healing relationship and template for secure attachment (Bachi, 2013; Godal-Kern, Brenna, Arnevik, & Ravndal, 2016). As SUD is likely related to heightened stress and dysregulation, an empathic, accepting relationship (with the equine) can decrease feelings of shame (Badenoch, 208). The relationship that forms as a result of interactions between the client and equine has several other benefits (Kern-Godal et al., 2016). Client can learn to experience positive emotions such as happiness and tranquility without the use of substances. Clients can also benefit from opportunities to practice communication, decision-making,

132 Different Client Populations

and problem-solving skills that arise both organically and through structured activities as the client works to gain the cooperation of the equine. Clients can also gain an increased sense of control, mastery usefulness, and accomplishment through such activities. The equine's feedback can help the client gain insight in the development of emotional and somatic awareness of their own experiences and as they learn self-regulation (Buzel, 2019; Kern-Godal et al., 2016). Finally, the client can work on building coping and calming skills using mindfulness, relaxation, and grounding to manage stress, increase regulation, and reduce the risk of relapse (Badenoch, 2008; Buzel, 2019).

Martin was a young adult who participated in group EACP as a part of his recovery from SUD from opioid addiction. During the initial intake, Martin reported several experiences of childhood trauma he believed had contributed to the development of his SUD. Martin had already done quite a bit of psychotherapeutic work in his office-based therapies as part of his recovery program and had realized that the opioids had initially been a way to self-medicate from stress or anxiety and later became an addiction. Martin reported that he still struggled to be present in the moment and wanted help finding "better" coping skills to manage stress. Martin chose a calm, gentle older mare named Cinnamon. While grooming Cinnamon, he noticed that she became increasingly restless. In checking with himself, Martin realized that his mind had been wandering and he not been focused on the grooming. With guidance from the treatment team, Martin practiced mindfulness-based skills while grooming to learn to be present and self-regulate. Martin commented on how much "better" the skills seemed to work for him while practicing with Cinnamon, as he felt comforted by her presence. He also reported that this experience created a strong memory to think back to when practicing the skills outside of session, leading to Martin's improved ability to apply such skills in managing stress and trauma triggers.

Military Clients

Military servicemember clients (including veterans, active duty, and reservists) represent a unique group of individuals who often have similar presenting concerns. The military background of these servicemembers contributes to differences in the way they experience specific mental health concerns such as PTSD, depression, traumatic brain injuries, anxiety, and others in comparison to civilian clients that have not served. However, it is important to also keep in mind that even among servicemembers, unique lived experiences both prior to, during, and after military service result in different experiences and impacts of similar diagnoses and traumas.

Researchers have found EACP and the therapeutic impact of the client-equine relationship to provide unique benefits to military servicemembers (Abrams, 2013; Mayfield, 2016; Sheade, 2015) such as reduced distress related to PTSD (Romaniuk et al., 2018; Sheade, 2015; Wharton et al., 2019),

Different Client Populations   133

improvements in mood and anxiety (Monroe, Whitworth, Wharton, & Turner, 2019; Romaniuk et al., 2018) and psychosocial benefits (Ferruolo, 2015). Mayfield (2016) identified specific intrapersonal benefits (e.g., increased self-awareness and self-regulation) and interpersonal benefits (e.g., building trust and improving communication) for military clients participating in EACP. For the REPC approach in particular, there are several specific benefits for servicemembers (Sheade, 2015). First, the REPC approach is well-equipped to meet servicemembers' mental health needs through the establishment of healthy relationships and relational skills, development of social supports, and increases in motivation to participate in counseling and psychotherapy. Furthermore, observation of the client's interactions with the equine and the associated meaning identified during processing can provide the therapist with valuable information regarding the client's functioning, especially for clients who feel uncomfortable talking about past trauma or current difficulties.

Many servicemembers feel that they are better able to relate to equines than to people. The equines' social organization and associated hierarchies may feel familiar to the servicemember and thus provide opportunities for the service-member to process personal experiences indirectly. Many servicemembers, especially those suffering from PTSD, can understand and feel understood by the equine's fight-or-flight mentality. This shared understanding can help the servicemember feel accepted and identify healthy strategies to function in the world by using the equine's way of operating as a model. Finally, given the significant events that many servicemembers have experienced, they may feel numb or feel that there is nothing left to fear or accomplish. Interaction with such a large animal can provoke a strong emotional response and lead to an increased sense of empowerment.

The Military Culture

First and foremost, it is important to be aware that there are distinct cultural differences in working with military clients in comparison to civilian clients. Competence in understanding the military culture is a necessity for any thera-pist seeking to work with military clients (Atuel & Castro, 2018). For a review on cultural competence, see Chapter 11. From both an ethical and best practice standpoint, both the therapist and equine specialist should receive specialized training in understanding military culture and related client needs. Without this understanding and knowledge, treatment team members who have not served will have difficulty gaining the trust of military clients (Atuel & Castro, 2018). Unfortunately, I often hear stories of well-intentioned individuals and organizations wanting to help military clients but attempting to do so without the appropriate training and tools. Too often this results in many vulnerable servicemembers becoming discouraged at best and re-traumatized at worst.

In order to understand military culture, it is important to understand the reasons why servicemembers choose to join the military. These reasons can

134 Different Client Populations

differ across clients, but generally include family encouragement or legacy, feeling called to serve, interest in excitement and adventure, desire for discipline and structure, financial stability, escape from an unstable or negative environment, or educational and vocational opportunities (Helmus et al., 2018). The reasons that a servicemember chooses to join the military has a critical impact on how they experience their service and on their recovery from mental health struggles, particularly for conditions as such as PTSD and depression. A client's specific military occupational specialty (MOS) can also greatly impact these experiences. Furthermore, servicemembers of different eras can have vast differences in their experiences and perceptions of their service based on the combat theater, the nature of warfare, their age, and their reception upon arriving home from deployment. Finally, it is also important to be aware that even servicemembers who have never deployed to a warzone can also develop non-combat posttraumatic stress, depression, or suicidal ideation connected to their service. It is important to understand that despite a shared military culture, no two servicemembers are the same, nor will their experiences of and recovery from mental health struggles be the same.

It is also important to understand various aspects of military culture including chain of command structure, military norms, and military identity (Atuel & Castro, 2018; Meyer, Writer, & Brim, 2016). The chain of command refers to the ordered power hierarchy that informs decision-making, transmission of information, authority, and responsibility. Upon joining the military, servicemembers learn about the beliefs, values, traditions, events, and behaviors to be expected with military service and life. Conformity to these norms is required and expected. Servicemembers experience a shift from an individualistic way of life to a collectivistic one and adopt an honor-based value system. Military service is not just a job—it is a way of life. Therefore, the chain of command and norms provide the basis of the military identity (Atuel & Castro, 2018). Additionally, military culture can also differ within the military itself across different branches of service, MOS, era, and rank (Meyer et al., 2016). To provide culturally competent services, treatment team members should reflect on their attitudes and values about military service and stereotypes, and understand how these factors may influence the service provided.

Mental Health Concerns of Servicemembers

Military servicemembers of all eras have a heightened risk of mental health issues, especially posttraumatic stress, depression, suicidality, and traumatic brain injury. Many more servicemembers, ranging from 27% to 44%, encounter significant transitional and reintegration stress when returning to civilian life or leaving the military. Such issues may be related to employment, housing, health, and self-concept (Atuel & Castro, 2018; Morin, 2011).

Many military servicemembers that do not respond to or avoid traditional office-based therapies seek EACP. As pointed out by Mobbs and Bonanno

(2017), servicemembers may face barriers that limit treatment such as perceived stigma, difficulty accessing quality care, and discomfort with treatment approaches available from the Department of Veterans Affairs (VA) or other military installations. An alternative approach, such as EACP, can minimize these barriers. Many of my military clients report choosing EACP because it did not "feel" like therapy. These clients often feel discomfort sitting in an office that can feel sterile and artificial. Servicemembers report preference for EACP due to it being outdoors and feelings of peace and calm generated by being with the equines.

Social connectedness is an important protective factor in recovery for all servicemembers with mental health issues. Servicemembers who report loneliness reported more severe depression symptoms, increased suicidality, and decreased help-seeking behaviors (Teo et al., 2018). In my clinical experience using REPC, many of the servicemembers I have worked with have reported strong feelings of disconnection, detachment, or distrust in others. Facilitating the servicemember's connection with their chosen equine can be a crucial first step in supporting recovery from depression and reducing risk of suicidality. These clients often form strong bonds and attachments with their chosen equine. Over time, this bond helps them feel safe to process distressing thoughts and feelings (including trauma) and take risks to initiate connections with other people. As I discuss mental health conditions commonly experienced by servicemembers in the following sections, I will follow the discussion with mention of benefits of EACP in treating such conditions.

Posttraumatic Stress (PTSD)

Posttraumatic stress disorder (PTSD) is considered to be one of the signature wounds of war for servicemembers who have deployed to locations in the Middle East such as Iraq and Afghanistan. The prevalence of PTSD in these servicemembers varies widely across different studies, ranging from 4% to 30% (Hepner et al., 2017a; Hepner et al., 2017b; Reisman, 2016). The prevalence of PTSD in Gulf War veterans is estimated to be 10.1% (Kang, Natelson, Mahan, Lee, & Murphy, 2003). In a recent study on PTSD prevalence in Vietnam veterans, Marmar and colleagues (2015) found the current prevalence of PTSD to be 4.8%, current plus threshold rate to be 10.8%, and lifetime prevalence to be 17.0%. It is important to keep in mind that there are likely many servicemembers who do not meet full criteria for PTSD but experience subthreshold PTSD (in which they meet some criteria for most symptom clusters and experience emotional distress and/or functional impairment comparable to other servicemembers who do meet the full criteria) (Marmar et al., 2015). There are several mental health conditions that often co-occur with PTSD in military clients including depression, mild traumatic brain injury, anxiety, and substance use disorder (Reisman, 2016).

136   Different Client Populations

In working with servicemembers, I have found that REPC and the associated bond formed between the equine and servicemember can be beneficial in reducing intrusion symptoms, especially physiological distress; reducing avoidance of distressing thoughts and feelings; reducing symptoms relating to negative alterations in cognitions and mood, especially in reduction of negative feelings and detachment and increases in interest and positive feelings; and reducing symptoms related to arousal and reactivity, especially irritable and aggressive behavior, hypervigilance, and sleep problems (Sheade, 2015).

Moral Injury (MI)

Many servicemembers with PTSD also experience moral injury (MI). However, many therapists are unaware that servicemembers can experience a MI without experiencing PTS or PTSD. A client suffering from a MI may experience feelings of guilt, betrayal, grief, shame, sense of meaningless, or spiritual struggle (Koenig, Youssef, & Pearce, 2019). Although distinct from PTSD, the presence of MI can interfere with treatment of PTSD if undetected. Koenig, Ames, and Büssing (2019) described the role of loss of trust, spirituality, and meaning in the treatment of MI. Through interaction with the equine, a servicemember has the opportunity to not only express and process thoughts and feelings directly related to the MI, they can also explore themes related to building trust. Furthermore, the spiritual domain of the REPC approach for EACP allows for exploration of the client's spiritual identity and challenges within the client's own spiritual framework while also enabling the client to connect with a sense of meaning or purpose through experiences with the equine.

Frank's experience with Grande illustrates the power of the human-equine relationship in promoting healing from MI. Frank was a Navy SEAL who had completed numerous deployments during the Gulf War. He presented for EACP after experiencing debilitating symptoms of PTSD and depression that had culminated in a suicide attempt. Frank reported that he no longer knew who he was, and was unable to make even simple decisions such as which cereal to eat for breakfast. Frank had few personal connections with friends or family. He stated that he trusted no one, not even himself. During his first visit to the pasture, Grande approached Frank from across the pasture. He stopped a few feet away from Frank, and reached his nose out to smell Frank. Frank started to reach to pet Grande but stopped himself. He said he did not know if that would be the right decision even though he wanted to touch Grande. Frank was paralyzed by his own indecision and lack of trust in himself. When asked if he wanted to work with Grande again the next week, Frank said he didn't know. During the next session, Grande once again approached Frank from across the pasture. Frank said that although he couldn't trust himself, he wanted to trust Grande's judgment and agreed to work with him. Over time, Frank began to take risks to initiate physical contact and later structured activities with Grande. Frank struggled to stay present during the sessions, as his mind raced with thoughts and worries about how to manage his daily life. Grande responded to Frank's agitation by becoming restless and disengaged himself. Frank and Grande spent weeks working together to help Frank become present. On one particularly challenging day, Frank suddenly stopped and turned to Grande. He said "I heard him! I don't know how but I feel like I just heard Grande's voice telling me that I can do this". Frank reported feeling comforted and encouraged by this experience and that he felt a new level of closeness with Grande. After this experience, Frank turned a corner in EACP and reported a significant decrease in negative thoughts and feelings about himself and worked towards the creation of a new meaning and narrative for all of his deployment-related experiences.

Depression

Depression is another significant mental health concern for servicemembers. Estimates of depression range from 1% up to 60% in servicemembers presenting with post-deployment health concerns (Hepner et al., 2017b). Furthermore, approximately 55% of servicemembers with PTSD also experience depression. Regarding suicidality, servicemembers who have deployed to Iraq and Afghanistan have a heightened risk compared to the U.S. general population, with deployed servicemembers having a 41% higher suicide risk of suicide than the general population and non-deployed servicemembers having a 61% higher suicide risk (Kang et al., 2018). The number of servicemembers who die by suicide each day has increased since 2005. According to the U.S. Department of Veterans Affairs (2019), 16.8 servicemembers died by suicide each day in 2017. Servicemembers who experience moral injury may have a heightened suicide risk (Koenig et al., 2019b). The presence of the equines can enable the clients to feel safe when processing distressing thoughts, feelings, and experiences. The relationship with their chosen equine can enable the client to feel safe and accepted while working to create new meaning and self-identity.

Mild Traumatic Brain Injury (mTBI)

Mild traumatic brain injury (mTBI) is also considered to be a signature wound for Iraq an Afghanistan veterans, with 15–25% sustaining an mTBI (Davenport, 2016). The majority of mTBIs are sustained following exposure to an explosive blast. However, as many symptoms of mTBI overlap with that of PTSD, accurate diagnosis can be difficult (Hayes, 2019). Clients who experience comorbid PTSD and mTBI can experience compounding of symptoms and impairment, especially in areas related to daily functioning and self-concept. Interventions in EACP that focus on promoting cognitive skills (e.g., decision-making, social skills, and problem-solving) while also addressing client identity and self-concept are especially helpful. In working with clients with service-connected mTBI, I have found the equines to be particularly helpful in assisting these clients in

138 Different Client Populations

relearning facial cues and social skills, building confidence and decision-making skills, and making connections between bodily sensations and emotional experiences. For many such servicemember clients, the equine's accepting, empathic, and authentic way of being enables these clients to feel a sense of worthiness in navigating life's new challenges and redefining self-identity.

Military Sexual Assault (MST)

Military sexual assault (MST) is defined as "both sexual harassment and sexual assault that occurs in military settings" (Street & Stafford, n.d.). Clients who have experienced MST are more likely to experience mental health concerns such as PTSD, eating disorders, dissociative disorders, personality disorders, anxiety, and depression (Kimerling, Gima, Smith, Street, & Frayne, 2007). The prevalence of MST is difficult to identify, but it is estimated that between 23.6% to 52.5% of female servicemembers and between 1.9% to 8.9% of male servicemembers have been the victims of MST (Wilson, 2018). Survivors of MST face unique challenges such as not being believed or blamed by others, and/or having to continue working in proximity to their perpetrator. Furthermore, MST survivors may feel a heightened sense of betrayal, especially if they worked closely with or perceived the perpetrator as family. This experience can lead to numerous interpersonal difficulties with trust, feeling safe, and setting boundaries. MST survivors often experience self-blame, shame, low self-worth, difficulty with decision-making, and guilt. The primary needs of an MST survivor are to experience safety, feel in control, and find meaning (Foynes, 2016).

The relational focus of the REPC approach makes this a useful intervention in meeting many of the needs of MST survivors. For many MST clients, the presence of the equine can enable the client to experience a sense of safety and protection. In fact, many of my clients with MST have deliberately chosen the largest equine in the herd, citing an increased feeling of protection. Additionally, interaction with their chosen equine can provide opportunities for the client to practice relational skills, such as building trust and setting boundaries, leading to a sense of empowerment and control by being able to communicate with and gain cooperation from such a large animal. The equine's interest in and acceptance of the client can challenge negative self-perceptions and strengthen the client's self-concept.

Mental Health Concerns in Military Dependents

It important to keep in mind that military dependents (i.e., children and spouses) are also at a heightened risk for mental health problems including anxiety, depression, behavioral problems, and psychological stress (Esposito-Smythers et al., 2011). Military families experience unique challenges associated with the deployment cycle. For this reason, group counseling formats may be especially helpful for some clients to help them build connections with others who have shared experiences. Military children and teenagers benefit most from approaches that focus on building support and coping skills (Esposito-Smythers, 2011). Additionally, spouses and children of servicemembers with PTSD may be at risk of developing secondary traumatic stress (Diehle, Brooks, & Greenberg, 2017) or child behavior problems (DeVoe, Kritikos, Emmert-Aronson, Kantor, & Paris, 2018). The REPC approach's focus on the relationship with the equine can enable children to experience a greater sense of support and acceptance through this relationship. The child has the opportunity to practice a wide range of skills in working with the equine, such as problem-solving, communication, conflict resolution, and calming to help manage stressors and mental health problems associated with the deployment cycle. Finally, it is important to consider that surviving spouses and children of deceased servicemembers are more likely to experience complex grief and have unique needs that differ from other types of grieving clients, especially in the case of loss due to combat (Cozza et al., 2017) or suicide (Harrington-LaMorie, Jordan, Ruocco, & Cerel, 2018).

Mental Health Concerns Related to COVID-19

At the time of writing this section (May 2020), restrictions in the United States are becoming increasingly relaxed while projected cases of and deaths from COVID-19 continue to rise. Pandemics have much in common with other types of disasters such as impacting entire communities, being unpredictable, resulting in fatalities, and continuing effects after the immediate danger has passed. However, unlike other disasters that encourage communities to physically come together for support and rebuilding, pandemic response is marked by separation and isolation (Sprang & Silman, 2013). COVID-19 is a global pandemic impacting individuals across ethnicity and socioeconomic status worldwide. It is crucial that attention to mental health needs is not overlooked. It is likely that the mental health impacts will be both acute and also long-lasting after life begins to normalize again (Galea, Merchant, & Lurie, 2020).

There is currently a limited amount of literature on the mental health needs of people experiencing a pandemic than other types of disaster-related mental health research and resources. Previous epidemics have been correlated to increases in posttraumatic stress disorder, stress, anxiety, and psychological distress (Galea et al., 2020). Individuals with preexisting mental health conditions are especially vulnerable to increased emotional distress and maladaptive behaviors (Cullen, Gulati, & Kelly, 2020). Societies are also at risk of increases in substance abuse, domestic violence, and child abuse (Galea et al., 2020). Loneliness is another significant threat to mental health and may be especially pronounced in older adults who practice social distancing more stringently (Galea et al., 2020). It is likely that many clients will also experience grief and loss not only from the death of and separation from loved ones but also for the loss of daily life and routines during times in which local restrictions and

140 Different Client Populations

social distancing measures are in place. However, even after these measures are relaxed or lifted, life may not return to the way it previously was and many clients will grieve this loss as well.

The impact of quarantine itself can lead to stress, depression, difficulty sleeping, fear, and confusion among children, adolescents, and adults (Golberstein, Wen, & Miller, 2020; Pfefferbaum & North, 2020; Wang, Zhang, Zhao, Zhang, & Jiang, 2020). These effects may be more pronounced due to prolonged quarantine periods, financial stress, and fear of not having adequate supplies to meet basic needs. Finally, it is important to note that the secondary effects of social distancing may influence an increased rate of suicide. Reger, Stanley, and Joiner (2020) identified factors influencing risk of suicide as economic stress, social isolation, decreased access to community and religious support, barriers to mental health treatment, illness and medical problems, national experience of anxiety, and an increase in firearms sales.

Individuals most at risk for the psychological distress related to the pandemic include those who contract the disease, older and/or immunocompromised individuals, individuals with preexisting mental health conditions, and essential workers (Pfefferbaum & North, 2020). Individuals who contract and recover from pandemic diseases are at greater risk of developing PTSD. Survivors with pandemic-related PTSD are also more likely to experience psychological distress and impaired social functioning years after receiving treatment (Hong et al., 2009).

Healthcare professionals, especially those working in emergency or critical care facilities, are especially vulnerable to negative impacts on mental health due to anxiety and fear of contracting the virus or passing it on to significant others, feeling stigmatized, negative feelings about their job, and high stress (Cullen et al., 2020; Lai et al., 2020). Nurses may be at an even higher risk given that they tend to have the most frequent close contact with patients. These healthcare professionals are also at risk of experiencing moral injury (MI). As described in the section on military clients, MI results from experiences or actions that violate an individual's sense of their moral code and places these professionals at an even higher risk of depression, PTSD, and suicide (Greenberg, Docherty, Gnanapragasam, & Wessely, 2020). These professionals may experience profound feelings of sadness, guilt, shame, and anger. It is critical that therapists working with frontline healthcare professionals are experienced in identifying and treating trauma. Based on research on military families, it is likely that family members of healthcare and other essential workers are at a heighted risk for secondary trauma based on the essential worker's exposure to stressful experiences (Dirkzwager, Bramsen, Adèr, & van der Ploeg, 2005; Herzog, Everson, & Whitworth, 2011). In the case of a pandemic and associated quarantine, these effects may be magnified due to lessened social support for both essential workers and their families.

As COVID-19 has impacted people worldwide, it would be prudent for all therapists practicing EACP to be trained in trauma-informed approaches.

Different Client Populations   141

All clients should be screened for presence of PTSD due to COVID-19. UCLA (2020) released a free screening tool to evaluate the presence of COVID-19-related PTSD in children and adolescents. Assuming it can be provided safely with proper sanitizing and social distancing procedures in place as needed (see Chapter 12), EACP may provide a less risky alternative to receiving office-based counseling as EACP sessions take place outdoors with greater opportunities for social distancing. Facilitating opportunities for clients to build connection with the equines can increase perceived social support and reduce loneliness. In addition, EACP can help clients to develop coping skills and providing opportunities for self-care (Pfefferbaum & North, 2020). For children, interventions focused on encouraging expression of feelings and strengthening the parent-child relationship can best support child clients and reduce the risk of developing or worsening serious mental health issues (WHO, 2020).

Finally, therapists should be aware of the potential for impacts on the session itself. For example, clients may feel more on edge or anxious while onsite if they are worried about contracting a disease. As many organizations highly recommend wearing masks when providing in-person services, the therapist should consider how restricting facial expressions may impede the counseling process as the client cannot read the therapist's facial expressions and the therapist cannot read the client's as accurately. The result may be increased misunderstandings and frustration on the part of both the client and therapist. However, as pointed out to me by an intern, wearing a mask may have a silver lining in that it may encourage some clients to verbalize their thoughts and feelings more directly in order to be understood.

Chapter 11

Ethical Considerations in Equine-Assisted Counseling and Psychotherapy

There are numerous ethical considerations in the practice of equine-assisted counseling and psychotherapy (EACP). Although some considerations are not unique to EACP, this modality presents challenges that would not be encountered in a traditional office-based setting related to multiple relationships and therapeutic boundaries, transference and countertransference, client screening, termination, multicultural and diversity considerations, and in-session crises. Other considerations are wholly unique to EACP such as maintaining client physical safety, limit-setting, equine welfare, and session debriefing and supervision. In this chapter, I provide a review of these considerations and suggestions to manage potential ethical issues that arise.

Multiple Relationships and Therapeutic Boundaries

The relationship between the client and the treatment team (i.e., therapist and equine specialist) is a professional one. Any relationships that occur outside of this relationship in EACP can create multiple relationships between the client and the treatment team. In order to best protect the client, neither the therapist nor the equine specialist should have a personal, social, or business relationship with clients receiving EACP and, in some cases, after EACP has ended. Whether or not it is acceptable to engage in a new type of relationship after EACP has ended is informed by the therapist's code of ethics, licensing board rules, and the client's best interest.

Welfel (2010) identified three dynamics that occur in multiple or dual relationships between the client and the treatment team: the fiduciary relationship, the client's emotional involvement, and the power differential. The term "fiduciary relationship" refers to the therapist's obligation to ensure the client's best interests are the focus of the relationship, and multiple relationships that could compete with the client's best interests should be avoided (p. 225). The client also has a high level of emotional involvement with the treatment team. The client is inherently placed in a more vulnerable position in the relationship than the treatment team—the client seeks help; the treatment team provides it.

Interactions with members of the treatment team in other contexts can confuse or threaten the client's well-being and therapeutic relationship overall.

It is the therapist's responsibility to establish clear and consistent boundaries and ensure that all other facility personnel (including the equine specialist) understand and abide by these boundaries. These boundaries protect the client's welfare and best interests. When these boundaries are not enforced, it can lead to dual or multiple relationships between the client and treatment team. Therapists in office-based practices establish boundaries with clients to prevent multiple relationships by avoiding certain activities such as accepting gifts or social invitations, engaging in sexual relationships, writing references, or interacting on social media. These boundaries should be similarly established and enforced in the EACP setting.

Certain types of multiple relationships may be encountered in EACP that are not present in a traditional office-based practice. If either member of the treatment team owns (or has a close relationship with) any of the equine(s) in the session, the treatment team member may have a more difficult time remaining objective (Wycoff, 2019). Additionally, therapists who also serve in the role of equine specialist play a dual role in both providing clinical services and maintaining client physical safety with the equines (Wycoff, 2019).

As noted by Welfel (2010), the relationship between the client and the treatment team is characterized by a power differential. As the client is inherently in a more emotionally vulnerable position than the treatment team, they have a higher risk of emotional harm. Clients may have difficulty saying no to requests or fear rejection by the treatment team. This power differential is often magnified in EACP due to the fact that the client not only has more emotional vulnerability, but also that the client is relying on the treatment team to protect their physical safety during the session as well. Furthermore, the experience of EACP taking place outside in a natural environment can shift the dynamics of the power differential, as nature interacts with all counseling participants, not just the client. Therefore, the treatment team members may be just as impacted as the client in coping with uncomfortable weather conditions, bee stings, or other unexpected or unpleasant events. Although the potential blurring of boundaries should be carefully considered and managed, it is also important to note the benefits of this shift in promoting the "real relationship" between the client and the treatment team and the client's ability to witness more of the treatment team member's humanity as individual people, not just the treatment team (Jordan, 2013).

In EACP, there are other types of potential multiple relationships that should be approached with caution. Oftentimes, the facilities where EACP takes place offer other types of activities such as riding lessons, horse boarding, or volunteer activities. It is imperative the therapist carefully consider the potential risks to the client and the impact on the therapeutic relationship with not only the therapist but also the equine specialist and other facility personnel in determining the appropriateness of the client's participation in other activities.

144 Ethical Considerations

The therapist must carefully consider all of the possible ways in which the client's concurrent or consecutive participation in other activities may negatively impact the client. First, allowing clients to participate in other facility activities may risk the client's confidentiality, as there a higher risk of an inadvertent disclosure. Furthermore, should the client experience difficulty in this new role, confidential information may be shared carelessly or unintentionally. Due to the client's high level of emotional vulnerability from participation in EACP, the client may have trouble emotionally distinguishing between the boundaries of psychotherapy and other non-psychotherapy activities. It is also important to consider the nature of the client's participation and how much benefit they may gain. Allowing current clients to volunteer can very easily create multiple relationships, as the client is now in a role to serve the treatment team or the facility. Due to the power imbalance inherent in EACP, clients may have trouble saying no or communicating discomfort when asked to complete tasks as part of their volunteer work. There is also a strong risk of role slippage in which a treatment team member who interacts with the client outside of an EACP session can further endanger the therapeutic relationship and the client's best interests (Welfel, 2010). Even allowing clients to volunteer after termination of counseling should be approached with caution. Any decision to allow a client to participate in other facility activities should be considered on a case-by-case basis and carefully weighed in accordance with the risks and benefits to the clients. I will discuss several cautionary tales that illustrate the risks of multiple relationships and the care that must be taken in making ethical decisions.

Nancy was a client who I had been seeing in counseling for quite some time. She initiated counseling to work on posttraumatic stress related to childhood sexual abuse. Early in her therapy work, she bonded with a draft horse named Jock. Jock was calm, quiet, and docile in her sessions. Nancy spent hours brushing Jock and processing her trauma in his presence. After counseling ended, and without my knowledge, Nancy requested permission from the therapeutic horseback riding program to volunteer as a side-walker for children with disabilities. Nancy was elated to be able to continue to work with Jock. As time progressed, Nancy began to struggle in her role as a volunteer, and it became evident that her intention was to spend time with Jock, not support the riding students. Nancy struggled to manage Jock in this new context. In riding lessons, Jock was stubborn and prone to refusing to cooperate with the volunteers. One day, Nancy was bringing Jock from the pasture to the barn for a riding lesson. Instead of refusing to move, Jock turned the other way and dragged Nancy down the driveway almost to the busy road at the facility entrance. From then on, Nancy and Jock's relationship was never the same. She lost all trust in him and the sacredness of the healing relationship she had established with him in EACP. Her posttraumatic symptoms resurfaced and she refused to return to the facility.

Another example of the risks of multiple relationships involves the story of Michael, a military veteran. Michael had been participating in EACP for over

Ethical Considerations 145

a year and wanted to begin participating in the veteran's therapeutic riding class as well. Given Michael's lack of social support and overall progress in EACP, he was approved to participate as a rider in the military riding class. His regular instructor was actively involved in the EACP program as an equine specialist (although not in Michael's EACP sessions) and consulted closely with his therapist to ensure the two services were supporting Michael in a complementary fashion. One day, Michael's instructor was absent and the program director decided to fill in rather than to cancel the class. The director had a limited understanding of EACP and was unaware of Michael's specific needs. Michael felt uncomfortable but decided to stay for the lesson anyway. At one point during the lesson, Michael felt so overwhelmed that he decided to dismount from the horse. The director later reported that Michael had a great lesson and dismounted because he felt tired. When Michael returned to EACP the following week, he reported that it had been the worst riding lesson that he had ever had. He stated that he felt judged and misunderstood by the director during the lesson. After his EACP session, he decided to approach the director to express his feelings. Following this conversation, Michael walked away feeling criticized and shut down. Michael spent the next several EACP sessions processing his feelings about his experience with the director and his newfound discomfort with the facility overall.

Transference and Countertransference

As discussed in Chapter 3, transference and countertransference processes are inherent in all forms of psychotherapy. These processes may be magnified in EACP due to higher client emotionality and feelings of attachment to the equines by both the client and treatment team members. It is critical that the therapist possesses a deep understanding of these processes as well as competence in managing them ethically and effectively for all involved. Due to the presence of the equines, treatment team members have a heightened risk transference associated with protectiveness for the animals. Observation of the client interacting with the equines in a way that may be uncomfortable or stressful to the equine may provoke negative feelings towards the client. The treatment team members should both engage in self-reflection to evaluate their own internal reactions to the client (Karol, 2007). The manner in which the treatment team interacts with the equine, both positively and negatively, will have a strong influence on the client's level of trust towards the treatment team members and nature of the therapeutic relationship. While the client's observation of the treatment team interacting in a way that seems positive can help build trust, the treatment team's response to inappropriate equine behaviors may do damage to the relationship should the client misunderstand or feel a strong emotional attachment to the equine. These clients may not be capable of understanding a "logical" explanation for the treatment team member's response to the equine as a result of the client's functioning and level of emotionality in the

146 Ethical Considerations

moment. If this transference is not appropriately attended to and managed, irreparable harm may be done to both the therapeutic relationship and the client's progress.

Client Screening: Precautions and Contraindications

As work with equines includes inherent risk of injury or even death to all personnel involved with the program—including the treatment team and the client—there are several factors to consider when screening a client for participation in EACP. A precaution may exist if a potential client has a condition (or develops a condition) that may interfere with their participation or require modifications to be made to create a safe environment. It should also be noted that a safe environment may not be possible with certain client conditions and therefore the client should not be allowed to participate in EACP. These conditions are called contraindications and may be brief and time-limited, or may preclude participation completely.

There are a number of precautions that clients should be screened for prior to participation in EACP including allergies, medication side-effects, physical and movement limitations, immunocompromised conditions, asthma, pregnancy, or seizures. As EACP typically takes place in outdoor environments, clients may be exposed to allergens that could otherwise be avoided in an office such as plants, hay, bedding, and animal dander (including equines, cats, dogs, and wildlife). Additionally, it is important to be aware if the client has any life-threating allergies, such as bee stings, and to create a safety plan with the client to respond in the case of exposure.

Many clients with mental health concerns take psychotropic medications. It is important to be aware of all of the client's medications (including non-psychotropic ones) and their associated side-effects. Such medications can affect the client's tolerance of temperature extremes, sensitivity to sunlight, risk of dizziness, cause immunosuppression, or impact their ability to stand or walk for extended periods of time.

The therapist should also carefully consider any physical limitations. For example, will a client with a broken foot be able to move quickly out of an equine's way? Can the treatment team make modifications to the environment to make it safe? It is also important to consider the client's weight and overall size. Clients who are obese may have less physical stamina and may have more difficulty moving themselves (or being moved) out of a potentially dangerous situation quickly. Additionally, for clients with physical disabilities that require accommodations (e.g., wheelchair), are the facility and working areas accessible to meet the client's needs?

Immunocompromised clients, such as individuals acquired immune deficiency syndrome (AIDS), cancer or undergoing chemotherapy, older adults, or clients with autoimmune, congenital, or chronic diseases, may have a higher

Ethical Considerations 147

risk of contracting illnesses from others, both human and equine. These clients may be more susceptible to zoonoses or infectious diseases that can be spread from equines to humans (Dwyer, 2015) such as the skin infection, methicillin-resistant Staphylococcus aureus (MRSA) (Weese et al., 2006), and other equine influenza viruses (Xie, Anderson, Dramragchaa, Chuluunbaatar, & Gray, 2016). It is crucial that all program equines are current on vaccinations and de-worming medications to minimize risk to these clients. These clients may require precautions in place to limit their contact with animal dander, saliva, manure, and urine. It is important to provide an opportunity for clients to wash their hands and any other part that came into contact with the equines and other barn animals (Murthy et al., 2015).

It is also important to note that the natural environment may present a challenge for some clients independent of any specific health conditions. Clients who have difficulty tolerating adverse weather conditions or fear of components of the natural environment (e.g., stinging insects) may have difficulty making progress in EACP if they are overly distracted by their concerns. For other clients with significant trauma or anxiety, certain aspects of the natural environment (e.g., a loud thunderclap) could become triggering or even re-traumatizing. Therefore, the therapist should carefully consider the client's history and functioning in light of these considerations (Berger, 2010). However, if these challenges can be overcome, they can provide rich opportunities for the client to gain insight and valuable skills that can be generalized to coping with life's daily challenges.

The severity of a client's mental health concerns should also be evaluated. First and foremost, the client's presenting concerns should not interfere with the treatment team's ability to keep the client safe during sessions. Clients with severe mental health concerns resulting in increased risk of danger to themselves or others should be carefully evaluated before participation in EACP based on the individual client's presentation and needs (PATH Intl., 2017). For example, many clients with suicidal ideation benefit significantly from participation in EACP. However, clients who are actively suicidal may require a higher level of care and safety protocols than can be provided, depending on the nature of the facility. It is also important for clients to be capable of taking some responsibility for their own safety in interacting with the equines. Some clients who have experienced trauma or severe depression may struggle to appropriately set boundaries or assert themselves when needed. For example, I have worked with several trauma survivors who experienced significant difficulty in moving the equine off their foot when stepped on, or even alerting the treatment team that the equine was stepping on their foot. It is important to be especially vigilant for these types of risks when working with certain types of trauma survivors. Clients who are actively under the influence of a substance, actively experiencing hallucinations or delusions, or not oriented to time, place, or person should be restricted from participation in EACP, as they will pose a significant risk to themselves and others during these times. However, that is

148 Ethical Considerations

not to say that clients with schizophrenia, substance use disorder, or trauma-related dissociation should not be accepted into the program. Instead, these clients should be evaluated at the start of each session and alternative activities not involving the equines should be planned in the case that it is unsafe for the client to work with the equines. Each treatment team should establish evaluation criteria and policies and procedures to handle such cases.

Clients should also be screened for high-risk behaviors such as animal abuse and fire-setting (PATH Intl., 2017). Ascione, McCabe, Phillips, and Tedeschi (2010) provided considerations and recommendations for evaluating and accepting clients with a history of animal abuse into animal-assisted therapy programs. In some cases, participation in EACP can be very helpful in building empathy and treating clients with conduct problems or antisocial behaviors. However, the treatment team is also responsible for maintaining the equines' welfare and not placing them at risk of harm. Children with a history of exposure to domestic violence, neglect, parent substance abuse, or physical, sexual, or emotional abuse have an elevated risk of animal abuse. Therefore, it is important to carefully evaluate clients with these types of histories for past animal abuse prior to providing EACP. In determining whether or not to accept a client with a history of animal abuse or fire-setting behavior, it may be useful to evaluate the client's level of impulse control, empathy towards others, willingness to follow directions, and self-awareness. Once accepted into EACP, the client should be closely monitored for signs of maltreatment that may escalate to animal cruelty or abuse such as over-vigorous grooming (PATH Intl., 2017).

Client Physical Safety

It is interesting to note that researchers have found injuries associated with working with equines to be more related to the frequency and amount of interactions with equines rather than an individual's level of competency in working with equines. Therefore, both the therapist and equine specialist should be knowledgeable of equine behavior and possess strong observation skills when in session to clients and themselves safe. Many potentially dangerous situations can be avoided simply by observing equine behavior to determine the safest human positioning and angle of approach. Interactions or activities occurring between the client and equine in which the equine displays conflictual or flight behaviors may indicate increasing stress and therefore increased risk of danger to both the client and equine. This risk may be more pronounced in lunging or round pen activities involving higher speeds. These activities should be facilitated intentionally and with caution (Fenner, McLean et al., 2019).

The strength of the relationship between the treatment team and equines, especially the equine specialist, is crucial to minimizing safety risks to the client (McBride & Mills, 2012). Furthermore, as the quality of past interactions with equines can predict the nature of future interactions, it is crucial for the treatment team to have a positive, trusting relationship with any equines to be

Ethical Considerations 149

included in sessions (Hausberger et al., 2008). In many sessions, the equines often approach and stand close to me when something unusual or potentially stressful is occurring in session, especially in play therapy sessions. As my relationship with the equines participating in play therapy progresses, I often observe that rather than walking away during a high-energy moment, such as a ball being thrown near the equine, the equine will instead walk to me and continue to observe the child's behavior from a closer distance than if they had decided to remove themselves from proximity to the child's behavior.

As the quality of equine husbandry can impact client safety, it is important to carefully evaluate the ongoing physical care of the equines and herd management procedures. The equine specialist should establish and maintain policies and procedures to minimize risk of client injury and illness, including zoonosis transmission (IAHAIO, 2019). Equines who are physically unhealthy or mentally stressed are more likely to engage in aggressive or dangerous behaviors towards humans such as biting or kicking. Equines who are experiencing pain, even if unrelated to the session, are also more likely to demonstrate aggressive behaviors towards humans (Fureix et al., 2010). In addition, equines kept in stalls for longer times may have more unspent energy and therefore may demonstrate more anxious, aggressive, or inattentive behaviors (Rivera et al., 2002). Equines kept in smaller paddocks may be more likely to demonstrate aggressive and stress-related behaviors than equines keep in a larger pasture (Hogan, Houpt, & Sweeney, 1988). It is important to note, in some cases, play behavior may indicate higher levels of stress and function as a coping mechanism to manage chronic stress by eliciting positive feelings, as equines who demonstrate more play behaviors also may demonstrate more aggression (Blois-Heulin et al., 2015; Hausberger et al., 2012). When grouping or selecting equines for activities, it is important to select equines who spend a considerable amount of time together outside of sessions. Equines who are less familiar with each other (especially those who interact across stalls or fences) are more likely to engage in aggressive behaviors, thus posing more of a safety risk to clients (Fureix et al., 2012).

It is important that the treatment team carefully consider how to best respond to inappropriate equine behaviors in session such as nipping, kicking, pushiness, or other undesirable or unsafe behaviors. The way in which the equine specialist responds to these behaviors can have a significant impact on both the client and equine(s). For example, smacking an equine on the nose for becoming too pushy or nipping can impact the client in a negative way, especially clients who have experienced trauma or abuse. Even the most logical explanation will have no effect on a client who has become triggered or overwhelmed by negative emotions such as fear. This client will not be capable of hearing or understanding the equine specialist's explanation. The client may lose trust in the equine specialist at best or become re-traumatized at worst. In addition, the use of positive punishment (e.g., smacking the equine on the nose) has been linked to several negative outcomes in equines such as decreased motivation, learned

150 Ethical Considerations

helplessness, increased fear responses, disruption in the relationship with the equine specialist, learning deficits, aggression, and even posttraumatic stress (Hartmann et al., 2017; McLean & Christensen, 2017). The equine specialist should consider the equine's inappropriate behavior in the context of what is happening in the session to try to understand why the equine is engaging in that particular behavior. If the behavior cannot be managed safely, the equine should be removed from the session.

Limit-Setting

At times, the treatment team will need to set safety limits regarding the client-equine interaction to protect all involved. General procedures for limit-setting, including the specific limits and manner in which they will be set, should be discussed and agreed upon in advance by the treatment team. Of course, it is also important for treatment team members to be flexible, as unique, unanticipated occurrences will happen. Generally speaking, the therapist is responsible for deciding and setting limits regarding the client's emotional safety, and the equine specialist is responsible for deciding and setting limits for physical safety for all involved (both people and equines) and the emotional safety of the equines. Limit-setting can be a delicate balance between managing safety risks and promoting equine welfare while also honoring the client's autonomy and discovery-based process. As there is an inherent risk of danger anytime anyone interacts with an equine (regardless of setting), the treatment team should work to manage potential safety issues and be prepared to take immediate action should an imminent physical safety risk arise. In other cases, the equine specialist may determine limits in the moment based on the specific client, equine, and contextual factors. For example, one of my non-negotiable safety limits relates to how the client holds the lead rope. In my sessions, the treatment team will immediately intervene and set a limit anytime a client has the rope in a loop, wrapped around their hand, or over any part of their body such as their shoulder. In my opinion, these ways of holding the lead rope pose an imminent risk of serious harm to the client should the equine spook or move suddenly. In another example, several of the equines that we work with have been trained and desensitized to stepping on their own lead rope. For example, Petey, an older Welsh pony gelding, will simply stand and wait to be moved. In contrast, Raven, a younger Thoroughbred mare, will have a huge reaction that could result in danger to the client should she step on her rope. In this case, the equine specialist may use different limits based on the different equines. For example, Petey's client may have more leeway to take time to notice and rectify the situation if Petey steps on his rope, whereas the equine specialist is likely to take action to prevent Raven from stepping on her rope in the first place. It is also important to consider each client's age and cognitive development in deciding when and how to set limits, as well as the knowledge of the specific equine's behavior and tolerance and behavior in the moment with the client.

Ethical Considerations 151

There may also be occurrences in which the equine must be removed from the session entirely due to a change in the equine's behavior resulting in heightened risk for the client, equine illness or injury, or the client's refusal or inability to comply with previously set limits.

There are many ways to set limits. All methods should convey inherent respect for the client and their autonomy. Treatment team members should communicate limits in a way that is matter-of-fact and nonjudgmental. It is also important to attend to language and tone used to communicate the limit, especially with older adolescents and adults to avoid appearing condescending or judgmental. The imminence and severity of the current risk also determine the manner in which the limit will be set. In most cases, clients who are behaving in ways that create emotional stress for the equines should be given the opportunity to understand the equine's experience and modify their behavior. I have found limit-setting methods based in play therapy, such as the A-C-T and choice-giving methods, to be useful in working with clients of all ages (Landreth, 2012; Sheade, 2019b). Both methods communicate respect for the client's thoughts and feelings, provide opportunities for the clients to better understand the equine's needs, and enable the client's autonomy in making choices. These methods can also help clients learn valuable skills such as decision-making, self-control, and self-monitoring, and can be especially helpful in building empathy with clients with development delays, oppositional behavior or conduct disorder, or clients with impaired social skills and engagement (Sheade, 2019a).

Termination

In all forms of counseling and psychotherapy, termination is the ultimate goal and indicative that the client has met their treatment goals and objectives. A planned and agreed upon termination is in the best interest of the client to ensure the client is well-equipped to manage without therapy and has closure on the relationships formed with the treatment team and equines. I believe that the termination process in ending the relationship between client and equine should be taken just as seriously as between the client and therapist in an office-based setting. Many clients form emotional bonds and attachments that are just as strong with the equine, if not more so, than with the treatment team. Likewise, as the equine specialist is also considered a part of the therapeutic relationship, the client should have the opportunity to have a healthy termination process with them as well, should the equine specialist be unable to continue working with a particular client.

Termination of the relationship with a specific equine can also occur even if the client remains in EACP. In some cases, the client decides that a particular equine is no longer a good fit for their needs and requests a new equine. In these cases, the treatment team should carefully process and explore the client's thoughts and feelings to ensure that the client is not repeating maladaptive

152 Ethical Considerations

relational patterns that parallel unhealthy interactions with people. In the case that the treatment team and client agree to switch equines, the treatment should still facilitate a healthy termination between client and equine. In other cases, the termination between client and equine may be unwanted or unexpected, such as in the case of the equine being sold, re-homed, or passing away.

Death of an Equine

It is an unfortunate but likely occurrence that, at some point, a client will have to mourn the loss of a program equine. Many equine-assisted activities and therapies programs work with older equines or those with preexisting health conditions. These equines often have a temperament more suitable for therapy work and can participate in therapy work even if they can no longer perform in their previous jobs. Given these factors, it is likely that you will experience the loss of a therapy equine. As most clients form close bonds with the equines, this loss is likely to have a significant impact on the client (Beck & Katcher, 2003).

Clients may grieve the loss in any number of ways, just as they would with their own pet or human significant other (Cohen, 2010). Most clients are sad, some more outwardly so than others. It is both likely and expected that clients will mourn and grieve the equine (Walsh, 2009). The client's grief may be influenced by factors surrounding the loss, such as a sudden and unexpected loss versus an equine that had been in ill health (Cohen, 2010). Additionally, for children in particular, the loss of an equine may be the child's first experience with death and loss. Clients who have experienced other significant losses or who feel more isolated and disconnected in their day-to-day lives are likely to be more affected by the loss of the equine. This loss is likely to elicit strong feelings, even if the client only knew the equine tangentially.

The therapist and equine specialist should collaborate to decide how to inform the client of the loss and help the client process. If possible, some clients may benefit from being able to say goodbye to the equine. Of course, allowing the client to say goodbye will be contingent on the equine's condition and current quality of life. In some cases, the facility has noticed a gradual deterioration in the equine's quality of life and made the decision to euthanize the equine. In these cases, clients often have the opportunity to say goodbye. In other cases, the equine sustained a sudden injury or serious colic in which keeping the equine alive would result in suffering and be traumatizing to the client. It is important for the treatment team to work closely in consulting with the facility to be thoughtful and intentional in considering both the needs of the equine and of the client. In addition, the therapist should be well-prepared to support the client in mourning the loss of an equine and well-versed in understanding the grief process.

Although most clients experience sadness, some may also experience anger. One such client became enraged upon learning that one of the equines in the herd had been euthanized following a serious, unexpected illness. This client had formed a strong attachment to the equine and viewed him as a "grandfatherly" figure. In my role as a contracting therapist, I was not involved in the difficult decision to euthanize the equine. However, the client became enraged at me for "not doing enough" to save the equine. Despite the difficulty of the situation for both the client and me, it provided an opportunity to process issues related to grief and loss. The client not only grieved the loss of the equine but was also able to grieve and process the loss of a significant family member. Up until this time, the client had avoided all thoughts and feelings about the family member and was finally able to grieve both losses.

To best support the client, I have found it is important to be honest and truthful in communicating the loss to the client. If a therapist were to simply inform the client that the equine had moved to another facility and the client were to later find out that the equine had passed away, trust would be broken in the therapeutic relationship, possibly irreparably. Although the treatment team should be open and honest, the therapist's clinical judgment will inform the level of detail provided to the client. The therapist should also be prepared to process the client's grief during the session, and in some cases, across numerous sessions. Allowing the client to have a token memory of the equine, such as piece of tail hair or a mold of the equine's hoof print, can help the client to gain closure while preserving the equine's memory. The therapist and equine specialist were also in a relationship with the equine and also need to grieve the loss. Treatment team members should ensure they have appropriate outlets to grieve and process the loss. If they do not grieve the loss themselves, they are likely to interfere with the client's grief process and even do damage the client.

It is also important to prepare for the equines themselves to grieve the loss of a fellow herd member. I have witnessed several cases in which the equine who seemed to have the strongest bond with deceased equine becomes listless and appears depressed. It is important for the treatment team to not only attend to the needs of the client but also the needs of the equine. Oftentimes, when a client's chosen equine has passed away, they begin working with the equine's closest herd mate and reported comfort in experiencing shared grief and support.

Re-Homing or Selling Equines

As previously described, most clients experience emotional closeness and attachment with their chosen equine. Therefore, termination due to the equine leaving the property or being no longer able to participate in sessions should be handled intentionally with understanding of the client's needs. The nature of the facility and its other programs will determine policies and procedures in place to address issues of equine re-homing. Should the treatment team have advance knowledge of the possibility of an equine becoming unavailable, this knowledge should be communicated to the client when they are first meeting the equines. In other cases, I have found it extremely useful to have agreements with facilities and equine owners regarding a notice period prior to an equine leaving the

154 Ethical Considerations

property if they are to be sold or re-homed. This notice period provides time to notify and prepare clients for an impending termination of their relationship with the equine. If a facility cannot provide a notice period, it is important for the therapist to carefully consider the potential risk of emotional harm to clients in working with equines who may be abruptly pulled from the program.

In-Session Crisis

In any counseling or psychotherapy practice, in-session crisis is a likely occurrence. It is important for the treatment team to be prepared to deal with different forms of in-session crises including outbursts or aggressive behavior, suicidality, homicidality, disclosures of child abuse or maltreatment, or client injuries. The therapist should also be knowledgeable regarding state reporting laws including mandated reporter laws.

The experiential nature of EACP can elicit strong feelings from clients, especially clients with limited capacity for emotional regulation. Young children and clients diagnosed with oppositional behavior disorder or conduct disorder may be more likely to demonstrate outbursts or aggressive behaviors in session than older clients. The therapist should ensure that equine specialists and volunteers are trained to recognize and respond to signs of crisis including oppositional or aggressive behavior, prevention and planning strategies to reduce the likelihood of these behaviors, and de-escalation strategies to respond to clients who have escalated (Haseman, 2017). Formal crisis intervention and de-escalation training for both the therapist and equine specialist can be invaluable in learning established techniques to manage behaviors and physically intervene if necessary. Please review Couvillon, Peterson, Ryan, Scheuerman, and Stegall (2010) for the different types of training programs available for this purpose.

All crises should be reported to and managed by the therapist. The equine specialist and volunteers should be trained to never agree to keep secrets from the therapist under any circumstances, especially in the case of client safety. It is also important to note that some clients are more inclined to make a disclosure to someone other than the therapist. In group settings with volunteers, some clients may feel a stronger sense of trust and connection with a volunteer who spends the entire session with them than with a therapist who checks in intermittently. Some children and adolescents may be more likely to confide in the equine specialist who may seem less intimidating than the therapist, especially because the therapist typically receives reports from and consults with the child's parents.

Given the prevalence of suicidality in certain populations commonly served in EACP programs such as at-risk youth and military veterans, it is the therapist's responsibility to train all personnel involved to understand the nature of suicide and appropriate ways to respond (Sheade & Ziehe, 2018). Without proper training, many people with the best of intentions often respond in counterproductive ways that increase client distress. Trainings such as Applied

Suicide Intervention Skills Training (ASIST) and online trainings through the Suicide Prevention Resource Center are helpful resources in training equine specialists and volunteers. Clients who report homicidal ideation should be taken just as seriously as clients who report suicidal ideation. Any disclosures of homicidal ideation should be immediately reported to the therapist. Laws related to reporting and duty to warn vary by state. Equine specialists and volunteers should make sure to notify the therapist of the client's disclosure prior to the client leaving the property. Please consult with an attorney regarding your state's specific reporting laws.

Certain types of vulnerable clients qualify for additional protections by law from abuse, neglect, and exploitation. These groups include minors under 18 years of age, older adults or adults with disabilities, or clients living in a healthcare or treatment facility. It is important to be well-versed in your state's reporting laws. In many states, all session personnel (including equine specialists and volunteers) qualify as mandated reporters and are legally obligated to report suspicion or knowledge of abuse, neglect, or exploitation. All reports should be made with the therapist's knowledge. Again, please consult with an attorney regarding your state's specific reporting laws.

Finally, a crisis may arise as a result of client or equine illness or injury. Both members of the treatment team should maintain CPR and first aid certification. The program should maintain up-to-date first aid kits for both humans and equines. The program should also establish policies and procedures to respond to health emergencies and complete occurrence reports. PATH Intl. (2018b) outlined detailed standards for preventing and responding to human or equine illness or injury.

Equine Welfare

First and foremost, the equines participating in EACP should consent to participation and benefit from this participation, just like the client does (Hatch, 2007). The nature of the equine's interactions with humans in and out of session will influence the equine's overall functioning and comfort level with humans (Hausberger et al., 2008). Animal welfare includes attention to equine physical and mental health, ability to cope, and overall quality of life (Webster, 2016). Acknowledgement of animal sentience is a crucial first step to maintaining welfare. It is important to be aware that many people, including some clients, may disregard or discount the equines' sentience (Proctor et al., 2013). Therefore, it is the treatment team's responsibility to model and advocate respecting and honoring the equines' emotional experiences and responses during the session. Ignoring or disregarding these experiences can lead to not only stress and burnout for the equines involved, but also elevate the risk of physical harm to the human participants. Attention to equine responses during session enable the equine to have a voice in consenting to participate in the session and the nature of such participation.

156 Ethical Considerations

A key component of animal welfare is to minimize negative experiences and promote positive ones. Mellor (2016a) adapted the Five Provisions and their associated Animal Welfare Aims from Webster's (2016) Five Freedoms. These provisions include: good nutrition, good environment, good health, appropriate behavior, and positive mental experiences. To provide good nutrition, the equine specialist should ensure the equines have access to fresh water and adequate food. Based on how the session is structured, equines might experience thirst or hunger during EACP sessions. If access to forage is limited during the session, the equine specialist should ensure the equine has breaks for forage throughout the day. To provide a good environment, the equine specialist should ensure equines have access to shade or shelter and comfortable resting areas. Physical discomfort during and outside of session should be minimized. Additionally, the equine specialist should assess potential environmental hazards in the working areas on an ongoing basis to minimize the risk of injury or illness. To provide good health, the equine specialist should confirm that the animals receive regular veterinary care and be capable of recognizing overt and subtle signs of illness and injury. To ensure appropriate behavior, the equine specialist should ensure that the equine feels safe and comfortable in their environment. Access to open space and interaction with other herd members is crucial to establishing a positive experience for the equines. Finally, the equine specialist should facilitate positive mental experiences for the equines by allowing for positive interaction with other equines, engaging in their own positive interactions with the equine in and out of session, and allowing the equine to have physical space to respond naturally and organically in session. A key to this provision is to allow the equines to have freedom of choice to express natural behaviors to meet their own needs and maintain their own quality of life (Webster, 2016). PATH Intl. (2018b) provided a comprehensive set of standards to ensure high welfare standards for equines participating in equine-assisted activities and therapies. It is important to have an emergency plan in place should there be an emergency, disaster, or sudden disruption in the ability to provide care to the equines. Gimenez Husted (2020) recommended that facilities should identify potential dangers, list all needed supplies and equipment to respond, create a plan and communication protocols, and practice the plan.

It is important that the treatment team members have positive working relationships with each equine. There are many ways to build these relationships, starting by simply observing and standing quietly in the pasture. The human team member's calm, quiet, non-demanding presence can help the equine feel safe. Activities designed to provide nurturing, such as grooming, while observing and responding to the equine's behavioral cues of pleasure or displeasure also build the relationship. It is also important that each human team member establishes respectful boundaries within their relationships with the equines. Depending on the equine, this process may require more or less assertiveness. The focus of these activities should not be to establish dominance and control over the equine, as that runs counter to the Relational Equine-Partnered

Counseling (REPC) and Equine-Partnered Play Therapy (EPPT) approaches for EACP. Instead, the focus should be on establishing necessary and healthy boundaries to protect the physical and emotional well-being of all involved, including the equines, to establish a positive working relationship.

The treatment team, especially the equine specialist, should be attuned to notice signs of evasive behaviors that may indicate stress in sessions such as head tossing or shaking, tail wringing or swishing, defecating, rearing, bucking, or backing away (Visser et al., 2008). Like people, equines are vulnerable to work-related stress and burnout. The equine specialist should establish and maintain equine workload limits so as to minimize stress and burnout (Iannuzzi & Rowan, 1991). PATH Intl. (2018b) suggested that each equine works no more than six hours per day, with no more than three sessions back to back. I have found that in certain cases, even this limit may be too much for some equines. In EACP it is also important to define "work". For example, does it count as work if the equine is simply in the pasture but not an active participant in the session? What if the herd as a whole is responding to the session? Does that count as an hour for each equine? Do the equines have access to food or forage during the session? If not, the equines are likely to have a lower threshold for stress tolerance. These are important questions to consider in structuring a program and scheduling sessions.

It is important that the equipment selected for use in a session does not cause pain or put undue pressure on the equine, especially in the hands of a client who is inexperienced with equines. For example, a halter used incorrectly that creates pain for the equine may result in increased danger to both the client and the equine (Equisearch, 2017. It is important to be aware of the way a client's anxiety and associated physical tension may be transferred to the equine via the rope. The use of rope halters should be carefully evaluated based on the client's experience, kinesthetic self-awareness, level of supervision by the equine specialist, and goal of the activity. For most activities, a nylon or leather halter has less potential to cause inadvertent harm to the equine. The equine specialist should monitor the equine's behavior for signs of discomfort and anticipate and address things that may cause discomfort, even if the equine is not showing overt signs. A stoic equine may not outwardly react to discomfort associated with a twisted halter strap. Ill-fitting equipment can lead to significant physiological stress for the equine and interfere with their participation in the session.

During a counseling session, equines experience the least amount of stress when they are able to move freely, interact with other equines, and have free access to food. The more limitations on food and water (or access to food and water), the more likely the equines are to demonstrate aggressive behaviors towards other equines in session (Goodwin, 1999). Interaction with other equines during sessions can reduce stress by enabling the equines to receive and provide social support to each other. Although these conditions may not be met in every session every time, it is important that these conditions are upheld outside of session to maintain happy and healthy equine partners in session. Equines do not generally show sudden aggressive behavior and instead usually provide warning signals that escalate in intensity. It is important to carefully interpret and respond to equine aggression towards humans. Aggression towards humans can be a sign of an overall deterioration of the human-equine relationship or a sign of physical pain. It is crucial to have an equine specialist who can not only recognize the initial signs of equine displeasure but can also notice them before the equine escalates to aggressive behavior (Goodwin, 1999). In many cases, communication of the equine's feelings and needs provides therapeutic benefits for the client.

Tommy's story is illustrative of this concept. Tommy, a 13-year-old client with autism, attended EACP to work on improving social skills, empathy, and reducing aggression towards peers. One day, Tommy was brushing an older Palomino Quarter Horse named Vince. As Tommy brushed Vince's neck, he stated that it felt "hard". A moment later, Vince showed Tommy his teeth. Tommy immediately stopped brushing Vince and thanked him for letting him know that he did not want his neck brushed. During processing, Tommy discussed that he realized Vince had initially tensed his neck because he did not want to be brushed on his neck and, when he continued, Vince tried to communicate his displeasure more directly. Tommy stated that he knew Vince could have bitten him if he wanted to, and that he learned enough about Vince to know Vince did not typically show his teeth. Rather than reprimand Vince for threatening to bite (something even the most seasoned equine expert may do), Tommy recognized Vince's attempt to communicate his wishes. Tommy stated that had he continued to brush Vince's neck, he would not have gotten mad at Vince for biting because he understood Vince had tried to tell him to stop in a "nice way" and he had not listened. This example demonstrates the importance of carefully considering the possible reasons for equine aggressive behaviors rather than immediately interpreting them as naughty or misbehaving.

Other equine stress can result from training to suppress emotional responses, conflict with human handlers or riders, physical demands, or lack of positive rewards (Hausberger et al., 2009). As a prey animal, equines may also conceal certain emotional experiences and responses which may make it more difficult to accurately identify signs of stress (Hall et al., 2018). Equines who demonstrate conflictual or flight behaviors during interaction with clients may be experiencing heightened emotional arousal and stress. Activities involving lunging or round pen work at higher speeds may create additional stress for equines and should be approached intentionally and with careful monitoring of the equine's responses during EACP sessions (Fenner, Caspar et al., 2019). To best minimize stress, positive experiences in session should outweigh negative or stressful ones (Mellor, 2016a). Certain types of client behaviors, attitudes, or emotions may add additional stress for equines. It is important for the equine specialist to consider the impact of client affect or attitude on the equine. As equines have demonstrated emotional transmission of both positive and negative feelings among other equines, they likely experience a similar transmission with people (Hall et al., 2018). Furthermore, equines have demonstrated increased stress when interacting with a person with a negative attitude. Therefore, the equine specialist should carefully monitor the equine's response and tolerance when interacting with clients with negative emotional or attitudinal states (Hama et al., 1996; Smith et al., 2016). Additionally, clients who present for issues related to impulsive, aggressive, inattentive/hyperactive, oppositional, or antisocial behaviors may be more likely to create stressful experiences by engaging in direct negative behaviors such as teasing or applying unnecessary pressure to the equine, or indirect negative behaviors such as inattentiveness, impatience, negative emotions, or abrupt movement (Kaiser, Heleski, Siegford, & Smith, 2006). It is important to note that children experiencing difficulties in family functioning may be more likely to demonstrate these behaviors (Luk, Staiger, Wong, & Mathai, 1999).

When considering equine work limits, the equine specialist should also consider each equine's caseload and types of clients. Following an especially stressful session, it is important for the equine specialist to "debrief" the equine by initiating activities that promote relaxation and nurturing. Depending on the equine and associated time constraints, these activities can be stroking or grooming the equine, walking around the pasture, providing forage, or providing access to friendly herd members. In particular, grooming or scratching just above the withers may promote a relaxation response in the equine (Feh & De Mazieres, 1993).

The environment where the session is taking place can also influence the equine's stress level during the session. For example, equines have the most freedom of choice in interacting with clients in a large pasture. In contrast, the equine's choices are much more restricted when interacting in a stall. It is important for the equine specialist to consider the impact of the session setting on the equine's welfare and potential stress. Each setting should also be considered based on capacity to allow access to water and opportunities to forage (Hatch, 2007). Regardless of the setting, the equine should always have an "out" to leave the session, whether the equine is physically able to walk away or the equine specialist advocates for the equine's needs by recognizing signs of stress and taking action to remedy the situation or allow the equine to end participation in the session (Serpell, Coppinger, Fine, & Peralta, 2010).

It is important to protect against animal exploitation, even inadvertent, when the client's needs overshadow the equine's and place the equine in the role of serving the client (Wycoff, 2019). It is important that the equine specialist is competent in inferring the equine's emotional state based on observable behaviors to best balance the equine's welfare with the client's needs. Some equines, especially older equines, may demonstrate less behavioral reactivity to stressful situations despite experiencing stress and negative emotions (Baragli et al., 2014). For some equines, this lack of outwardly displayed behavior may

160 Ethical Considerations

be a result of learned helplessness (Hall et al., 2008) or the equine equivalent of depression (Fureix et al., 2012).

For other equines, behaviors such as pushiness or dominance behaviors may indicate the equine is feeling emotionally overwhelmed by the session or the client's presentation, as equines are likely capable of recognizing both positive and negative human emotional states (Hama et al., 1996; Lanata et al., 2018; Smith et al., 2016). This response is best illustrated in my work with a young Appaloosa gelding named Rambo. Early on, I noticed Rambo would often become nippy and overly pushy with certain clients. I later realized there was a pattern to Rambo's behavior—anytime a client became incongruent or avoided acknowledging negative emotions, Rambo displayed these behaviors. Once the client acknowledged the emotions and became more authentic, Rambo immediately lowered his head, closed his eyes, and went to sleep. His behavior became an indicator of the client's state and helped the client become more aware of their emotions and learn to express them in a healthy way. But, what about Rambo? What about clients who did not have the ability to become more congruent and the "emotional pressure" continued? In these cases, we not only processed what was happening with Rambo, but also worked to create physical and emotional space between Rambo and the client. The equine specialist would often move closer to Rambo and stroke him in a soothing way. We would also encourage the client to take a break from Rambo. After session, the equine specialist would return to Rambo to spend some time grooming, stroking, or talking to him to help him "debrief" after such sessions.

There are four main indicators of global stress in equines as "stereotypies, aggressiveness towards humans, unresponsiveness to the environment, and [other] stress-related behaviors" (Ruet et al., 2019, p. 622). Even when displayed infrequently, stereotypic behaviors such as cribbing or weaving should be interpreted as signs of stress. Equines who crib may also demonstrate more tactile sensitivity and therefore be more reactive to touch or pressure (Briefer Freymond et al., 2019). In many cases, equines who appear "bomb proof" are, in fact, shut down and experiencing high levels of stress despite a calm outward appearance (Hall et al., 2008; Hausberger et al., 2009). Many such equines experience high anxiety and can react more strongly to new stimuli than would be expected. It is important that the equine specialist can recognize the difference between a truly "bomb proof" equine versus a withdrawn one (Fureix et al., 2012). Furthermore, certain breeds, such as Thoroughbreds and Warmbloods, may be more likely to experience anxiety and depression and will require closer monitoring (Bachmann et al., 2003).

There are several factors that influence equine stress (and associated stress behaviors) and their ability to manage stress. Equines that spend more time in stalls are likely to demonstrate more stereotypic (i.e., stress-related) and problem behaviors than equines who spend more time in the pasture during both sessions and during non-working times. Equines living in consistent herds are often more cooperative and easier to handle (Hausberger et al., 2008) and

Ethical Considerations 161

demonstrate less aggression (Goodwin, 1999). They may also be better able to cope with stress and challenging situations (Rivera et al., 2002). Amount of space, availability of food and other resources, group size, and consistency of herd mates influences levels of aggression and stress in individual equines, but also in the herd as a whole. Providing adequate roughage (i.e., hay) or access to quality grass, maintaining a consistent herd of the same equines, and pairing older equines with younger equines can reduce stress and problem behaviors (Fureix et al., 2012). By observing equines' behaviors and personality characteristics, you will learn which equines are friends and which ones do not get along. Pairing friendly equines together will result in less stress and conflict within the herd.

It is also important to consider the other types of work the equine participates in outside of session and how this work can contribute to overall stress. For example, equines participating in dressage may be more reactive and demonstrate more anxiety behaviors in response to stress in session than vaulting horses (Hausberger et al., 2011). For more information on this topic, see Hausberger and colleagues (2009, 2011). Equines who participate in programs for beginner or unbalanced riders (such as therapeutic riding) may experience more vertebral problems (e.g., back pain) and therefore more overall stress (Lesimple, Fureix, Menguy, & Hausberger, 2010).

Due to the potential for heightened stress during EACP sessions, equine schooling or training should be characterized by positive, relationship-strengthening interactions with the treatment team, especially the equine specialist, to offset potentially negative or stressful interactions during session (Mellor, 2016b). The therapist should also participate in schooling, as the equine does not discriminate between the specifics of the roles of the therapist versus the equine specialist. To the equine, both are part of the interaction and both should be included in such activities. Schooling methods should focus on strengthening the relationship between the equine and people, especially personnel participating in EACP sessions. Equines will benefit more from methods based on learning theory and positive reinforcement (McGreevy et al., 2018). Demonstration of conflictual or defensive behaviors during a training session may indicate the equine is overly stressed and the current training methods are not conducive to the equine's welfare or meeting schooling goals (Fenner, Caspar et al., 2019).

Multicultural and Diversity Considerations

Any therapist practicing any type of counseling or psychotherapy must possess cultural competency in working with diverse clients. It is essential that treatment teams providing EACP possess an understanding and skill set to provide culturally sensitive services to diverse clients (Sheade & Chandler, 2014). Diversity can take many forms across clients' identities such as race and ethnicity, religion, gender, or socioeconomic status. Cultural identity can also include age,

162 Ethical Considerations

sexual or affectional orientation, disability state, residence, language, or marital status (Remley & Herlihy, 2007). It is also important to be aware of dynamics of power, privilege, and oppression occurring between majority groups and minority groups (Welfel, 2010). All major mental health professional organizations, such as the American Counseling Association, American Psychological Association, and National Association of Social Workers, emphasize the importance of cultural competency in working with diverse clients (American Counseling Association, 2014; American Psychological Association, 2017; National Association of Social Workers, 2015). According to Remley and Herlihy (2007), "all counseling is cross-cultural" and therefore therapists should understand the manner in which cultural identities influence both their view and the client's view of the world, values, and beliefs (p. 51). As the therapeutic relationship also includes the equine specialist, the therapist should ensure the equine specialist also understands the impact of cultural identity on client worldview and interactions with the treatment team and equines. Without this understanding, the equine specialist risks causing harm to the client by engaging in unintentional or unconscious stereotyping, prejudice, microaggressions, or discrimination (Remley & Herlihy, 2007; Welfel, 2010).

Sue, Arredondo, and McDavis (1992) identified three qualities of culturally competent practice: understanding of beliefs and attitudes, knowledge of diversity considerations, and development of culturally sensitive skills with culturally diverse clients. Each characteristic is further comprised of the therapist's beliefs and attitudes, knowledge, and skills related to each characteristic. The treatment team members should work to develop greater self-awareness and understanding of their own beliefs and attitudes regarding own cultural identities and those of others with diverse identities. The treatment team can actively work to strengthen understanding of their own worldviews as well as the worldviews of others. Finally, the treatment team should work to understand the needs of diverse clients, including the interaction of social systems and societal issues influencing client needs and presenting concerns (Remley & Herlihy, 2007).

As interest in EACP grows, its practice is expanding worldwide. Because equines are naturally nonjudgmental, authentic, and empathic, the client is likely to feel accepted and understood by the equines even if they have a cultural identity different from the treatment team (Cohen, 2011). This experience can help build trust in the treatment team and bridge the gap of cultural differences. Observations of the equines and herd dynamics can enable clients to process cultural differences and experiences related to power, privilege, and oppression in ways that may feel less threatening (Cohen, 2011).

Client comfort with and perceptions of equines and EACP can vary both between and within different cultures. Sheade and Chandler (2014) provided a comprehensive review of diversity considerations for animal-assisted interventions based on considerations related to race, religion, socioeconomic status, and gender in the United States. Valiyamattam, Yamamoto, Fanucchi, and

Wang (2018) reviewed cultural considerations for animal-assisted interventions for cultures outside of the United States and Europe, including South America and Southeast Asia. People of different cultures may also have different preferences and levels of comfort with different types of outdoor environments (Hägerhäll et al., 2018). Serpell (2004) proposed that attitudes towards animals are influenced by two motivational considerations: affect (i.e., emotional responses towards animals) and utility (i.e., perception of the animal's instrumental value). In many cases, people who assign a high utility value to an animal experience difficulty with emotional closeness with animals, whereas people with strong emotional connections to animals tend not to view them with as strong of a utilitarian view. Serpell (2004) also identified cultural factors influencing client perception of and interaction with animals including "history, cultural/religious beliefs and values, culturally defining practices, and cultural representations" (p. S148). There is also an intersection between cultural views of animals and cultural views of science, including views on and acceptance of animal sentience and health practices such as psychotherapy (Serpell, 2004).

Cultural identity and associated experiences with equines plays an important role in client perceptions and feelings towards animals. In the United States and other Western countries, recreational interaction and experience with equines is often represented as a symbol of wealth (Robinson, 1999). However, in some cultures, such as Amish communities in the United States and nomadic peoples in Mongolia, work with equines is essential to community survival and livelihood. In some countries, equines are a source of national pride, such as the Icelandic Horse in Iceland and the Irish National Stud owned by the Irish government. In Native American, First Nations, and other indigenous groups, equines may be viewed as sacred leaders and healers (Dell, Chalmers, Dell, Sauve, & MacKinnon, 2008). Clients with limited exposure to equines may experience more fear in interacting with them. The equine likely has a different representation and value in each of these groups. Therefore, it is important to consider not only a client's past experience with equines but also the meaning or significance of that experience, or in some cases, lack thereof.

Beliefs about equines are not only likely to influence the client's view of the equine but also the nature of the relationship the client establishes with the equine. For example, although many religious traditions honor the human-animal relationship, specific teachings can influence vastly different experiences. Whereas some religions, such as Hinduism and Buddhism, tend to emphasize the importance of balance and interdependence of all species (Kesner & Pritzker, 2008), others, such as Islam, may teach that animals are unclean (Matuszek, 2010). Clients of certain Christian belief systems may perceive animals as placed on a lower moral plane than people, and therefore have less faith in the equine's capability of helping the client move towards therapeutic goals (Lawrence, 1995). Finally, a client's religious identity and associated beliefs

164 Ethical Considerations

can also influence the nature of anthropomorphic interactions and associated views of the equines (Epley, Waytz, Akalis, & Cacioppo, 2008).

Female clients may find it easier to bond with equines than male clients (Carter, 1998). This experience may be due in part to physiological differences related to the fact that females release higher amounts of oxytocin than males do (Miller et al., 2009). These differences may also be due to perceived cultural norms and expectations. In Western cultures, the nature of the client's relationship with the equine, including acknowledgment of the equine's sentience, may also be influenced by gender differences (Cornish, Wilson, Raubenheimer, & McGreevy, 2018). Birke & Brandt (2009) presented a thorough review on the role of gender on the formation of relationships and experience of intimacy between people and equines in Western culture, and how these relationships are experienced both similarly and differently by males and females. Whereas female clients may have a stronger affect motivation or experience emotional closeness with animals, male clients may hold a more utilitarian view and have more difficulty establishing an emotional connection with the equines (Herzog, Betchart, & Pittman, 1991; Kellert & Berry, 1987). Furthermore, some female clients may feel intimidated by the equines or struggle to communicate assertively, whereas male clients may demonstrate difficulty relinquishing control and desire to control or be dominant over the equine (Taylor, 2001). In addition, some male clients may struggle to express thoughts and feelings openly due to perceived stigma. The client's unique cultural identities and experiences can also influence client comfort and preferences in interactions with the equine.

Finally, it is also important to note that clients may have gendered ideas about equines and may perceive or relate differently to male versus female equines (Fenner, Caspar et al., 2019). These differences can impact the client's choice in equine partner as well the nature of their interactions with specific equines and associated thoughts, feelings, and creation of meaning during processing. I once worked with an adolescent named Jenna who had witnessed several episodes of domestic violence between her parents. At her first session, Jenna was adamant that she would only work with a mare (i.e., female horse) because they were "smaller and safer." When the smallest equine in the herd, a pony named Casper, approached Jenna, she chose him immediately, stating "she's the one!" When the equine specialist gently informed Jenna that Casper was, in fact, a male pony, Jenna was in disbelief. In her experience, females were always smaller than males. This size difference was particularly poignant in the interactions that she had witnessed at home. Jenna was equally amazed to learn that the largest equine, who was also the most dominant equine, was a female horse. As Jenna spent more time in the herd, her observations of the herd enabled her to express herself and process the trauma she had experienced.

Clients of some cultures, such as collectivistic cultures, may feel uncomfortable with directive or leadership-oriented activities, and may prefer activities focused on understanding the herd and promoting harmony within the herd. Additionally, clients of diverse backgrounds can benefit from engaging in touch and other nonverbal ways of relating to the equines outside of traditional Westernized talk therapy (Brandt, 2004). For example, in many Latino cultures, touch and physical contact are important ways of relating and connecting with others (Burleson, Roberts, Coon, & Soto, 2019). In my work with some clients from Latino cultures, they often engage in higher levels of physical contact and affection with the equines. In processing their experiences, all of these clients affirm the importance of this touch in feeling connected to the equine. In each of the cases described, it is important to try to understand the client in the context of their experiences and cultural backgrounds while also understanding each client is a unique individual to avoid sweeping generalizations based on cultural identity (Brown, 2002).

Finally, it is important to consider the implications of multicultural and diversity considerations in EACP practice (Sheade & Chandler, 2014). First and foremost, it is important to acknowledge the role of privilege and how cost can act as a barrier for clients, especially those of lower socioeconomic status or clients with disabilities. As the costs associated with EACP programs are higher than office-based practice, programs that operate on a fee-for-service basis may inadvertently restrict access for such clients due to cost and transportation accessibility (Cohen, 2011). Therefore, EACP programs should consider seeking external funding sources so as to not exclude these clients from receiving services. For clients with disabilities, especially physical limitations, the facility's setup may pose barriers for clients to participate. The treatment team should strive to create suitable alternative working areas to accommodate clients with physical disabilities and limitations.

Treatment Team Supervision and Consultation

It is crucial that the therapist, equine specialist, and any other personnel directly involved in the session engage in regular supervision, consultation, or client staffing (PATH Intl., 2018b). Non-clinical personnel, such as equine specialists and volunteers, may be more likely to experience negative emotional effects following an intense session, as they generally do not have the mental health education and training to understand the complexities of psychotherapy and mental health in the same way as the therapist. The therapist has a responsibility to attend to non-clinical personnel's responses and reactions to the session and provide support if needed after the session. However, it is also important to note that the therapist should not provide therapy to non-clinical personnel. If resolution of the equine specialist's or volunteer's distress cannot be resolved during debriefing, the therapist should provide a recommendation for another therapist. During these debriefings, the treatment team and other personnel discuss the session including the client's presentation and behaviors, equines' behaviors, the plan for future sessions, and evaluate the session overall. Support personnel outside of the treatment team, such as volunteers, should be given the opportunity to contribute and ask questions. These meetings are especially important following sessions that are emotionally intense or involve any type of incident or crisis.

The treatment team should also engage in more in-depth supervision and consultation alone without support personnel. During this time, the treatment team meets to discuss transference or countertransference reactions that arose during the session to protect not only the client's interests but also to protect the emotional safety of the non-clinical personnel. This debriefing should focus on increasing awareness of the team member's reaction, understanding the reaction, and ensuring that it does not negatively impact the client. It is important for the treatment team members to be aware of their own triggers and find ways to manage them productively during the session.

The treatment team should also use this time to discuss the client's presentation in session, new or unusual behaviors, progress towards goals, and ongoing treatment planning. The treatment team should discuss the client's and equines' interactions. It is important for the equine specialist to initiate discussions related to any concerning behaviors or indications of equine stress and work with the therapist to understand and plan to manage the equines' behavior or stress in future sessions. The equine specialist should advocate for the equines' needs both in the session and outside of session by addressing welfare concerns and discussing potential limits that may need to be set in future sessions.

During these meetings, it is essential that the therapist and equine specialist can communicate openly and honestly. Prior to seeing their first client together, the treatment team should discuss how they will handle potential conflict or disagreements. Both members of the treatment team should be comfortable in addressing potential conflict and using appropriate communication and conflict resolution strategies. Any concerns or negative feelings should be brought up immediately and discussed rather than left unspoken. I have witnessed several cases in which the therapist and equine specialist did not feel comfortable speaking openly with each other when they were frustrated or upset. This avoidance of conflict often results in an increasingly strained relationship within the treatment team that eventually impacts clients' experiences in negative ways.

Chapter 12

Risk Management Considerations in Equine-Assisted Counseling and Psychotherapy

There are risks in the practice of equine-assisted counseling and psychotherapy (EACP) not present in traditional office-based therapy due the inclusion of the equine and the outdoor nature of therapy. **It is essential to consult with an attorney with experience in this area of the law** who can provide advice on setting up a new EACP program, ensuring legal risks are assessed and addressed, drafting documentation that is properly prepared and complies with state and federal laws, and providing advice on the types of insurance needed to cover risks associated with EACP practice. **This section is not intended to be comprehensive or to provide legal advice and therefore should not be relied on as such**. This section merely highlights some areas to consider discussing with your attorney and insurance company.

Confidentiality, Privacy, and Therapist-Client Privilege

Just as in any form of counseling and psychotherapy, the client's expectation of privacy of personal information is critical to their emotional safety and enables them to be open during psychotherapy. Confidentiality refers to "an ethical duty to keep client identity and disclosures secret and a legal duty to honor the fiduciary relationship with the client" (Welfel, 2010, p. 116). Confidentiality pertains not only to the words spoken during the session, but all client records and documentation, and even their identity as a client (Welfel, 2010). The ethical codes of all major counseling and psychotherapy professions emphasize the importance of maintaining client confidentiality (American Counseling Association, 2014; American Psychological Association, 2017; National Association for Social Workers, 2015). Equine specialists and other personnel directly involved in the session (e.g., equine specialists and volunteers) and facility personnel with indirect involvement should all receive training to understand confidentiality and how to maintain confidentiality for clients.

Given the outdoor EACP environment, it is more vulnerable to threats to privacy, as clients may be easily seen or heard by others. It is imperative that the treatment team identify potential threats to privacy in advance and inform

168 Risk Management Considerations

the client of these threats during the informed consent process. The treatment team should collaborate with other facility personnel to minimize threats to privacy such as designating counseling areas, communicating facility rules, and limiting free access to different areas for visitors, other clients, and training facility staff to limit interaction with EACP clients.

It is imperative that the privacy of minor clients is respected, just the same as in an office-based setting. Therefore, the decision to allow the minor client's parents or family members to observe or participate should be informed by the client's wishes and therapist's clinical judgment related to the client's specific needs. In most cases, we do not even allow the client's parents to meet their chosen equine unless requested by the client. Many children, especially those experiencing high conflict with their parents, choose to keep their relationship with the equine private. Alternatively, for clients who do wish to have their parents meet the equine, this introduction can provide an opportunity for connection between the parent and the client. Again, it is important for the client to initiate the request and not be pressured by the parent or treatment team.

Therapist-client privilege and privileged communication is often misunderstood by therapists. Privileged communication is defined as "the client's right to prevent a court from demanding that a mental health professional reveal material disclosed in a confidential professional relationship" (Welfel, 2010, p. 116). Logically, one would think that the privilege is not lost as a result of the presence of the equine specialist in the therapy session, as they are a critical part of the session—similar to essential personnel in a law office, like an expert, brought in to assist in a case. But it is critical to consult with a qualified attorney on this issue. Each state differs as to the extent of the privilege and when it is lost. It is important to note, however, that there may be a greater risk of loss of the therapist-client privilege, if one exists in your state, in an EACP setting due to the possibility of third parties who are not directly involved in the session overhearing session content. For example, a barn manager who passes outside the pasture during a session and overhears a part of the session may therefore result in loss of privilege. It is important that the therapist collaborates with the facility to reduce risk of threats to therapist-client privilege and adequately acknowledges and explains such risks in the informed consent.

The Health Insurance Portability and Accountability Act (HIPAA) is a federal law which establishes basic standards for protecting private healthcare information (PHI), whether oral or written (Hartsell & Bernstein, 2013). Every state has their own unique set of laws related to protection of confidentiality of mental health care information and exceptions to confidentiality. HIPAA is a methodology to protect PHI and maintain privacy and security standards for PHI, including how information is stored and communicated with others. The therapist should collaborate with the facility to ensure that client documentation is stored in accordance with HIPAA requirements. Individuals or entities that you know or suspect may come into possession of PHI should be required to sign a Business Associate Agreement (BAA) and agree to protect client PHI in accordance with HIPAA requirements (equine specialists, facility personal, payroll service companies, software companies, etc.). It is suggested that equine specialists, staff, and facility personnel be trained on HIPAA requirements and compliance to avoid unintentional breaches, as such breaches can result in significant consequences such as loss of therapist licensure (Sheade & Box, 2017). Again, I recommend consultation with an attorney regarding questions related to any aspect of HIPAA compliance in the EACP setting.

Informed Consent

Informed consent is a practice requirement for all counseling and psychotherapy services to protect clients from medical abuse and enable them to have active participation in their own care and to make informed decisions about their care. The therapist is ethically and legally obligated to engage in both verbal and written informed consent with the client in which the client signs the consent documents after verbal and written review. In addition, the informed consent process should be ongoing throughout the psychotherapeutic process, not just during the intake or first session (Welfel, 2010). In EACP, the therapist has an obligation to address issues specific to EACP in both oral and written form using language that is easily understandable by the client. The informed consent should involve discussion of the nature of EACP, including, but not limited to, the therapist's training and qualifications to provide EACP; potential risks and benefits of participation in EACP, such as the risk of physical injury by the equines; risks associated with sessions being held outdoors; potential threats to privacy, confidentiality, and therapist-client privilege due to psychotherapy taking place in a more open area; and the role and qualifications of the equine specialist or any volunteers present in the session. The client should have the opportunity to ask questions regarding any part of the informed consent during this process. **It cannot be overemphasized that it is important to have the attorney review the informed consent document, as therapists providing animal-assisted interventions are more at risk of negligence claims than office-based providers due to issues related to inadequate informed consent** (Hartsell & Bernstein, 2013).

Voluntary Waiver and Release

It is common practice to have a client execute a "Voluntary Release and Waiver", or a liability release, in which the client waives all rights to claims against the therapist, equine specialist, facility owners, etc. for injury that may be caused by the equine. Most states have laws that recognize the need for this document. This form should comply with state laws regarding warning notices and acknowledgment of the risk of interacting with equines should the client sustain significant injury or death as a result of interaction with the equines

170 Risk Management Considerations

during EACP (PATH Intl., 2018b). A qualified attorney should assist in the drafting of this document to ensure it meets state requirements.

Clinical Documentation

Clinical documentation in EACP is just as important as in an office-based practice. You can use your standard documentation practices as a starting point and expand based on the unique aspects of EACP. One of the biggest challenges for EACP therapists is finding ways to document the equine-assisted components of the session while maintaining what I like to call a "clinical lens." What does that mean? A clinical lens refers to the ability to describe and interpret client processing and interactions with the equines from the standpoint of how these activities relate to presenting problems and progress. For example, a managed care provider is not going to care that a client brushed a horse during the session. In fact, they may question how brushing a horse is even therapy! Instead, focus on what the client brushing the horse means or indicates about the client or their progress. Was the client brushing the horse to avoid talking? Or perhaps the client was brushing the horse to self-soothe. Depending on the client and context, the meaning can be very different. It is important to be intentional about which parts of the session you choose to describe, how you choose to describe them, and the meaning you assign to their inclusion in your documentation. Many of the therapists that I have trained struggled to effectively document the equine-assisted portions of the session and oftentimes end up writing lengthy notes. It takes practice to learn how to identify the meaning and clearly communicate it in writing. One activity that we have found to be helpful is to review notes together during group supervision. This activity can help therapists clarify their intent and meaning by explaining their note to others not present in the session. For additional information and to ensure that your clinical documentation complies with state and federal laws, please consult with your attorney.

Initial Assessment

In your initial assessment, I recommend inclusion of additional components to document the client's past experience with animals (specifically equines), any potential allergies or physical health conditions that may interfere with the client's participation, and any high-risk behaviors such as fire-setting or animal abuse. It is also important to note initial observations of the client's interactions with the equines and the client's response to the equines using your "clinical lens." For example, what is the significance of the client approaching the equine from a clinical standpoint? Finally, the therapist should also document justification or rationale for why the specific client is a good candidate for EACP (Hartsell & Bernstein, 2013).

Treatment Plan

It is important to be thoughtful in designing your treatment plan to meet best practice standards, regardless of the presence of the equines. The treatment plan should reflect the specific goals and objectives associated with inclusion of equines to justify use of an animal-assisted intervention (Beck & Katcher, 2003). It can be helpful to include the equine specialist in treatment planning to identify how best to integrate equines in addressing specific clinical goals.

Clinical Assessments

It is important to use clinical assessments to gather information about the client's presenting concerns and overall functioning, just as in any office-based practice. Shockingly, Gergley (2012) found that more than 42% of EACP clinicians reported using no assessments at all. This finding is concerning given the importance of assessment in making clinical decisions and in justifying the use of animal-assisted intervention (Beck & Katcher, 2003). Assessments help determine whether the current course of treatment is benefiting the client or whether the treatment approach needs to be reviewed. Assessments used in EACP should be informed by your client's presenting concerns and your scope of practice. You may choose to include human-animal bond assessments in addition to your clinical assessments to gather information and evaluate the impact of the relationship with the equines for the client (Anderson, 2007).

Progress Notes

It is important to use established best practices for progress notes such as DAP (data, assessment, plan) or SOAP (subjective, objective, assessment, plan) formats. Which note you choose will depend on your clinical training and nature of your practice. You may choose to add additional fields to your notes such as the names of the equines involved, the location of the session, and the names of the other treatment team members such as the equine specialist. Whichever note format you choose, it is important to once again use your "clinical lens" when describing the client's interactions with and processing about the equines, especially when writing the progress section. For example, imagine that your client, Betsy, has chosen to approach and pet Gator. Later, Betsy brushed Gator with several different brushes. Afterward, Betsy reported she felt "better" and proud of herself. If you were to read this, would you have any idea what the clinical significance of this interaction was? To provide context, let's imagine that Betsy is a client presenting with high social anxiety. Up until today, she has never touched an equine during her sessions. Before brushing, the therapist had provided guidance to Betsy to observe Gator's responses to the different brushes. In the descriptive section of your note, you might write about how Betsy spent time observing the herd prior to approaching Gator. She chose

Gator because he stopped eating when she approached and made her feel the most comfortable. When Betsy first petted Gator, she appeared tense and noticeably anxious. However, as the session progressed, Betsy became more talkative and appeared less tense. Betsy later used different brushes on Gator while observing his responses to her and the different brushes.

In the progress section of your note, you may choose to write about Betsy having touched an equine for the first time as an indication of progress. While yes, this may be progress, what does it signify from a clinical standpoint? A possible elaboration would be to state something along the lines of "Betsy demonstrated evidence of progress in managing her social anxiety by approaching and petting Gator despite her reported fear of angering the equine by touching him". Keeping the client's presenting concerns and treatment goals in mind when writing these notes can be helpful in seeing the session through the clinical lens.

Client Injury Report

It is important to have documentation related to the occurrence of accidents or injuries as result of interaction with the equines or being in a less controlled, outdoor environment (PATH Intl., 2018b). Unlike office-based practices, the risk of injury is higher when working with equines. Your liability insurance carrier or attorney can advise you in the creation of an incident report form.

Equine Files

Finally, you may consider maintaining individual equine files. In these files you can include both equine-related session notes and schooling/training notes for each equine. I also recommend maintaining basic information about each equine such as age, breed, medical history, etc. The equine specialist (or therapist if acting in dual role) can complete session notes for each equine's contributions in the session including behaviors towards the client and other equines, potential indicators of stress, methods in which stress or inappropriate behaviors were managed, and ongoing welfare recommendations. As these notes are outside of client files, it is important to remove the client's identifying information or personal details and use a coding system to mask client identity. Schooling or training notes can complement session notes by describing training objectives and interventions, the equine's response to such interventions, and recommendations relation to participation in EACP.

Insurance

As noted in the previous section, there are risks in the practice of EACP not present in traditional office-based therapy as a result of the inclusion of the equine and the outdoor nature of therapy. Insurance can be obtained to cover these risks. An insurance company that writes policies for equine liability should be contacted to discuss the nature of your practice and the appropriate policy for your protection as therapist and for the protection of the facility and equine specialist.

Professional Liability (Malpractice) Insurance

As required in any psychotherapy practice, the therapist must acquire a policy or ensure that they are covered under the facility's policy to cover professional liability claims. This insurance protects the therapist against liability risks related the work they do as a licensed mental health professional. Often, the facility owner will be made an "additional insured" on this policy to protect them from the actions of the therapist.

Equine Liability Insurance

The Professional Liability Insurance described in the previous paragraph does not generally cover physical injuries or property damage sustained as a result of actions of the equine in a session. Equine liability insurance covers this risk. As with professional liability insurance, the facility owner will often be made an "additional insured" under this policy as well.

Considerations in Light of Pandemics and COVID-19

At the time of writing this section (May, 2020), COVID-19 continues to spread in the United States and elsewhere around the world. At the time of publication, it is likely that therapists will still be impacted by the effects of COVID-19. The following information will hopefully be helpful in decision-making and risk management related to services provided during the COVID-19 pandemic, as well as possible future pandemics. This information is not intended to be comprehensive or even necessarily relevant to the conditions in your location, but rather it is intended to emphasize the need to investigate the possible risks associated with conducting EACP during a pandemic, to inform your client of the risks, and to take reasonable steps to minimize the risk. It is highly recommended that you consult with a professional who can help you navigate and address the risks. For example, it is recommended that you consult with your professional liability insurance and/or equine insurance provider for guidance and to ensure that you are covered in providing in-person EACP services.

First, therapist and facilities should ensure compliance with all government mandates and guidelines. If guidelines from different entities appear to be in conflict (e.g., the state guidelines differ from the federal guidelines), it would be advisable to consult with a qualified attorney.

174 Risk Management Considerations

Therapist should carefully consider the risks and benefits, as well as any potential liabilities, for holding in-person EACP sessions in light of COVID-19. Trust Insurance (n.d.) recommended that therapists take the following actions in making the decision to hold in-person sessions: consultation (with qualified professionals), engagement in an ethical and risk analysis process, documenting the reasoning and conclusions for course of action, and a thorough informed consent process with clients. All of these actions should be carefully documented.

It is likely that you will want to amend to your existing client informed consent or service agreement to address issues related specifically to pandemics, including COVID-19, if not already addressed. The items that may be relevant will be dependent on your unique situation at your location and may include, but are not limited to, the following: onsite COVID-19 session safety procedures (such as wearing a face mask, social (physical) distancing, waiting in the car until the session begins, etc.); client agreement to inform therapist of any recent illness or illness of someone who they have been in close contact with; client waiver of liability if the client becomes infected; informing clients of the risks of contracting COVID-19 by choosing to attend face-to-face sessions; risks and benefits of in-person versus telehealth services; and a description of the facility's COVID-19 cleaning and sanitization procedures. Please consult with your attorney to ensure that your document contains all needed information and complies with relevant laws for your location.

At the time of writing, it is believed that equines are not at risk from COVID-19 (Equine Disease Communication Center, 2020). Nevertheless, it is also important to consider strategies to reduce risk for all human participants when clients and facility personnel are onsite. Some considerations may include, but are not limited to, structuring client scheduling so that clients working the same equines are not scheduled back-to-back; the risks of group EACP sessions; procedures to disinfect all equipment used by clients (e.g., tack and grooming tools); facility and/or therapist cleaning, sanitization, and biosecurity procedures. Lyman (2020) provided a detailed overview of biosecurity and sanitation protocols in light of COVID-19. PATH Intl. (2020) provided an abundance of resources for managing equine facilities in response to COVID-19. The Association for Play Therapy (2020) provided detailed guidelines for cleaning play rooms and toys used for play therapy. For general biosecurity considerations, Flynn (2020) provided a detailed overview on procedures in equine facilities in order to ensure health for both people and animals such as screening new equines for illness or infection, ensuring all equines are current on vaccinations and checkups, having an emergency plan for ill or injured equines, and following appropriate procedures for stall sanitation and food storage.

Chapter 13

Program Design in Equine-Assisted Counseling and Psychotherapy

Establishing an equine-assisted counseling (EACP) practice, and even practicing in an established EACP practice, are accompanied by many challenges (Gergley, 2012). In my experience, most counseling and psychotherapy training or educational programs lack information on the business and legal considerations in establishing and running a practice. As a result, therapists establishing EACP practices face steep learning curves. It is important to develop a support system of mentors and personal cheerleaders to help navigate the challenges associated with starting an EACP practice. There can be significant financial expenses for the facility and/or the therapist in providing EACP that can sometimes make providing these services cost-prohibitive. Many therapists identify insufficient funding as a primary challenge (Schlote, 2009). It can be difficult for some therapists to practice EACP full-time and many provide EACP as an adjunct to office-based practice. As a result, session fees may be higher, making these services financially inaccessible for some clients. Depending on the state, psychotherapy approach, and insurance provider, it can be difficult to obtain insurance reimbursement for EACP. Weather can also interfere with the ability to provide services. Additionally, it can be difficult to find qualified therapists and equine specialists to act as co-facilitators given the specialized training needed. Finally, therapists who do not have their own equines and facilities may struggle to find suitable facility partners equipped to meet the needs of mental health practice.

Starting a Program

First, the therapist and/or treatment team should create a business plan or program plan. This plan should include a description of the need for the business or program (market analysis), types of clients (target market), personnel and resources needed, funding sources, a marketing plan, and detailed budgets. Strozzi (2009) provided recommendations for creating a business plan in the equine-assisted activities and therapies industry. Accountants and attorneys can be invaluable in assisting with incorporating and establishing a new EACP practice. In the United States, organizations such as SCORE and the

176 Program Design

Small Business Administration provide free or low-cost resources and training designed to help small businesses.

Additionally, the therapist and/or treatment team must choose a business structure such as for-profit or non-profit. If you incorporate as a for-profit entity, your accountant and attorney can advise you on the most appropriate business structure given the nature of your specific type of practice. Unlike a for-profit entity, non-profits do not belong to a single individual or group of individuals. Instead, non-profits require oversight by a board of directors to ensure the non-profit acts in accordance with state and federal law. Depending on your client populations, a non-profit can enable you to raise additional funds through tax-deductible donations and grants to support clients who cannot afford to pay for services. These opportunities are much more limited for for-profit entities. It is important to note that non-profit entities are subject to extensive state and federal reporting requirements. In some cases, the presence of the board of directors can also create challenges, as the treatment team or program staff has less control over major decisions for the program. I recommend consultation with an accountant to learn about the requirements for establishing and managing a non-profit.

Practice Settings

In any practice setting, it is important to assess and evaluate the facility's ability to not only provide an environment conducive to client welfare, but also to maintain high standards for equine welfare. Therapists and/or treatment teams should evaluate potential settings based on client privacy, accessibility and comfort (e.g., restrooms, indoor temperature control, parking), condition of existing facilities (barns, fencing, pastures, pens, arenas, etc.), and maintenance or renovation needs. It is important to answer the following questions:

- Is there a completely private space to meet with clients where the session cannot be interrupted?
- Where will the equines be kept during sessions? Where will sessions occur?
- How will space be scheduled or reserved for sessions?
- Where will client documentation and records be kept? Does this space comply with HIPAA requirements?
- Where will sessions be held during inclement weather?
- What is the safety plan in case of fire or severe weather?
- Is there adequate pasture to meet ethical and legal equine management requirements?
- How many equines can be kept on the property?
- Where is feed kept and what is the feeding protocol?
- Where do clients go when they arrive for a session? Is there a waiting area for parents?

Many people want to practice EACP at their own privately owned facilities. Although there are a number of benefits to this arrangement, there are also a number of costs. Some of the benefits to acquiring your own facility and equines include complete control of equine care, improved client privacy, and avoidance of scheduling conflicts. In most cases, sessions fees alone are unlikely to cover the costs associated with high-quality equine care and facility maintenance while also providing a living wage for the therapist and equine specialist. Raising session fees to account for costs may make services inaccessible for many clients who would most benefit from these services. It is also important to note that there is no such thing as a "free horse", even when one is donated. The lifetime cost to care for an equine almost always exceeds the purchase cost. Many people who have not previously kept equines are unaware of the significant (and often unexpected) financial costs of equine care. I recommend creating a detailed budget including costs related to veterinary care, farrier, feed, hay, bedding, insurance, and unexpected costs. Many people acquire equines with the best of intentions but are woefully unprepared for high costs associated with an unexpected bout of colic requiring an emergency farm call or fluctuating hay costs based on drought conditions in another state thousands of miles away. In other cases, individuals are inexperienced in recognizing signs of serious medical emergencies and in knowing how to handle such emergencies. These deficits in equine experience and financial preparation result in compromised welfare and even outright neglect of countless equines worldwide.

I once visited a facility that had been newly acquired by a therapist who, in my opinion, had minimal and insufficient equine experience. The therapist informed me that she "ridden her whole life" and often went trail riding with a friend. However, her actual experience was limited to horse camps as a child and occasional riding as an adult. During my visit, there were numerous safety issues and indications of compromised equine welfare. Upon first bringing her horse over to meet me, she had the lead rope wrapped around her hand—a safety risk to her and likely something she was unaware may be a safety risk to clients as well. She only had one full-size horse pastured separate from her three other ponies. As she brought the mare over, the horse demonstrated clear stress behaviors throughout our interaction. In interacting with the ponies, one showed clear signs of fear and past abuse while the other engaged in aggressive behaviors that the therapist labeled as "cute". As we talked, she eventually disclosed this pony had already bitten clients and that she had no idea what to do about it. When I inquired about the horses' feed, she stated that she only provides grass for grazing as they are all "fat and happy", pointing to their large bellies. However, despite their large bellies, all showed protruding hip bones with distended abdomens, a likely indication of "hay belly"—a condition resulting from a low-quality diet lacking protein. As a result of her inexperience, the therapist mistakenly attributed their large bellies to be an indication

178   Program Design

of health rather than a serious underlying health concern. Although she had good intentions in acquiring land and equines to begin EACP practice, her lack of knowledge resulted in compromised care to her equines and significant safety risks to her clients. As discussed in Chapter 11, compromises in equine welfare will result in compromised client care at best and potential client re-traumatization at worst. At minimum, individuals wanting to establish their own facility should meet the following conditions (or plan to hire or partner with someone who does):

- Expert level of experience in understanding equine psychology and behavior (see Chapter 5).
- Experience managing a herd at another facility or as a working student to learn how to provide equine first aid, recognize equine medical emergencies, develop individualized feeding regimens for each equine, manage herd dynamics, and create safe and hazard-free pastures, stables, and pens.
- Possession of adequate savings or reserves to offset unexpected costs.

I realize that, for many individuals, meeting these conditions may present significant barriers to starting their own practice. However, I believe that EACP should never compromise equine welfare or client safety. It is better that the treatment team takes the time to develop the needed experience and financial reserves than risk harm to clients or equines.

For a therapist starting out, it may be better for them to establish a partnership with an existing facility that will assume financial and management responsibilities for the equines. There are many different settings to practice EACP. Some settings are more equine-oriented such as private ranches, boarding barns, or therapeutic riding facilities. Other settings are more health-care focused such as residential treatment centers or group homes. In some cases, EACP is provided by transporting equines to a separate facility such as a school or behavioral health hospital. All of these settings have pros and cons in practice. In equine-oriented settings, the treatment team may not have as much responsibility in caring for the equines or addressing welfare issues. However, they may struggle to maintain a private environment conducive to mental health treatment. In contrast, practicing at a health-care focused facility may avoid problems related to privacy and interference with mental health practices, but may raise equine-related problems if the facility is not strictly focused on providing EACP. Equine specialists may find themselves advocating more frequently for equines' needs, as individuals in leadership and management roles may be less experienced in understanding equine husbandry and welfare. Regardless of the specific type of facility, I recommend retaining an attorney to draft a contract outlining the specific terms and expectations for the partnership. There are several PATH Intl. (2018b) standards describing how to establish this relationship.

The EACP Team

The EACP team is comprised of a small or large group of individuals, depending on the size of your program. These individuals consist of direct service personnel (e.g., hands-on in providing actual EACP services), indirect on-site personnel (e.g., facility managers and administrators), and indirect outside personnel (e.g., business or equine care professionals). An organizational chart is invaluable in outlining all of the personnel needed, their relationships to each other, and their role and responsibilities.

Direct Service Personnel

First and foremost, you will need an appropriately credentialed and competent therapist. I recommend that all programs are overseen by a fully and independently licensed therapist to ensure that they possess the competencies needed to manage clinical issues and supervise other personnel. If the therapist holds dual qualification as an equine specialist, they may choose to facilitate sessions independently (See Chapter 5). However, in most cases, the therapist will co-facilitate with an equine specialist. Depending on your program's needs and session structure, you may decide to have more than one therapist or equine specialist in the session. Some programs also utilize volunteers to maintain a safe environment. It is important to consider employment structure for all direct personnel. Will they be employees or independent contractors? There are distinct legal differences between each employment structure. I have come across many programs (both equine-related and psychotherapy-related) who hire personnel as independent contractors to cut costs. However, many such programs are unaware of the legal differences for employees and contractors regarding the level of control over or direction of work, financial considerations related to reimbursement of expenses and provision of tools/resources to complete the work, and the nature of the relationship itself. It is important to be very clear on the requirements and restrictions related to independent contractors in order to avoid significant costs to the practice or the program if the contractor were to later claim employee status. Any program considering hiring independent contractors should consult with an attorney to ensure that they are structuring the personnel's work-related responsibilities and expectations in a manner consistent with legal requirements.

Finally, it is important to establish employment or contractor contracts. The contract should be informed by your state's employment laws and outline personnel roles, responsibilities, and expectations. I recommend consultation with an attorney to draft these contracts to ensure adequate protection for both the practice and personnel working in the practice. There are many other questions to consider as well. Will direct personnel be paid an hourly rate per session or a salary? If clients do not show up for the session, will personnel forfeit

180 Program Design

payment? If not, where will the money to pay the personnel come from? Most outside funding sources (grants, insurance, contracted agencies, etc.) do not pay for cancelled sessions. What types of policies will the program establish regarding client cancellation and cancellation fees? With many outside funding sources, therapists can neither receive payment from the funding source for cancelled sessions nor are they allowed to charge clients cancellation fees. It is important to make sure all personnel agree on these policies prior to rendering services. Programs that have not answered these questions risk losing personnel resulting in compromised client care or client abandonment if services have to be terminated prematurely due to loss of key personnel.

Indirect Personnel

Depending on your program's size and personnel's experience, you may need a barn/facility manager, equine manager, administrative assistant, development director, or volunteer manager. You may need additional personnel outside of your organization to help maintain high standards of care for clients, equines, and the program itself. It is important to establish a relationship with a veterinarian to provide equine medical care, a farrier to care for the equines' hooves, an accountant to assist with bookkeeping and financial reporting (especially in a non-profit setting), and an attorney to review clinical documentation and contract and consult on legal issues as they arise.

Getting Funding and Clients

The majority of EACP services are funded by self-pay, followed by private insurance (Gergley, 2012). Other services are funded by public aid (e.g., Medicaid and Medicare), third-party payers, donations, grants, and military benefits. In a Canadian study, Schlote (2009) found services were funded most often by government or nonprofit funding. Your service rates will be influenced by program expenses and comparable market values. You may also contract with local community organizations to provide services, although many may not be able to pay the full service rate. In some cases, insurers may be willing to reimburse for services. Finally, many practices offer sliding scales to make the services more accessible to clients with limited financial resources. Prior to implementation of a sliding scale, I recommend consultation with an attorney, as many therapists (both office-based and EACP) unknowingly offer sliding scales that are not in compliance with state and federal law and run the risk of inadvertent discrimination.

Most clients learn about EACP services from marketing and word of mouth. Clients are also referred to EACP services from school, court, and religious groups (Gergley, 2012). Other clients are referred by other mental health professionals such as counselors, social workers, and psychologists (Schlote, 2009). It is crucial for therapists to develop marketing and networking skills to promote EACP services to increase awareness and access more potential clients,

To market and network effectively, it is important to create written materials (flyers, business cards, brochures, etc.) and online materials (websites, blogs, social media, etc.). It is essential that you are aware of and comply with state and federal laws as well as professional ethical codes regarding marketing and outreach. In the United States, organizations like SCORE and the Small Business Administration offer training and resources to learn these skills. Finally, it is important to note that even if a client signs a photo release or provides a testimonial, it may not be ethical to use it in your materials due to the risk of unintentional client harm or exploitation. For more information on this topic, please consult your state board rules and/or professional code of ethics.

Chapter 14

Research Issues in Equine-Assisted Counseling and Psychotherapy

One of the biggest criticisms of all animal-assisted therapy in counseling approaches is the scarcity of research demonstrating effectiveness of these modalities. The results of literature reviews indicate that EACP is a beneficial and promising intervention (Kendall et al., 2015; Lee, Dakin, & McLure, 2016; Lentini & Knox, 2015; Rothe et al., 2005). Much of the existing literature base on EACP relies on anecdotal reports and client stories (Bachi, 2012). Furthermore, the majority of research in broad field of equine-assisted activities and therapies focuses more on the physiological effects of therapeutic riding rather than the psychological effects of EACP. Of the existing EACP research base, the majority focuses on EACP with children and adolescents, despite the fact that it is likely that more than half of EACP providers serve adult clients (Lee et al., 2016; Schlote, 2009). Bachi (2012) and Lee and colleagues (2016) conducted comprehensive reviews of existing studies and highlighted specific methodological problems. The majority of existing research studies on EACP specifically are marked by problems such as small sample sizes that limit statistical power and generalizability, and lack of control groups to be able to demonstrate the true effectiveness of EACP. Other research design issues include problematic sampling methods, limited duration of observation, inconsistency between the findings and reports by participants and personnel, and overgeneralization of findings. Anestis, Anestis, Zawilinski, Hopkins, and Lilienfeld (2014) identified three significant methodological flaws common to most research studies on EACP as a lack of experimental controls, insufficient procedures to evaluate outcomes, and biased raters. However, despite these limitations, Serpell et al. (2017) argued that a lack of insufficient research alone does not indicate that animal-assisted interventions are ineffective and that the research base continues to grow and demonstrate increasing methodological rigor.

Lack of consistency of terminology further complicates efforts to evaluate existing research on EACP across different studies. (See Chapter 1 for a review on terminology.) Furthermore, in reviewing countless studies for this book, there were several researchers who did not clearly define the intervention being utilized, and it was unclear if the treatment was true EACP or a form of equine-assisted activities such as therapeutic riding or equine-assisted learning.

Some researchers even used the term "equine-assisted activities and therapies" to describe the treatment without further defining or elaborating on the specific nature of the modality under study. Therefore, it was impossible to determine if the intervention was true therapy facilitated by licensed mental health professionals or activities facilitated by equine professionals without the involvement of a licensed mental health professional. The terminology issue is not limited to research issues alone. Many providers use these terms casually or without fully understanding their meaning, thus adding to public confusion and resistance on the part of stakeholders to endorse or fund programming. Another limitation of much of the EACP research is the lack of consistency among study participants. Rather than conducting a study on a heterogeneous sample defined as "at-risk youth" with varied emotional and behavioral concerns, researchers should strive to design studies that examine the effects of EACP on clients with specific diagnoses in order to work towards EACP becoming an evidence-based practice (Serpell et al., 2017).

Finally, there is also a need for studies to establish the theoretical basis for EACP rather than relying on case studies and anecdotal reports (Bachi, 2012; Lee et al., 2016; Serpell et al., 2017). With the exception of a limited number of studies on the Equine Assisted Growth and Learning (EAGALA) approach (e.g., Trotter et al., 2008) and a single doctoral dissertation study on Relational Equine-Partnered Counseling (Sheade, 2015), most studies that do evaluate EACP specifically do not clearly delineate a structured protocol or manualized approach, thus further complicating understanding of the results, mechanisms of change, and ability to generalize the results. Although the results of many qualitative studies indicate the role of the human-equine relationship as an important factor in EACP, research on understanding the theoretical basis is still lacking (Bachi, 2012). Serpell and colleagues (2017) proposed several potential theories to explain the effects of animal-assisted interventions including theories related to animals as social catalysts and social capital; attachment, bonding and social support; animals as supernormal stimuli; attention, distraction, and biophilia; and biopsychosocial effects. Chandler (2017) has proposed a unified theory of animal-assisted therapy in counseling—Human-Animal Relational Theory (HART)—that encompasses many of the theoretical explanations described by Serpell and colleagues (2017). Similarly, the REPC approach for EACP also references many of potential theories proposed by Serpell and colleagues (2017) in the four philosophical domains and each domain's underlying theory, as described in Chapter 3. More research is needed using grounded theory methods or deductive methods to evaluate specific features in proposed approaches and theories (Bachi, 2012; Serpell et al., 2017). As the biopsychosocial effects of animal-assisted interventions are highlighted in both HART and REPC, studies examining the physiological effects of interaction with equines in EACP may help establish physiological benefits indicative of psychological benefits and positive change (Johnson, Odendaal, & Meadows, 2002).

184 Research Issues

There is still a long way to go to establish the credibility and effectiveness of EACP. Kazdin (2017) presented four recommendations to improve animal-assisted intervention research. Kazdin's first recommendation relates to the expansion of research methods and designs. Randomized clinical trials are highly recommended and considered to be the gold standard in evaluating intervention outcomes (Kazdin, 2017; Kendall et al., 2015; Lee et al., 2016). Other recommended research designs include single-case experimental designs, non-randomized group experimental designs, benchmarking reviews, qualitative research, and mixed methods (Kazdin, 2017). Such research studies should focus on exploring the effectiveness of single, specific interventions (rather than multiple types of equine-assisted activities and therapies) for a clearly defined clinical population (Lee et al., 2016). Additionally, the interventions used should be informed by manualized approaches with the inclusion of integrity or fidelity checks completed by impartial judges (Anestis et al., 2014).

Kazdin's second recommendation pertains to the establishment of a "small theory" or "treatment theory" that specifies "the clinical problem, what the treatment is, how or why that treatment can be expected to have impact on the problem, what the critical components of treatment area, and what outcomes best reflect therapeutic change" (p. 157). My hope is that this book can, in part, serve as a starting point in establishing a treatment theory for EACP that can be further developed and tested in specific clinical populations. Kazdin's third recommendation is to initiate laboratory-based studies to explore therapeutic processes in a controlled environment to better understand the specific effects of the human-animal interaction such as client self-reports, biological measures, and direct observations of the interaction. I believe that this particular recommendation can help fill a gap in better understanding the emotional impact of participation in EACP on the equines themselves. Gaining more knowledge in this area can not only improve the welfare of equines participating in EACP but also increase the effectiveness of EACP overall and contribute to the establishment of a unified grounded theory that incorporates the equines' experience in the relationship with clients. Finally, Kazdin recommended that the field of animal-assisted interventions, as a whole, develop a strategic, collaborative, and cooperative plan to expand the research base.

Despite these limitations, I believe that EACP remains a promising approach with numerous studies that indicate it can be beneficial for clients of varied mental health concerns. However, therapists are cautioned against overstating or misrepresenting the effects of EACP, as it has not yet been established as evidenced-based practice. In the meantime, it is important to integrate EACP into existing best practices in traditional psychotherapy rather than practicing EACP as a completely separate modality unrelated to traditional psychotherapy. In our practice, we often say that we are "psychotherapy first". Simply put, this statement refers to the fact that our approach is first grounded in best practices in psychotherapy (whether or not a therapy animal is involved) and informed by evidence-based approaches. When presenting to colleagues or discussing with stakeholders, I most often describe the integration of research related to outcome predictors in psychotherapy, interpersonal neurobiology, and the physiological and psychological benefits of interacting with animals as a way to explain the potential benefits and possible mechanisms of change in EACP. I will also describe methods to integrate EACP into established psychotherapy interventions to treat specific mental health concerns. This way of thinking is often a paradigm shift for many EACP practitioners who may struggle to find ways to conceptualize their approach in relation to best practices in the office. Using a theoretically grounded approach based on the different psychotherapy theories described in Chapter 7 can help the therapist practice within an established framework to inform clinical judgment and treatment planning.

References

Abrams, B. N. (2013). *Exploring therapists' conceptions of equine facilitated/assisted psychotherapy for combat veterans experiencing posttraumatic stress disorder.* (Doctoral dissertation). San Diego, CA: Northcentral University. ProQuest UMI No. 3569187.

Acharya, S., & Shukla, S. (2012). Mirror neurons: Enigma of the metaphysical modular brain. *Journal of Natural Science, Biology and Medicine, 3*(2), 118–124.

Alden, A. C. (2017). Qualities of a good therapy horse. In *PATH Intl. student manual: Equine specialist in mental health and learning workshop.* Denver: PATH Intl.

Allen, K. M., Blascovich, J., Tomaka, J., & Kelsey, R. M. (1991). Presence of human friends and pet dogs as moderators of autonomic responses to stress in women. *Journal of Personality and Social Psychology, 61*(4), 582–589.

Allen, K. M., Shykoff, B. E., & Izzo, J. L. (2001). Pet ownership, but not ACE inhibitor therapy, blunts home blood pressure responses to mental stress. *Hypertension, 38,* 815–820.

Alvarsson, J. J., Wiens, S., & Nilsson, M. W. (2010). Stress recovery during exposure to nature sound and environmental noise. *International Journal of Environmental Research and Public Health, 7,* 1036–1046.

American Counseling Association. (2014). *ACA code of ethics.* Alexandria, VA: Author.

American Psychological Association. (2017). *Ethical principles of psychologists and code of conduct.* Washington, DC: Author.

Anderson, D. C. (2007). *Assessing the human-animal bond: A compendium of actual measures.* West Lafayette, IN: Purdue University Press.

Anestis, M. D., Anestis, J. C., Zawilinski, L. L., Hopkins, T. A., & Lilienfeld, S. O. (2014). Equine-related treatments for mental disorders lack empirical support: A systematic review of empirical investigations. *Journal of Clinical Psychology, 70*(12), 1115–1132.

Anthony, D. W., & Brown, D. R. (2011). The secondary products revolution, horse-riding, and warfare. *Journal of World Prehistory, 24,* 131–160.

Ascione, F. R., McCabe, M. S., Phillips, A., & Tedeschi, P. (2010). Animal abuse and developmental psychopathology: Recent research, programmatic and therapeutic issues and challenges for the future. In A. H. Fine (Ed.), *Handbook on animal-assisted therapy: Theoretical foundations and guidelines for practice* (pp. 357–400). San Diego, CA: Academic Press.

Association for Play Therapy. (2020, May 7). *Tips for a clean play room.* Association for Play Therapy. Retrieved from https://www.a4pt.org/general/custom.asp?page=covidplayroomcare

References 187

Atuel, H. R., & Castro, C. A. (2018). Military cultural competence. *Clinical Social Work Journal, 46*, 74–82.

Axline, V. (1969). *Play therapy.* Boston, MA: Houghton-Mifflin.

Bachi, K. (2012). Equine-facilitated psychotherapy: The gap between practice and knowledge. *Society & Animals, 20*, 364–380.

Bachi, K. (2013). Application of attachment theory to equine-facilitated psychotherapy. *Journal of Contemporary Psychotherapy, 43*(3), 187–196. https://doi.org/10.1007/s10879-013-9232-1

Bachi, K., Terkel, J., & Teichman, M. (2011). Equine-facilitated psychotherapy for at-risk adolescents: The influence on self-image, self-control and trust. *Clinical Child Psychology and Psychiatry, 17*(2), 298–312. https://doi.org/10.1177/1359104511404177

Bachman, I., Audige, L., & Stauffacher, M. (2003). Risk factors associated with behavioural disorders of crib-biting, weaving, and box-walking in Swiss horses. *Equine Veterinary Journal, 35*(2), 158–163.

Badenoch, B. (2008). *Being a brain-wise therapist: A practical guide to interpersonal neurobiology.* New York: W. W. Norton & Company.

Baehr, G. O. (1954). The comparative effectiveness of individual psychotherapy, group psychotherapy, and a combination of these methods. *Journal of Consulting Psychology, 18*(3), 179–183.

Bailey, R. F., & Bailey, E. (2019). The transitioning families equine-assisted model for the treatment of anxiety. In K. S. Trotter and J. N. Baggerly (Eds.), *Equine-assisted mental health: Harnessing solutions to common problems* (pp. 51–57). New York: Routledge.

Banks, M. R., & Banks, W. A. (2002). The effects of animal-assisted therapy on loneliness in an elderly population in long-term care facilities. *Journal of Gerontology, 57A*(7), M428–M432.

Baragli, P., Vitale, V., Banti, L., & Sighieri, C. (2014). Effect of aging on behavioural and physiological responses to a stressful stimulus in horses (*Equus caballus*). *Behaviour, 151*, 1513–1533.

Barber, J. P., Connolly, M. B., Crits-Christoph, P., Gladis, L., & Siqueland, L. (2000). Alliance predicts patients' outcome beyond in-treatment change in symptoms. *Journal of Consulting and Clinical Psychology, 68*(6), 1027–1032.

Barker, S. B., Knisely, J. S., McCain, N. L., Schubert, C. M., & Pandurangi, A. K. (2010). Exploratory study of stress-buffering response patterns from interaction with a therapy dog. *Anthrozoös, 23*(1), 79–91.

Bartz, J. A., & Hollander, E. (2006). The neuroscience of affiliation: Forging links between basic and clinical research on neuropeptides and social behavior. *Hormones and Behavior, 50*, 518–528.

Bauducco, S. V. (2012). *Equine assisted psychotherapy with suicidal girls: Understanding the changes over time.* (Masters paper). Örebro, Sweden: Örebro University.

Baumeister, R. F., & Leary, M. R. (1995). The need to belong: Desire for interpersonal attachments as a fundamental human motivation. *Psychological Bulletin, 117*(3), 497–529. https://doi.org/10.1037/0033-2909.117.3.497.

Beauregard, M. (2012). *Brain wars: The scientific battle over the existence of the mind and the proof that will change the way we live our lives.* New York: HarperCollins Publishers.

Beck, A. M., & Katcher, A. H. (2003). Future directions in human-animal bond research. *American Behavioral Scientist, 47*(1), 79–93.

Beck, A. T., & Dozois, D. J. A. (2011). Cognitive therapy: Current status and future directions. *Annual Review of Medicine, 62*, 397–409.

188 References

Beetz, A. M. (2017). Theories and possible processes of action in animal assisted interventions. *Applied Developmental Science, 21*(2), 139–149.

Bekoff, M. (2006). Animal passions and beastly virtues: Cognitive ethology as the unifying science for understanding the subjective, emotional, empathic, and moral lives of animals. *Human Ecology Review, 13*(1), 39–59.

Bekoff, M. (2007). *The emotional lives of animals: A leading scientist explores animal joy, sorrow, and empathy—and why they matter.* Novato, CA: New World Library.

Bekoff, M. (2013, June 20). *A universal declaration on animal sentience: No pretending.* Retrieved from www.psychologytoday.com/us/blog/animal-emotions/201306/universal-declaration-animal-sentience-no-pretending

Bennett, B., & Woodman, E. (2019). The potential of equine-assisted psychotherapy for treating trauma in Australian Aboriginal peoples. *British Journal of Social Work, 49*, 1041–1058.

Berger, R. (2010). Nature therapy: Thoughts about the limitations of practice. *Journal of Humanistic Psychology, 50*(1), 65–76.

Berger, R., & McLeod, J. (2006). Incorporating nature into therapy: A framework for practice. *Journal of Systemic Therapies, 25*(2), 80–94.

Berget, B., & Braastad, B. O. (2011). Animal-assisted therapy with farm animals for persons with psychiatric disorders. *Annali dell'Istituto Superiore di Sanità, 47*(4), 384–390.

Bergman, H. E., Kline, A. C., Feeny, N. C., & Zoellner, L. A. (2015). Examining PTSD treatment choice among individuals with subthreshold PTSD. *Behaviour Research and Therapy, 73*, 33–41.

Berto, R. (2014). The role of nature in coping with psycho-physiological stress: A literature review on restorativeness. *Behavioral Sciences, 4*, 394–409.

Biedel, D. C., Christ, M. A. G., & Long, P. J. (1991). Somatic complaints in anxious children. *Journal of Abnormal Child Psychology, 19*(6), 659–670.

Birke, L., & Brandt, K. (2009). Mutual corporeality: Gender and human/horse relationships. *Women's Studies International Forum, 32*, 189–197.

Birke, L., & Hockenhull, J. (2015). Journeys together: Horses and humans in partnership. *Society & Animals, 23*, 81–100.

Blake, H. (1975). *Talking with horses.* London: Souvenir Press.

Blois-Heulin, C., Rochais, C., Camus, S. Fureix, C., Lemasson, C. L., Lunel, C., . . . Hausberger, M. (2015). Animal welfare: Could adult play be a false friend? *Animal Behavior and Cognition, 2*(2), 156–185.

Bohart, A. C. (1993). Experiencing: The basis of psychotherapy. *Journal of Psychotherapy Integration, 3*(1), 51–67.

Bokor, J., Broo, J., & Mahoney, J. (2016). Using fossil teeth to study the evolution of horses in response to a changing climate. *The American Biology Teacher, 78*(2), 166–170.

Boorstein, S. (1997). *Clinical studies in transpersonal psychotherapy.* Albany, NY: State University of New York Press.

Bordin, E. S. (1979). The generalizability of the psychoanalytic concept of the working alliance. *Psychotherapy: Theory, Research and Practice, 16*(3), 252–260.

Bradley, E. L. (2014). Choice theory and reality therapy: An overview. *International Journal of Choice Therapy and Reality Therapy, XXXIV*(1), 6–13.

Brandt, K. (2004). A language of their own: An interactionist approach to human-horse communication. *Society & Animals*, 299–316.

Briefer, E. F., Maigrot, A., Mandel, R., Freymond, S. B., Bachmann, I., & Hillmann, E. (2015). Segregation of information about emotional arousal and valence in horse whinnies. *Scientific Reports, 4*. https://doi.org/10.1038/srep09989

References 189

Briefer Freymond, S., Bardou, D., Beuret, S., Bachmann, I., Zuberbuhler, K., & Briefer, E. F. (2019). Elevated sensitivity to tactile stimuli in stereotypic horses. *Frontiers in Veterinary Science, 6*. https://doi.org/10.3389/fvets.2019.00162

Broesma, T. (2007). *Riding into your mythic life: Transformational adventures with the horse.* Novato, CA: New World Library.

Broom, D. M. (2007). Cognitive ability and sentience: Which aquatic animals should be protected? *Diseases of Aquatic Organisms, 75*, 99–108.

Brown, R. C., & Plener, P. L. (2017). Non-suicidal self-injury in adolescence. *Current Psychiatry Reports, 19*. https://doi.org/10.1007/s11920-017-0767-9

Brown, S. (2002). Ethnic variations in pet attachment among students at an American school of veterinary medicine. *Society & Animals, 10*, 249–266.

Brühwiller Senn, R. (2003). Personzentrierter Ansatz und körperorientierten Interventionen in der Reittherapie. In M. Gäng (Ed.), *Reittherapie* (pp. 56–66). Basel: Ernst Reinhardt Verlag.

Bugental, J. F. T. (1990). Existential-humanistic psychotherapy. In J. K. Zeig & W. M. Munion (Eds.), *What is psychotherapy: Contemporary perspectives* (pp. 189–193). San Francisco, CA: Jossey-Bass.

Bugental, J. F. T., & Bracke, P. E. (1992). The future of existential-humanistic psychotherapy. *Psychotherapy, 29*(1), 28–33.

Burgon, H. L. (2011). "Queen of the world": Experiences of "at-risk" young people participating in equine-assisted learning/therapy. *Journal of Social Work Practice, 25*(2), 165–183.

Burleson, M. H., Roberts, N. A., Coon, D. W., & Soto, J. A. (2019). Perceived cultural acceptability and comfort with affectionate touch: Differences between Mexican Americans and European Americans. *Journal of Social and Personal Relationships, 36*(3), 1000–1022.

Buzel, A. (2019). Equine-assisted mental health therapy and alcoholism: Issues in early sobriety. In K. S. Trotter & J. N. Baggerly (Eds.), *Equine-assisted mental health interventions: Harnessing solutions to common problems* (pp. 155–160). New York: Routledge.

Buzzell, L., & Chalquist, C. (Eds.). (2009). *Ecotherapy: Healing with nature in mind.* San Francisco, CA: Sierra Club Books.

Cacioppo, J. T., & Hawkley, L. C. (2003). Social isolation and health, with an emphasis on underlying mechanisms. *Perspectives in Biology and Medicine, 46*(3), S39–S52.

Cacioppo, J. T., & Hawkley, L. C. (2009). Perceived social isolation and cognition. *Trends in Cognitive Sciences, 13*(10), 447–454. https://doi.org/10.1016/j.tics.2009.06.005.

Cacioppo, J. T., Hawkley, L. C., Ernst, J. M., Burleson, M., Berntson, G. G., Nouriani, B., & Spiegel, D. (2006). Loneliness within a nomological net: An evolutionary perspective. *Journal of Research in Personality, 40*, 1054–1085. https://doi.org/10.1016/j.jrp.1005.11.007

Cacioppo, J. T., Norris, C. J., Decety, J., Monteleone, G., & Nusbaum, H. (2009). In the eye of the beholder: Individual differences in perceived social isolation predict regional brain activation to social stimuli. *Journal of Cognitive Neuroscience, 21*(1), 83–92. https://doi.org/10.1162/jocn.2009.21007

Cameron, J., & Robey, P. A. (2013). Healing through healing: The horse power of choice theory. *International Journal of Choice Theory and Reality Therapy, XXXIII*(1), 87–98.

Carlsson, C., Ranta, D. N., & Traeen, B. (2014). Equine assisted social work as a mean for authentic relations between clients and staff. *Human-Animal Interaction Bulletin, 2*(1), 19–38.

190 References

Carlsson, C., Ranta, D. N., & Traeen, B. (2015). Mentalizing and emotional labor facilitate equine-assisted social work with self-harming adolescents. *Child & Adolescent Social Work Journal, 32,* 329–339.

Carter, C. S. (1998). Neuroendocrine perspectives on social attachment and love. *Psychoneuroendocrinology, 23*(8), 779–818.

Castonguay, L. G., Goldfriend, M. R., Wiser, S., Raue, P. J., & Hayes, A. M. (1996). Predicting the effect of cognitive therapy for depression: A study of unique and common factors. *Journal of Consulting and Clinical Psychology, 64*(3), 497–504.

Center for Disease Control. (2019). *Data and statistics on children's mental health.* Retrieved from www.cdc.gov/childrensmentalhealth/data.html

Chalmers, D. J. (2014). *Fulfilling the fundamentals of life: A grounded theory of the process of human-horse relationship development.* (Doctoral dissertation). Calgary, Canada: University of Calgary.

Chandler, C. K. (2017). *Animal assisted therapy in counseling* (3rd ed.). New York: Routledge.

Chandler, C. K. (2018). Human-animal relational theory: A guide for animal-assisted counseling. *Journal of Creativity in Mental Health, 13*(4), 429–444.

Chandler, C. K., Potrie-Bethke, T. L., Barrio Minto, C. A., Fernando, D. M., & O'Callaghan, D. M. (2010). Matching animal-assisted therapy techniques and intentions with counseling guiding theories. *Journal of Mental Health Counseling, 32*(4), 354–374.

Chardonnens, E. (2009). The use of animals as co-therapists on a farm: The child-horse bond in person-centered equine-assisted psychotherapy. *Person-Centered and Experiential Psychotherapies, 8*(4), 320–332.

Cohen, R. A. (2011). *Exploring multicultural considerations in equine facilitated psychotherapy.* (Doctoral dissertation). ProQuest UMI No. 3516479.

Cohen, S. P. (2010). Loss of a therapy animal: Assessment and healing. In A. H. Fine (Ed.), *Handbook on animal-assisted therapy: Theoretical foundations and guidelines for practice* (pp. 441–456). San Diego, CA: Academic Press.

Cole, K. M., Gawlinski, A., Steers, N., & Kotlerman, J. (2007). Animal-assisted therapy in patients hospitalized with heart failure. *American Journal of Critical Care, 16,* 575–585.

Corey, G. (2009). *Theory and practice of counseling and psychotherapy* (8th ed.). Belmont, CA: Thomson Brookes/Cole.

Cornish, A., Wilson, B., Raubenheimer, D., & McGreevy, P. (2018). Demographics regarding belief in non-human animal sentience and emotional empathy with animals: A pilot study among attendees of an animal welfare symposium. *Animals, 8.* https://doi.org/10.3390/ani8100174

Correia, E. A., Cooper, M., & Berdondini, L. (2015). Existential psychotherapy: An international survey of the key authors and texts influencing practice. *Journal of Contemporary Psychotherapy, 45*(1), 3–10.

Couvillon, M., Peterson, R. L., Ryan, J. B., Scheuerman, B., & Stegall, J. (2010). A review of crisis intervention training programs for schools. *Teaching Exceptional Children, 42*(5), 6–17.

Coyne, J. C., & Liddle, H. A. (1992). The future of systems therapy: Shedding myths and facing opportunities. *Psychotherapy, 29*(1), 44–50.

Cozolino, L. (2016). *Why therapy works: Using our minds to change our brains.* New York: W. W. Norton & Company, Inc.

Cozza, S. J., Fisher, J. E., Zhou, J., Harrington-LaMorie, J., La Flair, L., Fullerton, C. S., & Ursano, R. J. (2017). Bereaved military dependent spouses and children: Those left behind in a decade of war (2001–2011). *Military Medicine, 182*(3/4), e1684–e1690.

Cullen, W., Gulati, G., & Kelly, B. D. (2020). Mental health in the Covid-19 pandemic. *QJM: An International Journal of Medicine*. doi: 10.1093/qjmed/hcaa110

Cumella, E. J., Lutter, C. B., Lutter, C. B., & Lutter, C. B. (2014). Equine therapy in the treatment of female eating disorder. *SOP Transactions on Psychology, 1*(1), 13–21.

Darwin, C. (1890/2009). *The expression of the emotions in man and animals* (2nd ed.). London: Penguin Books.

Davenport, N. D. (2016). The chaos of combat: An overview of challenges in military mild traumatic brain injury research. *Frontiers in Psychology, 7*. https://doi.org/10.3389/fpsyt.2016.00085

Davis, S. J. M., & Valla, F. R. (1978). Evidence for domestication of the dog 12,000 years ago in the Natufian of Israel. *Nature, 276*, 608–610.

De Barros Damgaard, P., Martiniano, R., Kamm, J., Moreno-Mayar, J. V., Kroonen, G., Peyrot, M., . . . Willerslev, E. (2018). The first horse herders and the impact of early Bronze Age steppe expansions into Asia. *Science, 360*. Retrieved from https://science.sciencemag.org/content/sci/360/6396/eaar7711.full.pdf

Dell, C. A., Chalmers, D., Bresette, N., Swain, S., Rankin, D., & Hopkins, C. (2011). A healing space: The experiences of First Nations and Inuit Youth with Equine-assisted learning (EAL). *Child Youth Care Forum*. https://doi.org/10.1007/s10566-011-9140-z

Dell, C. A., Chalmers, D., Dell, D., Sauve, E., & MacKinnon, T. (2008). Horse as healer: An examination of equine assisted learning in the healing of First Nations youth from solvent abuse. *Pimatisiwin: A Journal of Aboriginal and Indigenous Community Health, 6*(1), 81–106.

DeMala-Moran, C. L. (2019). The *Four Agreements* in equine-assisted therapy for relationships. In K. S. Trotter & J. N. Baggerly (Eds.), *Equine-assisted mental health interventions: Harnessing solutions to common problems* (pp. 233–237). New York: Routledge.

DeMayo, N. (2009). Horses, humans, and healing. In L. Buzzell & C. Chalquist (Eds.), *Ecotherapy: Healing with nature in mind*. San Francisco, CA: Sierra Club Books.

DePrekel, M., & Runge, N. (2019). Equine-facilitated psychotherapy for the treatment of depression. In K. S. Trotter and J. N. Baggerly (Eds.), *Equine-assisted mental health: Harnessing solutions to common problems* (pp. 27–41). New York: Routledge.

DeVoe, E. R., Kritikos, T. M., Emmert-Aronson, B., Kantor, G. K., & Paris, R. (2018). Very young child well-being in military families: A snapshot. *Journal of Child and Family Studies, 27*, 2138–2148. https://doi.org/10.1007/s10826-018-1069-5

Devon, J. M. (2011). *The therapist's description of the experience of equine assisted psychotherapy (EAP) as it pertains to youth with attention deficit disorder/attention deficit hyperactivity disorder: A qualitative study*. (Doctoral dissertation). Capella University. ProQuest UMI No. 3489636.

Diehle, J., Brooks, S. K., & Greenberg, N. (2017). Veterans are not the only ones suffering from posttraumatic stress symptoms: What do we know about dependents' secondary traumatic stress? *Social Psychiatry and Psychiatric Epidemiology, 52*, 35–44.

Diener, E., & Seligman, M. E. P. (2002). Very happy people. *Psychological Science, 13*(1), 81–84.

Dinkmeyer, D., & Sperry, L. (2000). *Counseling and psychotherapy: An integrated, individual psychology approach* (3rd ed.). Upper Saddle River, NJ: Prentice-Hall, Inc.

Dirkzwager, A. J. E., Bramsen, I., Adèr, H., & van der Ploeg, H. M. (2005). Secondary traumatization in partners and parents of Dutch peacekeeping soldiers. *Journal of Family Psychology, 19*(2), 217–226.

Donovan, A. (2017). *The effect of nontherapeutic interaction on college equestrian students' anxiety level*. (Unpublished masters paper). Baltimore, MD: Goucher College.

192   References

Dossey, L. (1989). *Recovering the soul.* New York: Bantam.

Dossey, L. (2015). Nonlocal mind: A (fairly) brief history of the term. *Explore, 11*(2), 89–101.

Doucette, P. A. (2004). Walk and talk: An intervention for behaviorally challenge youths. *Adolescence, 39*(154), 373–388.

Duncan, I. J. H. (2006). The changing concept of animal sentience. *Applied Animal Behaviour Science, 100*, 11–19.

Dunlop, K., & Tsantefski, M. (2018). A space of safety: Children's experience of equine-assisted group therapy. *Child & Family Social Work, 23*, 16–24.

Dwyer, R. M. (2015). Equine zoonoses: Consequences of horse-human interactions. In A. Sing (Ed.), *Zoonoses-infections affecting humans and animals* (pp. 643–657). New York: Springer.

Dziegelewski, N. (2014). *Trauma-focused equine assisted psychotherapy: A quantitative study of intervention effectiveness.* (Master thesis). Northampton, MA: Smith College.

Earles, J. L., Vernon, L. L., & Yetz, J. P. (2015). Equine-assisted therapy for anxiety and posttraumatic stress symptoms. *Journal of Traumatic Stress, 28*, 149–152.

Ecken, T. S. (2012). *An investigation of the adolescents' experience of EAT, a qualitative approach.* (Unpublished doctoral dissertation). London: Middlesex University.

Ecker, S., & Byrnes, J. (2019). Improving social and communication skills for participants with autism spectrum disorder through equine-assisted psychotherapy. In K. S. Trotter & J. N. Baggerly (Eds.), *Equine-assisted mental health interventions: Harnessing solutions to common problems* (pp. 114–121). New York: Routledge.

Eisenberger, N. I., Lieberman, M. D., & Williams, K. D. (2003). Does rejection hurt? An fMRI study of social exclusion. *Science, 302*, 290–292.

Elliot, A. J., Eder, A. B., Harmon-Jones, E. (2013). Approach-avoidance motivation and emotion: Convergence and divergence. *Emotion Review, 5*(3), 308–311.

Epley, N., Waytz, A., Akalis, S., & Cacioppo, J. T. (2008). When we need a human: Motivational determinants of anthropomorphism. *Social Cognition, 26*(2), 143–155.

Ernest, J. M., & Cacioppo, J. T. (1999). Lonely hearts: Psychological perspectives on loneliness. *Applied and Preventive Psychology, 8*, 1–22.

Equine Assisted Growth and Learning Association. (2018). *Certification.* Retrieved from www.eagala.org/certification

Equine Disease Communication Center. (2020, May 7). *Coronavirus disease resources and updates.* Equine Disease Communication Center. Retrieved from http://www.equinediseasecc.org/coronavirus-resources

Equisearch. (2017). *Your choice of horse halter matters.* Retrieved from www.equisearch.com/articles/your-choice-horse-halter-matters-21170

Ernst, J. M., & Cacioppo, J. T. (1999). Lonely hearts: Psychological perspectives on loneliness. *Applied and Preventive Psychology, 8*(1), 1–22.

Esposito-Smythers, C., Wolff, J., Lemmon, K. M., Bodzy, M., Swenson, R. R., & Spirito, A. (2011). Military youth and the deployment cycle: Emotional health consequences and recommendations for intervention. *Journal of Family Psychology, 25*(4), 497–507.

Eurodressage. (2019). *France bans the trimming of whiskers.* Retrieved from www.eurodressage.com/2019/04/03/france-bans-trimming-whiskers

Faa-Thompson, T. (2019). Equine-assisted play therapy for clients with autism spectrum disorder. In K. S. Trotter & J. N. Baggerly (Eds.), *Equine-assisted mental health interventions: Harnessing solutions to common problems* (pp. 109–113). New York: Routledge.

Falk, J. H., & Balling, J. D. (2009). Evolutionary influence on human landscape preference. *Environment and Behavior, 42*(4), 479–493. https://doi.org/10.1177/0013916509341244

References 193

Fall, K. A., Holden, J. M., & Marquis, A. (2010). *Theoretical models of counseling and psychotherapy* (2nd ed.). New York: Routledge.

Feh, C., & De Mazieres, J. (1993). Grooming at a preferred site reduces heart rate in horses. *Animal Behaviour, 46,* 1191–1194.

Felitti, V. J., Anda, R. F., Nordenberg, D., Williamson, D. F., Spitz, A. M., Edwards, V., . . . Marks, J. S. (1998). Relationship of childhood abuse and household dysfunction to many of the leading causes of death in adults: The Adverse Childhood Experiences (ACE) study. *American Journal of Preventive Medicine, 14*(4), 245–258.

Fenner, K., Caspar, G., Hyde, M., Henshall, C., Dhand, N., Probyn-Rapsey, F., . . . McGreevy, P. (2019). It's all about the sex, or is it? Humans, horses and temperament. *PLoS One, 14*(5). Retrieved from https://doi.org/10.1371/journal.pone.0216699

Fenner, K., McLean, A. N., & McGreevy, P. D. (2019). Cutting to the chase: How round-pen, lunging, and high-speed liberty work may compromise equine welfare. *Journal of Veterinary Behavior, 29,* 88–94.

Fernández, O. M., Krause, M., & Pérez, J. C. (2016). Therapeutic alliance in the initial phase of psychotherapy with adolescents: Different perspectives and their association with therapeutic outcomes. *Research in Psychotherapy: Psychopathology, Process and Outcome, 19.* https://doi.org/10.4081/ripppo.2016.180

Ferruolo, D. M. (2015). Psychosocial equine program for veterans. *Social Work, 61*(1), 53–60.

Filippides, N. C. (2016). *Beyond the couch: A psychoanalytic approach to equine assisted psychotherapy.* (Doctoral dissertation). ProQuest UMI No. 10261714.

Filippides, N. C. (2019). Beyond the couch: An object relations approach to EACP substance abuse treatment. In K. S. Trotter and J. N. Baggerly (Eds.), *Equine-assisted mental health: Harnessing solutions to common problems* (pp. 169–174). New York: Routledge.

Fine, A. H. (Ed.). (2010). *Handbook on animal assisted therapy: Theoretical foundations and guidelines for practice* (3rd ed.). San Diego, CA: Academic Press.

Fishman, M. A. (1999). Predator inspection: Closer approach as a way to improve assessment of potential threats. *Journal of Theoretical Biology, 2*(21), 225–235.

Flückiger, C., Del Re, A. C., Wampold, B. E., & Horvath, A. O. (2018). The alliance in adult psychotherapy: A meta-analytic synthesis. *Psychotherapy, 55*(4), 316–340.

Flynn, K. (2020). Biosecurity basics. *PATH Intl. Strides, 26*(1), 37–41.

Foynes, M. M. (2016). *PTSD & military sexual trauma* [PowerPoint Slides]. Retrieved from www.ptsd.va.gov/professional/consult/2016lecture_archive/02172016_lecture_slides.pdf

Frame, D. L. (2006). *Practices of therapists using equine facilitated/assisted psychotherapy in the treatment of adolescents diagnosed with depression: A qualitative study.* (Doctoral dissertation). ProQuest UMI No. 3204151.

Frederick, K. (2019). An Eagala model approach to using equine-assisted counseling with teens suffering from depression. In K. S. Trotter and J. N. Baggerly (Eds.), *Equine-assisted mental health: Harnessing solutions to common problems* (pp. 42–47). New York: Routledge.

Fredrickson, M., & Stewart, J. (2003). Partnership. *NARHA's Strides,* 120–122.

Froeschle, J. (2009). Empowering abused women through equine assisted career therapy. *Journal of Creativity in Mental Health, 4,* 181–190.

Fuhriman, A., & Burlingame, G. M. (1990). Consistency of matter: A comparative analysis of individual and group process variables. *The Counseling Psychologist, 18*(1), 6–63.

194 References

Fureix, C., Gorecka-Bruzda, Gautier, E., Hausberger, M. (2011). Cooccurrence of yawning and stereotypic behaviour in horses *(Equus caballus). ISRN Zoology*, Article ID 271209. https://doi.org/10.5402/2011/271209

Fureix, C., Jego, P., Henry, S., Lansade, L., & Hausberger, M. (2012). Towards an ethological animal model of depression? A study on horses. *PLoS One, 7*(6). https://doi.org/10.1371/journal.pone.0039280

Fureix, C., Menguy, H., & Hausberger, M. (2010). Partners with bad temper: Reject or cure? A study of chronic pain and aggression in horses. *PLoS One, 5*(8), e12434. https://doi.org/10.1371/journal.pone.0012434

Galea, S., Merchant, R. M., & Lurie, N. (2020). The mental health consequences of COVID-19 and physical distancing: The need for prevention and early intervention. *JAMA Internal Medicine*. Retrieved from https://jamanetwork.com/ on 05/05/2020

Gaunitz, C., Fages, A., Hanghøj, K., Albrechtsen, A., Khan, N., Schubert, M., . . . Orlando, L. (2018). Ancient genomes revisit the ancestry of domestic and Przewalski's horses. *Science, 360*, 111–114.

Gelso, C. J., & Carter, J. A. (1985). The relationship in counseling and psychotherapy: Components, consequences, and theoretical antecedents. *The Counseling Psychologist, 13*(2), 155–243.

Gendlin, E. T. (1973). Experiential psychotherapy. In R. Corsini (Ed.), *Current psychotherapies* (pp. 317–352). Itasca, IL: Peacock. Retrieved from www.focusing.org/gendlin/docs/gol_2029.html

Gergley, E. J. (2012). *Equien-assisted psychotherapy: A descriptive study*. (Doctoral dissertation). Kalamazoo, MI: Western Michigan University. Retrieved from https://scholarworks.wmich.edu/dissertations/107

Ghandour, R. M., Sherman, L. J., Vladutiu, C., Ali, M. M., Lynch, S. E., Bitsko, R. H., & Blumberg, S. J. (2019). Prevalence and treatment of depression, anxiety, and conduct problems in US children. *The Journal of Pediatrics, 206*, 256–267.

Gidlow, C. J., Jones, M. V., Hurst, G., Masterson, D., Clark-Carter, D., Tarvainen, M. P., . . . Nieuwenhuijsen, M. (2015). Where to put your best foot forward: Psychophysiological responses to walking in natural and urban environments. *Journal of Environmental Psychology, 45*, 22–29. https://doi.org/10.1016/j.jenvp.2015.11.003

Gilbert, R. (2013). *Equine assisted psychotherapy: Provider perspectives and beliefs*. (Doctoral dissertation). Indiana University. ProQuest UMI No. 3599176.

Gimenez Husted, R. (2020). Emergency planning: Forming a facility evacuation plan. *PATH Intl. Strides, 26*(1), 28–33.

Gladding, S. T. (2008). *Groups: A counseling specialty* (7th ed.). Upper Saddle River, NJ: Pearson Education, Inc.

Godal-Kern, A., Brenna, I. H., Arnevik, E. J., & Ravndal, E. (2016). More than just a break from treatment: How substance use disorder patients experience the stable environment in horse-assisted therapy. *Substance Abuse: Research and Treatment, 10*, 99–108.

Golberstein, E., Wen, H., & Miller, B. F. (2020). Coronavirus disease 2019 (COVID-19) and mental health for children and adolescents. *JAMA Pediatrics*. Retrieved from https://jamanetwork.com/ on 05/05/2020

Goldenberg, H., & Goldenberg, I. (2008). *Family therapy: An overview* (7th ed). Belmont, CA: Thomson Brooks/Cole.

Goodwin, D. (1999). The importance of ethology in understand the behaviour of the horse. *Equine Veterinary Journal, 28*, 15–19.

References 195

Górecka-Bruzda, A., Fureix, C., Ouvrard, A., Bourjade, M., & Hausberger, M. (2016). Investigating determinants of yawning in the domestic (Equus caballus) and Przewalski (Equus ferus przewalskii) horses. *The Science of Nature, 103*(72). https://doi.org/10.1007/s00114-016-1395-7

Gosling, S. D., & John, O. P. (1999). Personality dimensions in nonhuman animals: A cross-species review. *Current Directions in Psychological Science, 8*(3), 69–75.

Green, S., Rolleston, M., Schroeder, M. (2019). Equine-assisted psychotherapy with couples and families. In K. S. Trotter & J. N. Baggerly (Eds.), *Equine-assisted mental health interventions: Harnessing solutions to common problems* (pp. 238–247). New York: Routledge.

Green, S., Schroeder, M., Penalva, C., Rolleston, M., & Judd, V. B. (2019). Triggering transformations: An equine-assisted approach to the treatment of substance abuse. In K. S. Trotter & J. N. Baggerly (Eds.), *Equine-assisted mental health: Harnessing solutions to common problems* (pp. 161–168). New York: Routledge.

Greenberg, N., Docherty, M., Gnanapragasam, S., & Wessely, S. (2020). Managing mental health challenges face by healthcare workers during covid-19 pandemic. *British Medical Journal.* doi: 10.1136/bmj.m1211

Grier, K. C. (1999). Childhood socialization and companion animals: United States, 1820–1870. *Society and Animals, 7*(2), 95–120.

Griffin, D. (1976). *The question of animal awareness.* New York: Rockefeller University Press.

Guastella, A. J., Mitchell, P. B., & Mathews, F. (2008). Oxytocin enhances the encoding of positive social memories in humans. *Biological Psychiatry, 64*, 256–268.

Guo, X., & Slesnick, N. (2013). Family versus individual therapy: Impact on discrepancies between parents' and adolescents' perceptions over time. *Journal of Marital & Family Therapy, 39*(2), 182–194.

Hägerhäll, C. M., Sang, A. O., Englund, J., Ahlner, F., Rybka, K., Huber, J., & Burenhult, N. (2018). Do humans really prefer semi-open natural landscapes? A cross-cultural reappraisal. *Frontiers in Psychology, 9.* https://doi.org/10.3389/fpsyg.2018.00822

Hall, C., Goodwin, D., Heleski, C., Randle, H., & Waran, N. (2008). Is there evidence of learned helplessness in horses? *Journal of Applied Animal Welfare Science, 11*(3), 239–266.

Hall, C., Randle, H., Pearson, G., Prenshaw, L., & Waran, N. (2018). Assessing equine emotional state. *Applied Animal Behaviour Science, 205*, 183–193.

Hallberg, L. (2008). *Walking the way of the horse: Exploring the power of the horse-human relationship.* Bloomington, IN: iUniverse.

Halm, M. A. (2008). The healing power of the human-animal connection. *American Journal of Critical Care, 17*, 373–376.

Ham, T. M. (2013). *Equine assisted couples therapy: An exploratory study.* (Masters paper). Virginia Polytechnic Institute and State University.

Hama, H., Yogo, M., & Matsuyama, Y. (1996). Effects of stroking horses on both humans' and horses' heart rate responses. *Japanese Psychological Research, 38*(2), 66–73.

Hamilton, A. (2011). *Zen mind zen horse: The science and spirituality of working with horses.* North Adams, MA: Storey Publishing.

Harrington-LaMorie, J., Jordan, J. R., Ruocco, K., & Cerel, J. (2018). Surviving families of military suicide loss: Exploring postvention peer support. *Death Studies, 42*(3), 143–154. https://doi.org/10.1080/07481187.2017.1370789

Hartmann, E., Christensen, J. W., & McGreevy, P. D. (2017). Dominance and leadership: Useful concepts in human-horse interactions? *Journal of Equine Veterinary Science, 52*, 1–9.

196 References

Hartsell, T. L., & Bernstein, B. E. (2013). *The portable lawyer for mental health professionals.* Hoboken, NJ: John Wiley & Sons, Inc.

Haseman, S. (2017). Crisis: Preventing it, handling it. In *PATH Intl. student manual: Equine specialist in mental health and learning workshop* (pp. 83–87). Denver: PATH Intl.

Hatch, A. (2007). The view from all fours: A look at an animal-assisted activity program from the animals' perspective. *Anthrozoös, 20*(1), 37–50.

Hatcher, R. L., & Barends, A. W. (1996). Patients' view of the alliance in psychotherapy: Exploratory factor analysis of three alliance measures. *Journal of Consulting and Clinical Psychology, 64*(6), 1326–1336.

Hausberger, M., Bruderer, C., Le Scolan, N., & Pierre, J. (2004). Interplay between environmental and genetic factors in temperament/personality traits in horses (*Equus caballus*). *Journal of Comparative Psychology, 118*(4), 434–446.

Hausberger, M., Fureix, C., Bourjade, M., Wessel-Robert, S., & Richard-Yris, M. (2012). On the significance of adult play: What does social play tell us about adult horse welfare? *Naturwissenchaften, 99*, 291–302.

Hausberger, M., Gautier, E. Biquand, V., Lunel, C., & Jego, P. (2009). Could work be a source of behavioural disorders? A study in horses. *PLoS One, 4*(10), e7625. https://doi.org/10.1371/journal.pone.0007625

Hausberger, M., Muller, C., & Lunel, C. (2011). Does work affect personality? A study in horses. *PLoS One, 6*(2). https://doi.org/https://doi.org/10.1371/journal.pone.0014659

Hausberger, M., Roche, H., Henry, S., & Visser, E. K. (2008). A review of the human-horse relationship. *Applied Animal Behaviour Science, 109*, 1–24.

Hausberger, M., Stomp, M., Sankey, C., Brajon, S., Lunel, C., & Henry, S. (2019). Mutual interactions between cognition and welfare: The horse as an animal model. *Neuroscience & Biobehavioral Reviews, 107*, 540–559.

Hausman, G., & Hausman, L. (2003). *The mythology of horses: Horse legend and lore throughout the ages.* New York: Three Rivers Press.

Hayes, J. P. (2019). PTSD and TBI comorbidity. *PTSD Research Quarterly, 30*(2), 1050–1835.

Heinrichs, M., Baumgartner, T., Kirschbaum, C., & Ehlert, U. (2003). Social support and oxytocin interact to suppress cortisol and subjective responses to psychosocial stress. *Biological Psychiatry, 54*, 1389–1398.

Heinrichs, M., & Gaab, J. (2007). Neuroendocrine mechanism of stress and social interaction: Implications for mental disorders. *Current Opinion in Psychiatry, 20*, 158–162.

Helmus, T. C., Zimmerman, R., Posard, M. N., Wheeler, J. L., Olgetree, C., Stroud Q., & Harrell, M. C. (2018). *Life as a private: A study of the motivations and experiences of junior enlisted personnel in the U.S. Army.* Santa Monica, CA: RAND Corporation.

Henshall, C., & McGreevy, P. (2014). The role of ethology in round pen horse training—a review. *Applied Animal Behaviour Science, 155*, 1–11.

Hepner, K. A., Farris, C., Farmer, C. M., Iyiewuare, P. O., Tanelian, T., Wilks, A., . . . Pincus, H. A. (2017a). *Delivering clinical practice guide-concordant care for PTSD and major depression in military treatment facilities.* Santa Monica, CA: RAND Corporation.

Hepner, K. A., Roth, C. P., Sloss, E. M., Paddock, S. M., Iyiewuare, P. O., Timmer, M .J., & Pincus, H. A. (2017b). *Quality of care for PTSD and depression in the military health system.* Santa Monica, CA: RAND Corporation.

Herzog, H. A., Betchart, N. S., & Pittman, R. B. (1991). Gender, sex role orientation, and attitudes toward animals. *Anthrozoös, 4*(3), 184–191.

References   197

Herzog, J. R., Everson, R. B., & Whitworth, J. D. (2011). Do secondary trauma symptoms in spouses of combat-exposed National Guard soldiers mediate impacts of soldiers' trauma exposure on their children? *Child and Adolescent Social Work Journal, 28*, 459–473.

Hill, C. (2006). *How to think like a horse: The essential handbook for understanding why horses do what they do.* North Adams, MA: Storey Publishing.

Hinde, R. (1979). *Towards understanding relationships.* London, UK: Academic Press.

Hoehn-Saric, R., McLeod, D. R., Funderburk, F., & Kowalski, P. (2004). Somatic symptoms and physiology responses in generalized anxiety disorder and panic disorder: An ambulatory monitor study. *Archives of General Psychiatry, 61*, 913–921.

Hogan, E. S., Houpt, K. A., & Sweeney, K. (1988). The effect of enclosure size on social interactions and daily activity patterns it the captive Asiatic wild horse (*Equus przewalskii*). *Applied Animal Behaviour Science, 21*, 147–168.

Hollander, E., Bartz, J., Chaplin, W., Phillips, A., Sumner, J., Soorya, L., . . . Wasserman, S. (2007). Oxytocin increases retention of social cognition in autism. *Biological Psychiatry, 61*(4), 498–503.

Holloway, A. C. (2009). *Relationship enhancement for couples using equine facilitated psychotherapy techniques: A model program.* (Doctoral dissertation). San Francisco, CA: Alliant International University. ProQuest UMI No. 3417182.

Hong, X., Currier, G. W., Zhao, X., Jiang, Y., Zhou, W., & Wei, J. (2009). Posttraumatic stress disorder in convalescent severe acute respiratory syndrome patients: A 4-year follow-up study. *General Hospital Psychiatry, 31*, 546–554.

House, J. S., Landis, K. R., & Umberson, D. (1988). Social relationships and health. *Science, 241*, 540–545.

Howey, M. O. (1923). *The horse in magic and myth.* London: William Rider and Son Ltd.

IAHAIO. (2019). *IAHAIO position statement: Zoonoses and animal-assisted interventions.* Retrieved from http://iahaio.org/wp/wp-content/uploads/2019/10/zoonoses-and-aai-position-paper-final.pdf

Iannuzzi, D., & Rowan, A. N. (1991). Ethical issues in animal-assisted therapy programs. *Anthrozoös, 4*(3), 154–163.

Insel, T. R. (1997). A neurobiological basis of social attachment. *American Journal of Psychiatry, 154*(6), 726–735.

International Society for Equitation Science. (n.d.). *Position statement on the use/misuse of leadership and dominance concepts in horse training.* Retrieved from https://equitationscience.com/equitation/position-statement-on-the-use-misuse-of-leadership-and-dominance-concepts-in-horse-training

Irwin, C. (2005). *Dancing with your dark horse: How horse sense helps us find balance, strength, and wisdom.* New York: Marlowe & Company.

Ish-Lev, H., & Amit, R. (2013). Elements of group psychotherapy found in individual animal- assisted psychotherapy. In N. Parish-Plass (Ed.), *Animal-assisted psychotherapy.* West Lafayette, IN: Purdue University Press.

Ivey, A. E., & Ivey, M. B. (2007). *Intentional interviewing and counseling: Facilitating client development in a multicultural society* (6th ed.). Belmont, CA: Thomson Brooks/Cole.

Jang, B., Song, J., Kim, J., Kim, S., Lee, J. Shin, H., … & Joung, Y. (2015). Equine-assisted activities and therapy for treating children with attention-deficit/hyperactivity disorder. *The Journal of Alternative and Complementary Medicine, 00*(0), 1–8.

Jenkins, C. D., Laux, J. M., Ritchie, M. H., & Tucker-Gail, K. (2014). Animal-assisted therapy and Rogers' core components among middle school students receiving counseling services: A descriptive study. *Journal of Creativity in Mental Health, 9,* 174–187.

Johansen, S. G., Arfwedson Wang, C. E., & Biner, P. (2016). Facilitating change in a client's dysfunctional behavioural pattern with horse-aided psychotherapy. A case study. *Counselling and Psychotherapy Research, 16*(3), 222–231.

Johansen, S. G., Arfwedson Wang, C. E., Binder, P., & Malt, U. F. (2014). Equine-facilitated body and emotion-oriented psychotherapy designed for adolescents and adults not responding to mainstream treatment: A structured program. *Journal of Psychotherapy Integration, 24*(4), 323–335.

Johnson, P. J., Janvier, V., Luh, W., FitzMaurice, M., Southard, T., & Barry, E. F. (2019). Equine stereotaxtic population average brain atlas with neuroanatomic correlation. *Frontiers in Neuroanatomy, 13*(89). https://doi.org/10.3389/fnana.2019.00089

Johnson, R. A., Odendaal, J. S. J., & Meadows, R. L. (2002). Animal-assisted interventions research: Issues and answers. *Western Journal of Nursing Research, 24*(4), 422–440.

Jongsma, A. E., Peterson, L. M., & Bruce, T. J. (2014). *The complete adult psychotherapy treatment planner* (5th ed.). Hoboken, NJ: John Wiley & Sons, Inc.

Jordan, A. J., Litz, B. T. (2014). Prolonged grief disorder: Diagnostic, assessment, and treatment considerations. *Professional Psychology: Research and Practice, 45*(3), 180–187.

Jordan, M. (2013). *Taking therapy outside—A narrative inquiry into counselling and psychotherapy in outdoor natural spaces.* (Doctoral thesis). Brighton, UK: University of Brighton.

Kaiser, L., Heleski, C. R., Siegford, J., & Smith, K. A. (2006). Stress-related behaviors among horses used in a therapeutic riding program. *Journal of the American Veterinary Medical Association, 228*(1), 39–45.

Kaminski, M., Pellino, T., & Wish, J. (2002). Play and pets: The physical and emotional impact of child-life and pet therapy on hospitalized children. *Children's Health Care, 31*(4), 321–335.

Kang, H. K., Bullman, T. A., Smolenski, D. J., Skopp, N. A., Gahm, G. A., & Reger, M. A. (2018). Suicide risk among 1.3 million veterans who were on active duty during the Iraq and Afghanistan wars. *Annals of Epidemiology, 25*(2), 96–100.

Kang, H. K., Natelson, B. H., Mahan, C. M., Lee, K. Y., & Murphy, F. M. (2003). Posttraumatic stress disorder and chronic fatigue syndrome-like illness among Gulf War veterans: A population-based survey of 30,000 veterans. *American Journal of Epidemiology, 157*(2), 141–148.

Kaplan, S. (1995). The restorative benefits of nature: Toward an integrative framework. *Journal of Environmental Psychology, 15,* 169–182.

Karol, J. (2007). Applying a traditional individual psychotherapy model to equine-facilitated psychotherapy (EFP): Theory and method. *Clinical Child Psychology and Psychiatry, 12*(1), 77–90.

Karver, M. S., Handelsman, J. B., Fields, S., & Bickman, L. (2006). Meta-analysis of therapeutic relationship variables in youth and family therapy: The evidence for different relationship variables in the child and adolescent outcome literature. *Clinical Psychology Review, 26,* 50–65.

Kazdin, A. E. (2017). Strategies to improve the evidence base of animal-assisted interventions. *Applied Developmental Science, 21*(2), 150–164.

Kellert, S. R., & Berry, J. K. (1987). Attitudes, knowledge, and behaviors toward wildlife as affected by gender. *Wildlife Society Bulletin, 15,* 363–371.

Kellert, S. R., & Wilson, E. O. (1993). *The biophilia hypothesis.* Washington, DC: Island Press.

References 199

Kemp, K., Signal, T., Botros, H., Taylor, N., & Prentice, K. (2014). Equine facilitated therapy with children and adolescents who have been sexually abused: A program evaluation study. *Journal of Child and Family Studies, 23*, 558–566.

Kendall, E., Maujean, A., Pepping, C. A., Downes, M., Lakhani, A., Byrne, J., & Macfarlane, K. (2015). A systematic review of the efficacy of equine-assisted interventions on psychological outcomes. *European Journal of Psychotherapy & Counselling, 17*(1), 57–79.

Kern-Godal, A., Arnevik, E. A., Walderhaug, E., & Ravndal, E. (2015). Substance use disorder treatment retention and completion: A prospective study of horse-assisted therapy (HAT) for young adults. *Addiction Science & Clinical Practice, 10.* https://doi.org/10.1186/s13722-015-0043-4

Kern-Godal, A., Brenna, I. H., Kogstad, N., Arnevik, E. A., & Ravndal, E. (2016). Contribution of the patient-horse relationship to substance use disorder treatment: Patients' experiences. *International Journal of Qualitative Studies on Health and Well-being, 11*(1). https://doi.org/10.3402/qhw.v11.31636

Kesner, A., & Pritzker, S. R. (2008). Therapeutic horseback riding with children placed in the foster care system. *ReVision, 30*(1/2), 77–87.

Kimerling, R., Gima, K., Smith, M. W., Street, A., & Frayne, S. (2007). The Veterans Health Administration and military sexual trauma. *American Journal of Public Health, 97*(12), 2160–2166.

Kirby, M. (2010). Gestalt equine psychotherapy. *Gestalt Journal of Australia and New Zealand, 6*(2), 60–68.

Kirschenbaum, H., & Jourdan, A. (2005). The current status of Carl Rogers and the person-centered approach. *Psychotherapy: Theory, Research, Practice, Training, 42*(1), 37–51.

Klontz, B., T., Bivens, A., Leinart, D., & Klontz, T. (2007). The effectiveness of equine-assisted experiential therapy: Results of an open clinical trial. *Society & Animals, 15*, 257–267.

Koenig, H. G., Ames, D., & Büssing, A. (2019a). Editorial: Screening for and treatment of moral injury in veterans/active duty military with PTSD. *Frontiers in Psychiatry, 10.* doi: 10.3389/fpsyt.2019.00596

Koenig, H. G., Youssef, N. A., & Pearce, M. (2019b). Assessment of moral injury in veterans and active duty military personnel with PTSD: A review. *Frontiers in Psychiatry, 10.* https://doi.org/10.3389/fpsyt.2019.00443

Kohanov, L. (2001). *The Tao of Equus: A woman's journey of healing & transformation through the way of the horse.* Novato, CA: New World Library.

Korpela, K. M., Stengård, E., & Jusilla, P. (2016). Nature walks as a part of therapeutic intervention for depression. *Ecopsychology, 8*(1). Retrieved from https://doi.org/10.1089/eco.2015.0070

Kosfeld, M., Heinrichs, M., Zak, P. J., Fischenbacher, U., & Fehr, E. (2005). Oxytocin increases trust in humans. *Nature, 435*(7042), 673–676.

Krueger, K., & Flaunger, B. (2011). Olfactory recognition of individual competitors by means of faeces in horse (*Equus caballus*). *Animal Cognition, 14*, 245–257.

Krueger, K., Flauger, B., Farmer, K., & Maros, K. (2011). Horses (Equus caballus) use human local enhancement cues and adjust to human attention. *Animal Cognition, 14*(2), 187–201.

Kydd, E., Padalino, B., Henshall, C., McGreevy, P. (2017). An analysis of equine round pen training videos posted online: Differences between amateur and professional trainers. *PLoS One, 12*(9). Retrieved from https://doi.org/10.1371/journal.pone.0184851

200 References

Lac, V. (2019). The Human-Equine Relational Development (HERD) approach to working with clients suffering from bulimia nervosa. In K. S. Trotter & J. N. Baggerly (Eds.), *Equine-assisted mental health: Harnessing solutions to common problems* (pp. 149–152).

Lac, V., Marble, E., & Boie, I. (2013). Equine-assisted psychotherapy as a creative relational approach to treating clients with eating disorders. *Journal of Creativity in Mental Health, 8*(4), 483–498.

Lagarde, J., Peham, C., Licka, T., & Kelso, J. A. S. (2005). Coordination dynamics of the horse-rider system. *Journal of Motor Behavior, 37*(6), 418–424.

Lai, J., Ma, S., Wang, Y., Cai, Z., Hu, J., Wei, N., ... Hu, S. (2020). Factors associated with mental health outcomes among health care workers exposed to coronavirus disease 2019. *JAMA Network Open.* doi:10.1001/jamanetworkopen.2020.3976

Lambert, M. J., & Barley, D. E. (2001). Research summary on the therapeutic relationship and psychotherapy outcome. *Psychotherapy, 38*(4), 357–361.

Lampe, J. F., & Andre, A. (2012). Cross-modal recognition of human individuals in domestic horses (*Equus caballus*). *Animal Cognition, 15*, 623–630.

Lanata, A., Nardelli, M., Valenza, G., Baragli, P., D'Aniello, B., Alterisio, A., . . . Scilingo, E. P. (2018, July 18–21). *A case for the interspecies transfer of emotions: A preliminary investigation on how humans odors modify reactions of the autonomic nervous system in horses.* 40th Annual International Conference of the IEEE Engineering in Medicine and Biology Society (EMBC), Honolulu, HI, 2018, pp. 522-525.

Landreth, G. L. (2012). *Play therapy: The art of the relationship* (3rd ed.). New York: Routledge.

Lawrence, E. A. (1995). Cultural perceptions of differences between people and animals: A key to understanding human-animal relationships. *Journal of American Culture, 18*(3), 75–82.

Lee, P., Dakin, E., & McLure, M. (2016). Narrative synthesis of equine-assisted psychotherapy literature: Current knowledge and future research directions. *Health and Social Care in the Community, 24*(3), 225–246.

Lee, P., & Makela, C. (2015). Horses' role in equine-assisted psychotherapy: Perspectives of mental health professionals. *Journal of Psychology and Behavioral Science, 3*(1), 78–95.

Lentini, J. A., & Knox, M. S. (2015). Equine-facilitated psychotherapy with children and adolescents: An update and literature review. *Journal of Creativity in Mental Health, 10*, 278–305.

Lesimple, C., Fureix, C., Menguy, H., & Hausberger, M. (2010). Human direct actions may alter animal welfare on horses (*Equus caballus*). *PLoS One, 5*(4). https://doi.org/10.1371/journal.pone.0010257

Levine, G. N., Allen, K., Braun, L. T., Christian, H. E., Friedmann, E., Taubert, K. A., . . . Lange, R. A. (2013). Pet ownership and cardiovascular risk: A scientific statement from the American Heart Association. *Circulation, 127*, 2353–2363.

Levinson, B. M. (1962). The dog as a "co-therapist". *Mental Hygiene, 46*, 59–65.

Levinson, B. M., & Mallon, G. P. (1997). *Pet-oriented child psychotherapy* (2nd ed.). Springfield, IL: Charles C Thomas.

Lira, J., Linderholm, A., Olaria, C., Durling, M. B., Gilbert, T. P., Ellegren, H., . . . Götherström, A. (2010). Ancient DNA reveals traces of Iberian Neolithic and Bronze Age lineages in modern Iberian horses. *Molecular Biology, 19*, 64–78.

Lloyd, A. S., Martin, J. E., Bornett-Gauci, H. L., & Wilkinson, R. G. (2007). Evaluation of a novel method of horse personality assessment: Rater-agreement and links to behaviour. *Applied Animal Behaviour Science, 105*, 205–222.

References 201

Lloyd, A. S., Martin, J. E., Bornett-Gauci, H. L., & Wilkinson, R. G. (2008). Horse personality: Variation between breeds. *Applied Animal Behaviour Science, 112*, 369–383.

Low, P., Panksepp, J., Reiss, D., Edelman, D., Van Swinderen, B., & Koch, C. (2012, July). *The Cambridge declaration on consciousness.* Presented at the Francis Crick Memorial Conference on Consciousness in Human and Non-Human Animals, University of Cambridge, Cambridge, United Kingdom. Retrieved from http://fcmconference. org/img/CambridgeDeclarationOnConsciousness.pdf

Ludwig, A., Pruvost, M., Reissmann, M., Benecke, N., Brockmann, G. A., Castaños, P., . . . Hofreiter, M. (2009). Coat color variation at the beginning of horse domestication. *Science, 324*(5296). https://doi.org/10.1126/science.1172750

Luk, E. S. L., Staiger, P. K., Wong, L., & Mathai, J. (1999). Children who are cruel to animals: A revisit. *Australian and New Zealand Journal of Psychiatry, 33*, 29–36.

Lutter, C. B. (2008). *Equine assisted therapy and exercise with eating disorders: A retrospective chart review and mixed method analysis.* (Masters paper). Arlington, TX: University of Texas at Arlington.

Lyman, J. [ExtensionHorses]. (2020, April 15). *Horse biosecurity and facility sanitation.* [Video]. YouTube. Retrieved from https://www.youtube.com/watch?v=cuONqhw PlmQ&feature=youtu.be

Lynch, J. J., Fregin, G. F., Mackie, J. B., & Monroe, R. R. (1974). Heart rate changes in the horse to human contact. *Psychophysiology, 11*(4), 472–478.

Mader, D. R., & Price, E. O. (1980). Discrimination learning in horses: Effects of breed, age and social dominance. *Journal of Animal Science, 50*(5), 962–965.

Marmar, C. R., Schlenger, W., Henn-Haase, C., Qian, M., Purchia, E. Li, M., . . . Kulka, R. A. (2015). Course of posttraumatic stress disorder 40 years after the Vietnam War: Findings from the National Vietnam Veterans Longitudinal Study. *JAMA Psychiatry, 72*(9), 875–881. https://doi.org/10.1001/jamapsychiatry.2015.0803

Marx, R. D., & Cumella, E. J. (2003). Question: Is equine therapy useful in the treatment of eating disorders? *Eating Disorders, 11*, 143–147.

Matuszek, S. (2010). Animal-facilitated therapy in various patient populations. *Holistic Nursing Practice,* July/August, 187–203.

Mauss, I. B., & Robinson, M. D. (2009). Measures of emotion: A review. *Cognition and Emotion, 23*(2), 209–237.

Mayfield, M. A. (2016). *Equine-facilitated psychotherapy for veteran survivors with full or partial PTSD.* (Doctoral dissertation). Walden University. Retrieved from http://scholarworks. waldenu.edu/cgi/viewcontent.cgi?article=4148&context=dissertations

Maziere, C., & Gunnlaugson, O. (2015). A case for developing spiritual intelligence in leaders through equine facilitated learning. *The Journal of Values-Based Leadership, 8*(1). Retrieved from http://scholar.valpo.edu/jvbl/vol8/iss1/10

McBride, S. D., & Mills, D. S. (2012). Psychological factors affecting equine performance. *Veterinary Research, 8.* Retrieved from www.biomedcentral.com/1746-6148/8/180

McCormick, A. V., & McCormick, M. D. (1997). *Horse sense and the human heart: What horses can teach us about trust, bonding, creativity, and spirituality.* Deerfield Beach, FL: Health Communications, Inc.

McCullough, L., Risley-Curtiss, C., Rorke, J. (2015). Equine facilitated psychotherapy: A pilot study of effect on posttraumatic stress symptoms in maltreated youth. *Journal of Infant, Child, and Adolescent Psychotherapy, 14*, 158–173.

McDonnell, S. (2005, December 1). *Licking/chewing=Learning?* Retrieved from https:// thehorse.com/129051/lickingchewinglearning/

202 References

McGreevy, P. D., Christensen, J. W., von Borstel, U. K., & McLean, A. (2018). *Equitation science* (2nd ed.). Hoboken, NJ: John Wiley & Sons Ltd.

McGreevy, P. D., Oddie, C., Burton, F. L., & McLean, A. N. (2009). The horse-human dyad: Can we align horse training and handling activities with the equid social ethogram? *The Veterinary Journal, 181,* 12–18.

McKinney, B. L. (2011). *Therapist's perceptions of walk and talk therapy: A grounded study.* (Doctoral dissertation). New Orleans, LA: University of New Orleans.

McLean, A. N., & Christensen, J. W. (2017). The application of learning theory in horse training. *Applied Animal Behaviour Science, 190,* 18–27.

McLean, A. N., & McGreevy, P. D. (2010). Ethical equitation: Capping the price horses pay for human glory. *Journal of Veterinary Behaviour, 5,* 203–209.

McRoberts, C., Burlingame, G. M., Hoag, M. J. (1998). Comparative efficacy of individual and group psychotherapy: A meta-analytic perspective. *Group Dynamics: Theory, Research, and Practice, 2*(2), 101–117.

Mellor, D. J. (2016a). Moving beyond the "Five Freedoms" by updating the "Five Provisions" and introducing aligned "Animal Welfare Aims". *Animals, 6,* https://doi.org/10.3390/ani6100059

Mellor, D. J. (2016b). Updating animal welfare thinking: Moving beyond the "Five Freedoms" towards "A Life Worth Living". *Animals, 6.* https://doi.org/10.3390/ani6030021

Melson, G. F., & Fine, A. H. (2010). Animals in the lives of children. In A. H. Fine (Ed.), *Handbook of animal-assisted therapy: Theoretical foundations and guidelines for practice* (pp. 223–245). San Diego, CA: Academic Press.

Mendl, M., Burnman, O. H. P., & Paul, E. S. (2010). An integrative and functional framework for the study of animal emotion and mood. *Proceedings of The Royal Society, 277,* 2895–2094.

Meyer, E. G., Writer, B. W., & Brim, W. (2016). The importance of military cultural competence. *Current Psychiatry Reports, 18*(26). https://doi.org/10.1007/s11920-016-0662-9

Mikolajaczak, M., Gross, J. J., Lane, A., Corneille, O., de Timary, P., & Luminet, O. (2010). Oxytocin makes people trusting, not gullible. *Psychological Science, 21*(8), 1072–1074.

Miller, S. C., Kennedy, C., DeVoe, D., Hickey, M., Nelson, T., & Kogan, L. (2009). An examination of changes in oxytocin levels in men and women before and after interaction with a bonded dog. *Anthrozoös, 22*(1), 31–42.

Mills, D. S. (1998). Applying learning theory to the management of the horse: The difference between getting it right and getting it wrong. *Equine Veterinary Journal, 30,* 44–48.

Minatrea, N. B., & Wesley, M. C. (2008). Reality therapy goes to the dogs. *International Journal of Reality Therapy, XXVIII*(1), 69–77/

Mobbs, M. C., & Bonanno, G. A. (2017). Beyond war and PTSD: The crucial role of transition stress in the lives of military veterans. *Clinical Psychology Review.* https://doi.org/10.1016/j.cpr.2017.11.007

Monroe, M., Whitworth, J. D., Wharton, T., & Turner, J. (2019). Effects of an equine-assisted therapy program for military veterans with self-reported PTSD. *Society & Animals.* https://doi.org/10.1163/15685306-12341572

Morin, R. (2011). *The difficult transition from military to civilian life.* Washington, DC: Pew Research Center.

References 203

Murphy, J., Hall, C., & Arkins, S. (2009). What horses and humans see: A comparative review. *International Journal of Zoology.* http://doi.org/10.1155/2009/721798

Murthy, R., Bearman, G., Brown, S., Bryant, K., Chinn, R., Hewlett, A.,... Wieber, D. J. (2015). Animals in healthcare facilities: Recommendations to minimize potential risks. *Infection Control & Hospital Epidemiology, 36*(5). Retrieved from https://www.slu.se/globalassets/ew/org/inst/hmh/hmh-pdf/murthy-2015-animals_in_healthcare_facilities.pdf

NARHA. (n.d.). *NARHA/EFMHA: Integration faqs.* Retrieved from www.pathintl.org/images/pdf/about-narha/Integration-FAQ-web.pdf

Naste, T. M., Price, M., Karol, J., Martin, L., Murphy, K., Miguel, J., & Spinazzola, J. (2018). Equine facilitated therapy for complex trauma (EFT-CT). *Journal of Child & Adolescent Trauma, 11*, 289–303.

National Association for Social Workers. (2015). *Standards and indicators for cultural competence in social work practice.* Retrieved from www.socialworkers.org/LinkClick.aspx?fileticket=PonPTDEBrn4%3D&portalid=0

National Association of Social Workers. (2017). *Code of ethics.* Retrieved from www.socialworkers.org/about/ethics/code-of-ethics/code-of-ethics-english

National Institute of Mental Health. (2018a). *Any anxiety disorder.* Retrieved from www.nimh.nih.gov/health/statistics/any-anxiety-disorder.shtml

National Institute of Mental Health. (2018b). *Autism spectrum disorder.* Retrieved from www.nimh.nih.gov/health/topics/autism-spectrum-disorders-asd/index.shtml

National Institute of Mental Health. (2019a). *Child and adolescent mental health.* Retrieved from www.nimh.nih.gov/health/topics/child-and-adolescent-mental-health/index.shtml

National Institute of Mental Health. (2019b). *Suicide.* Retrieved from www.nimh.nih.gov/health/statistics/suicide.shtml

National Institute of Mental Health. (2019c). *Attention-deficit/hyperactivity disorder (ADHD).* Retrieved from www.nimh.nih.gov/health/topics/attention-deficit-hyperactivity-disorder-adhd/index.shtml

Nielsen, J. A., & Delude, L. A. (1989). Behavior of young children in the presence of different kinds of animals. *Anthrozoös, 3*(2), 119–129.

O'Callaghan, D. M., & Chandler, C. K. (2011). An exploratory study of animal-assisted interventions utilized by mental health professionals. *Journal of Creativity in Mental Health, 6*, 90–104.

Odendaal, J. S. J. (2000). Animal-assisted therapy—magic or medicine? *Journal of Psychosomatic Research, 49*, 275–280.

Odendaal, J. S. J., & Meintjes, R. A. (2003). Neurophysiological correlates of affiliative behaviour between humans and dogs. *The Veterinary Journal, 165*, 296–301.

Oetzel, K. B., & Scherer, D. G. (2003). Therapeutic engagement with adolescents in psychotherapy. *Psychotherapy: Theory, Research, Practice, Training, 4*(3), 215–225.

Olmert, M. D. (2009). *Made for each other: The biology of the human-animal bond.* Cambridge, MA: Da Capo Press.

Orlando, L. (2015). Equids. *Current Biology, 25*(20), R973–R978.

Outram, A. K., Stear, N. A., Bendrey, R., Olsen, S., Kasparov, A., Zaibert, V., . . . Evershed, V. (2009). The earliest horse harnessing and milking. *Science, 323*(6), 1332–1335.

Panksepp, J. (1998). *Affective neuroscience: The foundations of human and animal emotions.* New York: Oxford University Press.

204 References

Parish-Plass, N. (2013). The contribution of animal-assisted psychotherapy to the potential space in play therapy. In N. Parish-Plass (Ed.), *Animal assisted psychotherapy: Theory, issues, and practice*. West Lafayette, IN: Purdue University Press.

PATH Intl. (2017). *PATH Intl. student manual: Equine specialist in mental health and learning workshop*. PATH Intl.

PATH Intl. (2018a). *History: PATH Intl. history*. Retrieved from www.pathintl.org/about-path-intl/about-path-intl/history

PATH Intl. (2018b). *Professional Association of Therapeutic Horsemanship International standards and certification & accreditation* (2018 ed.). Denver, CO: Author.

PATH Intl. (2019, June 6). *Correct terminology for PATH Intl. member centers*. Email communication.

PATH Intl. (2020, May 7). *COVID-19 support resources*. Retrieved from https://www.pathintl.org/images/pdf/resources/COVID-Information/COVID-19-Support-Resources.pdf

Paul, E. S., Harding, E. J., & Mendl, M. (2005). Measuring emotional processes in animals: The utility of a cognitive approach. *Neuroscience and Biobehavioral Review, 29*, 469–491.

Payne, E., DeAraugo, J., Bennett, P., & McGreevy, P. (2016). Exploring the existence and potential underpinnings of dog-human and horse-human attachment bonds. *Behaviour Processes, 125*, 114–121.

Perry, B. D. (2009). Examining child maltreatment through a neurodevelopmental lens: Clinical applications of the Neurosequential Model of Therapeutics. *Journal of Loss and Trauma, 14*, 240–255.

Perry, B. D., Rubinstein, D., & Austin, J. (2012). Animal-assisted group therapy in mental health settings: An initial model. *Alternative and Complementary Therapies, 18*(4). https://doi.org/10.1089/act.2012.18403

Pet Partners. (n.d.). *The Pet Partners story*. Retrieved from https://petpartners.org/aboutus/petpartners-story/

Pfefferbaum, B. & North, C. S. (2020). Mental health and the Covid-19 pandemic. *The New England Journal of Medicine*. doi: 10.1056/NEJMp2008017

Piaget, J. (1951). *Play, dreams, and imitation in childhood*. New York: Norton.

Porges, S. W. (1995). Orienting in a defensive world: Mammalian modifications of our evolutionary heritage. A polyvagal theory. *Psychophysiology, 32*, 301–318.

Porges, S. W. (2011). The polyvagal theory: New insights into adaptive reactions of the autonomic nervous system. *Cleveland Clinic Journal of Medicine, 76*(S2), S86–S90.

Pos, A. E., Greenberg, L. S., & Elliott, R. (2008). Experiential therapy. In J. L. Lebow (Ed.), *Twenty-first century psychotherapies: Contemporary approaches to theory and practice* (pp. 80–122). Hoboken, NJ: John Wiley and Sons, Inc.

Proctor, H. S. (2012). Animal sentience: Where are we and where are we heading? *Animals, 2*, 682–639.

Proctor, H. S., Carder, G., & Cornish, A. R. (2013). Searching for animal sentience: A systematic review of the scientific literature. *Animals, 3*, 882–906.

Proops, L., Grounds, K., Smith, A. V., & McComb, K. (2018). Animals remember previous facial expressions that specific humans have exhibited. *Current Biology, 28*, 1428–1432.

Proops, L., & McComb, K. (2010). Attributing attention: The use of human-given cues by domestic horses (*Equus caballus*). *Animal Cognition, 13*, 197–205.

Proops, L., & McComb, K. (2012). Cross-modal individual recognition in domestic horses (*Equus caballus*) extends to familiar humans. *Proceedings of the Royal Society B, 279*, 3131–3138.

References   205

Proops, L., McComb, K., & Reby, D. (2009). Cross-modal individual recognition in domestic horses (*Equus caballus*). *PNAS, 106*(3), 947–951.

Ray, D. C, & McCullough, R. (2015; revised 2016). *Evidence-based practice statement: Play therapy*. Research report. Retrieved from Association for Play Therapy website www.a4pt.org/?page=EvidenceBased

Rector, B. K. (2005). *Adventures in awareness: Learning with the help of horses*. Bloomington, IN: AuthorHouse.

Reger, M. A., Stanley, I. H., & Joiner, T. E. (2020). Suicide mortality and coronavirus disease 2019-A perfect storm? *JAMA Psychiatry*. Retrieved from https://jamanetwork.com/journals/jamapsychiatry/fullarticle/2764584

Reichert, E. (1998). Individual counseling for sexually abused children: A role for animals and storytelling. *Child and Adolescent Social Work Journal, 15*(3), 177–185.

Reisman, M. (2016). PTSD treatment for veterans: What's working, what's new, and what's next. *P & T: A Peer-Reviewed Journal for Formulary Management, 41*(10), 623–634.

Remley, T. P., & Herlihy, B. (2007). *Ethical, legal, and professional issues in counseling* (2nd ed.). Upper Saddle River, NJ: Pearson Education, Inc.

Rice, S. S., Brown, L. T., & Caldwell, S. (1973). Animals and psychotherapy: A survey. *Journal of Community Psychology, 1*(3), 323–236.

Riede, D. 1987. The relationship between man and horse with reference to medicine, through the ages. *People-Animals-Environment, 5*, 26–28.

Rivera, E., Benjamin, S., Nielsen, B., Shelle, J., & Zanella, A. J. (2002). Behavioral and physiological responses of horses to initial training: The comparison between pastured versus stalled horses. *Applied Animal Behaviour Science, 78*, 235–252.

Robinson, I. H. (1999). The human-horse relationship: How much do we know? *Equine Veterinary Journal, Supplement, 28*, 42–45.

Rogers, C. R. (1964). Significant aspects of client-centered therapy. *The American Psychologist, 1*, 415–422.

Rogers, C. R. (1992). The necessary and sufficient conditions of therapeutic personality change. *Journal of Consulting and Clinical Psychology, 60*(6), 827–832.

Rogers, C. R. (2007). The necessary and sufficient conditions for therapeutic personality change. *Psychotherapy: Theory, Research, Practice, and Training, 44*(3), 240–248.

Romaniuk, M., Evans, J., & Kidd, C. (2018). Evaluation of an equine-assisted therapy program for veterans who identify as "wounded, injured or ill" and their partners. *PLoS One, 13*(9), e0203943. Retrieved from https://doi.org/10.1371/journal.pone.0203943

Rotenberg, K. J. (1994). Loneliness and interpersonal trust. *Journal of Social and Clinical Psychology, 13*(2), 152–173.

Rothe, E. Q., Vega, B. J., Torres, R. M., Soler, S. M. C., & Pazos, R. M. M. (2005). From kids and horses: Equine facilitated psychotherapy for children. *International Journal of Clinical and Health Psychology, 5*(2), 373–383.

Ruet, A., Lemarchand, J., Parias, C., Mach, N., Moisan, M., Foury, A., . . . Lansade, L. (2019). Housing horses in individual boxes is a challenge with regard to welfare. *Animals, 9*. https://doi.org/10.3390/ani9090621

Russell-Martin, L. A. (2006). *Equine facilitated couples therapy and solution focused couples therapy: A comparison study*. (Doctoral dissertation). Prescott, AZ: Northcentral University.

Sackman, J. E., & Houpt, K. A. (2019). Equine personality: Association with breed, use, and husbandry. *Journal of Equine Veterinary Science, 72*, 47–55.

Saslow, C. A. (2002). Understanding the perceptual world of horses. *Applied Animal Behaviour Science, 78*, 209–224.

206 References

Schlote, S. M. (2009). *Animal-assisted therapy and equine-assisted therapy/learning in Canada: Surveying the current state of the field, its practitioners, and its practices.* (Master's thesis). University of Victoria.

Schlote, S. M. (2018a). *List of EAPL trainings and certifications.* Retrieved from https://equusoma.com/wp-content/uploads/2018/10/List-of-Equine-Assisted-Practice-Trainings-and-Certifications-September-2018.pdf

Schlote, S. M. (2018b, January 15). *Why horses lick and chew – a polyvagal lens.* Retrieved from https://equusoma.com/why-horses-lick-and-chew/

Schlough, P. (2019). Equine-assisted psychotherapy, grief, and loss. In K. S. Trotter & J. N. Baggerly (Eds.), *Equine-assisted mental health interventions: Harnessing solutions to common problems* (pp. 81–88). New York: Routledge.

Schmidt, M. J., Knemeyer, C., & Heinsen, H. (2019). Neuroantaomy of the equine brain as revealed by high-field (3Tesla) magnetic-resonance-imaging. *PLoS One, 14*(4). https://doi.org/10.1371/journal.pone.0213814

Schroeder, K., & Stroud, D. (2015). Equine-facilitated group work for women survivors of interpersonal violence. *The Journal for Specialists in Group Work, 40*(4), 365–386.

Schultz, P. N., Remick-Barlow, G. A., & Robbins, L. (2007). Equine-assisted psychotherapy: A mental health promotion/intervention modality for children who have experienced intra-family violence. *Health and Social Care in the Community, 15,* 265–271.

Scopa, C., Contalbrigo, L., Greco, A., Lanatà, A., Scilingo, E. P., & Baragli, P. (2019). Emotional transfer in human-horse interaction: New perspectives on equine assisted interventions. *Animals, 9*(1030). https://doi.org/10.3390/ani9121030

Scotton, B. W. (1996). Introduction and definition of transpersonal psychiatry. In B. W. Scotton, A. B. Chinen, & J. R. Battista (Eds.), *Textbook of transpersonal psychiatry and psychology.* New York: Basic Books.

Scotton, B. W., Chinen, A. B., & Battista, J. R. (1996). *Textbook of transpersonal psychiatry and psychology.* New York: Basic Books.

Serpell, J. A. (2004). Factors influencing human attitudes to animals and their welfare. *Animal Welfare, 13,* S145–151.

Serpell, J. A., Coppinger, R., Fine, A. H., & Peralta, J. M. (2010). Welfare considerations in therapy and assistance animals. In A. H. Fine (Ed.), *Handbook on animal-assisted therapy: Theoretical foundations and guidelines for practice* (pp. 481–503). San Diego, CA: Academic Press.

Serpell, J. A., McCune, S., Gee, N., & Griffin, J. A. (2017). Current challenges to research on animal-assisted interventions. *Applied Developmental Science, 21*(3), 223–233. https://doi.org/10.1080/10888691.2016.1262775

Sexauer, A. M. (2011). *Equine embrace: Touch and the therapeutic encounter in equine facilitated psychotherapy from the perspective of the clinician.* (Unpublished masters paper). Smith College, Northampton, MA.

Sharpe, H. (2013). *Equine-facilitated counseling and women with eating disorders: Articulating bodily experiences.* (Doctoral thesis paper). Calgary, Alberta: University of Calgary.

Sheade, H. E. (2015). *Effectiveness of Relational Equine-Partnered Counseling (REPC) on reduction of symptoms of PTSD in military veterans: A single case design.* (Doctoral dissertation). Denton, TX: University of North Texas. ProQuest UMI No. 10034403.

Sheade, H. E. (2019a). *Equine-partnered play therapy: Training manual.* Fort Worth, TX: Equine Connection Counseling.

Sheade, H. E. (2019b). Equine-partnered play therapy™ for children with oppositional behavior. In K. S. Trotter & J. N. Baggerly (Eds.), *Equine-assisted mental health interventions: Harnessing solutions to common problems.* New York: Routledge.

References   207

Sheade, H. E. (2019c). *Relational Equine-Partnered Counseling: Practice Manual.* Fort Worth, TX: Equine Connection Counseling.

Sheade, H. E., & Box, L. (2014). Playtime with horses: Equine-partnered play therapy. *PATH Intl. Strides, 20*(3), 18–21.

Sheade, H. E., & Box, L. (2017). EFP ethics and skills for equine specialists. *PATH Intl. Strides, 23*(2), 22–28.

Sheade, H. E., & Chandler, C. K. (2014). Cultural diversity considerations in animal assisted counseling. *Ideas and Research You Can Use: VISTAS* (Article 76). Retrieved from www.counseling.org/docs/default-source/vistas/article_76.pdf?sfvrsn=f6117e2c_13

Sheade, H. E., & Ziehe, P. (2018, October). *Crisis in the Barn: EAAT participants and suicide.* Professional Association of Therapeutic Horsemanship International Conference and Annual Meeting, Orlando, FL.

Shear, K., Frank, E., Houck, P. R., & Reynolds, C. F. III (2005). Treatment of complicated grief: A randomized controlled trial. *JAMA: Journal of the American Medical Association, 293,* 2601–2608. https://doi.org/10.1001/jama .293.21.2601

Shear, M. K. (2010). Complicated grief treatment; The theory, practice and outcome. *Bereavement Care, 29*(3), 10–14.

Shedler, J. (2006). *That was then, this is now: Psychoanalytic psychotherapy for the rest of us.* Retrieved from http://psychsystems.net/shedler.html

Shedler, J. (2010). The efficacy of psychodynamic psychotherapy. *American Psychologist, 65*(2), 98–109.

Sheldrake, R. (1999). *Dogs that know when their owners are coming home and other unexplained powers of animals.* New York: Crown Publishers.

Shev, E. T. (2016). The introduction of the domesticated horse in southwest Asia. *Archaeology, Ethnology and Anthropology of Eurasia, 44*(1), 123–136.

Shevlin, M., McElroy, E., & Murphy, J. (2014). Loneliness mediates the relationship between childhood trauma and adult psychopathology: Evidence from the adult psychiatric morbidity survey. *Social Psychiatry and Psychiatric Epidemiology, 50*(4), 591–601. https://doi.org/10.1007/s00127-014-0951-8

Shiloh, S., Sorek, G., & Terkel, J. (2003). Reduction of state-anxiety by petting animals in a controlled laboratory experiment. *Anxiety, Stress, and Coping, 16*(4), 387–395.

Shultz-Jobe, B., McFarland, L., & Jobe, T. (2019). Natural lifemanship's trauma-focused equine assisted psychotherapy and treatment of anxiety disorders. In K. S. Trotter & J. N. Baggerly (Eds.), *Equine-assisted mental health interventions: Harnessing solutions to common problems* (pp. 58–69). New York: Routledge.

Siegel, D. J. (2001). Toward an interpersonal neurobiology of the developing mind: Attachment relationships, "mindsight," and neural integration. *Infant Mental Health Journal, 22*(1–2), 67–94.

Signal, T., Taylor, N., Botros, H., Prentice, K., & Lazarus, K. (2013). Whispering to horses: Childhood sexual abuse, depression, and the efficacy of equine facilitated therapy. *Sexual Abuse in Australia and New Zealand, 5*(1), 24–32.

Silvers, J. A., McRae, K., Gabrieli, J. D. E., Gross, J. J., Remy, K. A., & Ochsner, K. N. (2012). Age-related differences in emotional reactivity, regulation, and rejection sensitivity in adolescents. *Emotion, 12*(6), 1235–1247.

Skeen, J. (2011). Predator-prey relationships: What humans can learn from horses about being whole. In C. Blazina, G. Boyraz, & D. Shen-Miller (Eds.), *The psychology of the human-animal bond: A resource for clinicians and researchers.* New York: Springer.

208 References

Smith, A. V., Proops, L., Grounds, K., Wathan, J., McComb, K. (2016). Functionally relevant responses to human facial expressions of emotion in the domestic horse (*Equus caballus*). *Biology Letters, 12*. http://doi.org/10.1098/rsbl.2015.0907

Smith-Osbourne, A., & Selby, A. (2010). Implications of the literature of equine-assisted activities for use a complementary intervention in social work practice with children and adolescents. *Child and Adolescent Social Work Journal, 27*, 291–307.

Sobo, E. J., Eng, B., & Kassity-Krich, N. (2006). Canine visitation (pet) therapy: Pilot data on decreases in child pain perception. *Journal of Holistic Nursing, 24*(1), 51–57.

Sokolof, M., & Stuart, M. (2000). Mental health professional + Horse professional = Value greater than the sum of its parts. *Strides*, 8–9.

Souter, M. A., & Miller, M. D. (2007). Do animal-assisted activities effectively treat depression? A meta-analysis. *Anthrozoös, 20*(2), 167–180.

Spiedel, M. P. (1996). Roman cavalry training and the riding school of the Mauretanian Horse Guard. *Antiquités africaines, 32*, 57–62.

Sprang, G., & Silman, M. (2013). Posttraumatic stress disorder in parents and youth after health-related disasters. *Disaster Medicine and Public Health Preparedness, 7*(1). Retrieved from https://doi.org/10.1017/dmp.2013.22

Staudt, M., & Cherry, D. (2017). Equine facilitated therapy and trauma: Current knowledge, future needs. *Advances in Social Work, 18*(1), 403–414.

Stewart, L. A., Chang, C. Y., Parker, L. K., & Grubbs, N. (2016). *Animal-assisted therapy in counseling competencies*. Alexandria, VA: American Counseling Association, Animal-Assisted Therapy in Mental Health Interest Network.

Stewart, L. A., Chang, C. Y., & Rice, R. (2013). Emergent theory and model of practice in animal-assisted therapy in counseling. *Journal of Creativity in Mental Health, 8*, 329–348.

Street, A., & Stafford, J. (n.d.). *Military sexual trauma: Issues in caring for veterans*. Retrieved from www.ptsd.va.gov/professional/treat/type/sexual_trauma_military.asp

Strom, L., & Wilson, J. (2009, March). *Horses as healers: Equine facilitated therapy for grieving children*. Paper based on a program presented at the American Counseling Association Annual Conference and Exposition, Charlotte, NC.

Strozzi, A. (2009). *Planning your business in the horse as healer/teacher profession*. Author.

Substance Abuse and Mental Health Services Administration. (2014). *SAMHSA's concept of trauma and guidance for a trauma-informed approach*. HHS Publication No. (SMA) 14–4884. Rockville, MD: Substance Abuse and Mental Health Services Administration.

Substance Abuse and Mental Health Services Administration. (2017a). *Trends in substance used disorders among adults aged 18 or older*. Retrieved from www.samhsa.gov/data/sites/default/files/report_2790/ShortReport-2790.html

Substance Abuse and Mental Health Services Administration. (2017b). *Understanding child trauma*. Retrieved from www.samhsa.gov/child-trauma/understanding-child-trauma

Sue, D. W., Arredondo, P., & McDavis, R. J. (1992). Multicultural counseling competencies and standards: A call to the profession. *Journal of Counseling and Development, 70*, 477–486.

Swannell, S. V., Martin, G. E., Page, A., Hasking, P., & St John, N. J. (2014). Prevalence of nonsuicidal self-injury in nonclinical samples: Systematic review, meta-analysis and meta-regression. *Suicide and Life-Threatening Behavior, 44*(3), 273–303. https://doi.org/10.1111/sltb.12070

References 209

Symington, A. (2012). Grief and horses: Putting the pieces together. *Journal of Creativity in Mental Health, 7*, 165–174.

Taylor, A. F., & Kuo, F. E. M. (2009). Children with attention deficits concentrate better after walk in the park. *Journal of Attention Disorders, 12*(5), 402–409.

Taylor, A. F., & Kuo, F. E. M. (2011). Could exposure to everyday green spaces help treat ADHD? Evidence from children's play settings. *Applied Psychology: Health and Well-Being, 3*(3), 281–303.

Taylor, C. (2019). "Combing" through ADHD symptoms: Utilizing mindful grooming. In K. S. Trotter & J. N. Baggerly (Eds.), *Equine-assisted mental health interventions: Harnessing solutions to common problems* (pp. 91–105). New York: Routledge.

Taylor, S. M. (2001). *Equine-facilitated psychotherapy: An emerging field.* (Unpublished master's paper). Vermont, CA: Saint Michael's College.

Teo, A. R., Marsh, H. E., Forsberg, C. W., Nicolaidis, C., Chen, J. I., Newsom, J., . . . Dobscha, S. K. (2018). Loneliness is closely associated with depression outcomes and suicidal ideation among military veterans in primary care. *Journal of Affective Disorders, 230*(1), 42–49.

The Regents University of California. (2020). *UCLA brief COVID-19 screen.* Retrieved from https://istss.org/getattachment/Clinical-Resources/Assessing-Trauma/UCLA-Posttraumatic-Stress-Disorder-Reaction-Index/UCLA-Brief-COVID-19-Screening-Form-English-4-13-20.pdf?lang=en-US

Times Staff and Wire Reports (2009, February 15). Obituaries/Passings/Lis Hartel. *Los Angeles Times.* Retrieved from http://articles.latimes.com/2009/feb/15/local/me-passings15.S2

Torbett, D. (2017). *Exploring the experiences of adults after equine facilitated psychotherapy (EFP).* (Doctoral dissertation). Walden University.

Trotter, K. S., & Baggerly, J. N. (Eds.). (2019a). *Equine-assisted mental health for healing trauma.* New York: Routledge.

Trotter, K. S., & Baggerly, J. N. (Eds.). (2019b). *Equine-assisted mental health interventions: Harnessing solutions to common problems.* New York: Routledge.

Trotter, K. S., Chandler, C. K., Goodwin-Bond, D., Casey, J. (2008). A comparative study of the efficacy of group equine assisted counseling with at-risk children and adolescents. *Journal of Creativity in Mental Health, 3*(3), 254–284.

Trust Insurance. (n.d.). *The Trust's statement on in-person psychological services during the COVID-19 crisis.* Retrieved from https://parma.trustinsurance.com/Portals/0/documents/The%20Trust's%20Statement%20on%20In-person%20Psychological%20Services.pdf?ver=2020-04-24-200805-840

Ulrich, R. S. (1984). View through a window may influence recovery from surgery. *Science, 224*(4647), 420–421.

Ulrich, R. S., Simons, R. F., Losito, B. D., Fiorito, E., Miles, M. A., & Zelson, M. (1991). Stress recovery during exposure to natural and urban environments. *Journal of Environmental Psychology, 11*, 201–230.

Ung. E. M., Erichsen, E. B., Poulsen, S., Lau, M. E., Simonsen, S., & Davidsen, A. H. (2017). The association between interpersonal problems and treatment outcome in patients with eating disorders. *Journal of Eating Disorders, 5*(53). https://doi.org/10.1186/s40337-017-0179-6

U.S. Department of Health and Human Services. (2019). *What is the U.S. opioid epidemic?* Retrieved from www.hhs.gov/opioids/about-the-epidemic/index.html

210   References

U.S. Department of Veterans Affairs. (2019). *National veteran suicide prevention annual report.* Retrieved from www.mentalhealth.va.gov/docs/data-sheets/2019/2019_National_Veteran_Suicide_Prevention_Annual_Report_508.pdf

U.S. Department of Veterans Affairs. (n.d.). *Acute stress disorder.* Retrieved from www.ptsd.va.gov/professional/treat/essentials/acute_stress_disorder.asp

Valiyamattam, G., Yamamoto, M., Fanucchi, L., & Wang, F. (2018). Multicultural considerations in animal-assisted intervention. *Human-Animal Interaction Bulletin, 6,* Special Edition, 82.104.

Van der Kolk, B. (2014). *The body keeps score: Brain, mind, and body in the healing of trauma.* New York: Viking.

van Dierendonck, M., & Goodwin, D. (2005). Social contact in horses: Implications for human-horse interactions. In F. H. de Jonge & R. van den Bos (Eds.), *The human-animal relationship: Forever and a day* (pp. 65–81). Assen, Netherlands: Royal Van Gorcum.

VanDierendonck, M. C., & Spruijt, B. M. (2012). Coping in groups of domestic horses—Review from a social and neurobiological perspective. *Applied Animal Behaviour Science, 138,* 194–202.

VanFleet, R., & Thompson, T. (2010). The case for using animal-assisted play therapy. *British Journal of Play Therapy, 6,* 4–18.

Vidrine, M., Owen-Smith, P., & Faulkner, P. (2002). Equine-facilitated group psychotherapy: Applications for therapeutic vaulting. *Issues in Mental Health Nursing, 23,* 587–603.

Vila, C., Leonard, J. A., Götherström, A., Marklund, S., Sandberg, K., Lidén, K., . . . Ellegren, H. (2001). Widespread origins of domestic horse lineages. *Science, 291,* 474–477.

Virués-Ortega, J., & Buela-Casal, G. (2006). Psychophysiological effects of human-animal interaction theoretical issues and long-term interaction effects. *The Journal of Nervous and Mental Disease, 194*(1), 52–57.

Visser, E. K., Van Reenen, C. G., Blokhuis, M. Z., Morgan, K. M., Hassmén, P., Rundgren, M. M., & Blokhuis, H. J. (2008). Does horse temperament influence horse-rider cooperation? *Journal of Applied Animal Welfare Science, 11,* 267–284.

Visser, E. K., Van Reenen, C. G., Rundgren, M., Zetterqvist, M., Morgan, K., & Blokhuis, H. J. (2003). Responses of horses in behavioural tests correlate with temperament assessed by riders. *Equine Veterinary Journal, 35*(2), 176–183.

von Borstel, U. K. (n.d.). *Genetics of the horse-human interactions.* Retrieved from http://wcgalp.org/system/files/proceedings/2010/genetics-horse-human-interactions.pdf

Waite, C., & Bourke, L. (2013). "It's different with a horse": Horses as a tool for engagement in a horse therapy program for marginalized young people. *Youth Studies Australia, 32*(4). Retrieved from https://skerrettequine.com/wp-content/uploads/2016/08/Horse-therapy-for-young-people.pdf

Walsh, F. (2009). Human-animal bonds II: The role of pets in family systems and family therapy. *Family Process, 48,* 481–499.

Wang, G., Zhang, Y., Zhao, J., Zhang, J., & Jiang, F. (2020). Mitigate the effects of home confinement on children during the COVID-19 outbreak. *The Lancet, 395.* Retrieved from https://doi.org/10.1016/S0140-6736(20)30547-X

Wathan, J., Burrows, A. M., Waller, B. M., & McComb, K. (2015). EquiFACS: The equine facial action coding system. *PLoS One, 10*(9). https://doi.org/10.1371/journal.pone.0137818

References   211

Wathan, J., & McComb, K. (2014). The eyes and ears are visual indicators of attention in domestic horses. *Current Biology, 24*(15), R677–R679.

Wathan, J., Proops, L., Grounds, K., & McComb, K. (2016). Horses discriminate facial expressions of conspecifics. *Scientific Reports, 6*(38322). https://doi.org/10.1038/srep38322

Webster, J. (2016). Animal welfare: Freedoms, dominions, and "a life worth living." *Animals, 6*. https://doi.org/10.3390/ani6060035

Weese, J. S., Caldwell, F., Willey, B. M., Kreiswirth, B. N., McGeer, A., & Low, D. E. (2006). An outbreak of methicillin-resistant *Staphylococcus aureus* skin infections resulting from horse to human transmission in veterinary hospital. *Veterinary Microbiology, 114*, 160–164.

Welfel, E. R. (2010). *Ethics in counseling and psychotherapy: Standards, research, and emerging issues* (4th ed.). Belmont, CA: Brooks/Cole.

Wesley, M. C. (2012). *Animal assisted therapy and the therapeutic alliance in the treatment of substance dependence.* Martin Cortez Wesley.

Wharton, T., Whitworth, J., Macauley, E., & Malone, M. (2019). Pilot testing a manualized equine-facilitated cognitive processing therapy (EF-CPT) intervention for PTSD in veterans. *Psychiatric Rehabilitation Journal, 42*(3), 268–276.

Willerson, S. (2019). Walking with the wisdom of peace: A horse-guided practice to leave anxiety in the dust. In K. S. Trotter & J. N. Baggerly (Eds.), *Equine-assisted mental health interventions: Harnessing solutions to common problems* (pp. 70–78). New York: Routledge.

Wilsie, S., & Vogel, G. (2016). *Horse speak: An equine-human translation guide: Conversations with horses in their language.* North Pomfret, VT: Trafalgar Square Books.

Wilson, L. C. (2018). The Prevalence of Military Sexual Trauma: A Meta-Analysis. *Trauma, Violence, & Abuse, 19*(5), 584–597.

World Health Organization. (2018). *Depression.* Retrieved from www.who.int/news-room/fact-sheets/detail/depression

World Health Organization. (2019). *Suicide data.* Retrieved from www.who.int/mental_health/prevention/suicide/suicideprevent/en/

World Health Organization. (2020). *Mental health and psychosocial considerations during COVID-19 outbreak.* Retrieved from https://www.who.int/docs/default-source/coronaviruse/mental-health-considerations.pdf

Wycoff, K. (2019). Competencies and ethics involved with the counseling modality of animal-assisted interventions. In L. Kogan (chair), *Animal-assisted interventions: Competencies and ethics: APA 2019.* Chicago, IL: American Psychological Association. Retrieved from www.apa-hai.org/human-animal-interaction/wp-content/uploads/2019/08/APA-COMPETENCIES-AND-ETHICS.pdf

Xie, T., Anderson, B. D., Dramragchaa, U., Chuluunbaatar, M., & Gray, G. C. (2016). A review of evidence that equine influenza viruses are zoonotic. *Pathologens, 5*(50), https://doi.org/10.3390/pathogens5030050

Yalom, I., & Leszcz, M. (2005). *The theory and practice of group psychotherapy* (5th ed.). New York: Basic Books.

Yang, K. (2017). *Working alliance in equine assisted therapy from an attachment perspective.* (Doctoral dissertation). Los Angeles, CA: Alliant International University.

Yontef, G. (2002). The relational attitude in Gestalt therapy theory and practice. *International Gestalt Journal, 25*(1), 15–34.

212 References

Yorke, J. (2010). The significance of human–animal relationships as modulators of trauma effects in children: A developmental neurobiological perspective. *Early Childhood Development and Care, 180*(5), 559–570.

Yorke, J., Nugent, W., Strand, E., Bolen, R., New, J., & Davis, C. (2013). Equine-assisted therapy and its impact on cortisol levels of children and horses: A pilot study and meta-analysis. *Early Child Development and Care, 183*(7), 874–894.

Zeder, M. A. (2012). Pathways to animal domestication. In P. Gepts, T. R. Famula, R. L. Bettinger, Brush, S. B., Damania, A. B., McGuire, P. E., & Qualset, C. O. (Eds.), *Biodiversity in agriculture: Domestication, evolution, and sustainability* (pp. 227–259). New York: Cambridge University Press.

Zimring, F. (1994). Carl Rogers. *Prospects: The Quarterly Review of Comparative Education (Paris, UNESCO: International Bureau of Education), 24*(3/4), 411–422.

Index

AAT *see* animal-assisted therapy
AAT-C *see* animal-assisted therapy in counseling
abused equines 59–61
ACA *see* American Counseling Association
activity-focused clients 82–83
acute stress disorder 102, 129
ADHD *see* attention-deficit/hyperactivity disorder
Adlerian therapy 91–92
adolescents 151, 154, 164; and ADHD 122; and animals 104; and anxiety 127; and COVID-19-related PTSD 141; and depression 124; EACP for 106–109, 114, 182; mental health needs of 102; and substance use disorder 131
adults 41; attachment style 36; EACP for 109–111; and mental health concerns related to COVID-19 139–140; and substance use disorder 131–132
advocacy 65, 69
American Counseling Association (ACA) 10, 162
Animal-Assisted Therapy in Counseling (AATC) Competencies Framework 61–70
animal-assisted therapy (AAT) 23, 49, 89, 148
animal-assisted therapy in counseling (AAT-C) 10, 61, 182–183
anxiety 33–35, 79–80; different client populations 125–127, 138–140; ethical considerations 160–161; integration of counseling theory 97–98; practice across lifespan 102–104, 109–111; risk management considerations 171–172

arena 55
ASD *see* autism spectrum disorder
assessment: clinical 171; initial 170
attending skills 86
attention-deficit/hyperactivity disorder (ADHD) 122–123
attitude domain 65, 69–70
autism spectrum disorder (ASD) 121–122, 129

barn 53–54
behavioral therapy 93–94
boundaries, therapeutic 142–145

Chandler, Cynthia 10, 75–77, 162, 183; *see also* Human-Animal Relational Theory (HART)
chewing *see* licking and chewing
children 3–4, 144, 148, 168, 182; and animals 102–104; and attention-deficit/hyperactivity disorder 122–123; and autism spectrum disorder 121; and death of an equine 152; and Equine-Partnered Play Therapy 104–106; and equine welfare 159; and group EACP 116; and in-session crisis 154; mental health concerns related to COVID-19 139–140; mental health needs of 102; military dependents 138–139; and the natural environment 51; and the therapist 61
Choice Theory 98–99
client injury report 172
client physical safety 148–150
client presentations 82–83
client screening 146–148
clinical assessments 171
cognitive-behavioral therapy 95–96

214 Index

communication 4, 6–9; counseling and psychotherapy formats 114; different client populations 120–125; equine communication in session 78–81; ethical considerations 151, 158, 166; facilitating relational equine-partnered counseling 76–77, 84, **85**; nature of equines 15–17; philosophical domains 25–32, 36, 44–48; practice across lifespan 104–106; risk management considerations 167–168; the team approach 81; the treatment team 68, 72–73
competencies 10, 61–64, 67, 74, 148, 161–162, 179
confidentiality 167–169
confrontation 87–88
Constructivist Psychotherapy 99
constructivist therapies 99–100
consultation 165–166
contraindications 146–148
cooperation 47–48
cortisol 5, 34–35
counseling skills 63–64
countertransference 26, 28, 39; ethical considerations 142, 145–146, 166; the treatment team 58, 67, 71
couple counseling and/or psychotherapy 80, 112–115
COVID-19 139–141, 173–174
crisis, in-session 154–155

death of equine 18, 152–153
debriefing 62, 69, 73–74, 142, 159–160, 165–166
depression 123–125, 134–138
direct service personnel 179–180
documentation 72, 167, 170–172, 176, 180
dominance: in equines 19–20, 33, 160; human dominance over equines 47–48, 156
domination 47–48

EAAT *see* equine-assisted activities and therapies
EAC *see* equine-assisted counseling
EACP *see* equine-assisted counseling and psychotherapy
EAL *see* equine-assisted learning
eating disorders 120–121
EFP *see* equine facilitated psychotherapy
emotional safety 74, 150, 166–167

emotions 13–15
enlargement of the meaning 87
EPPT *see* Equine-Partnered Play Therapy
equine advocacy 69
equine-assisted activities and therapies (EAAT) 9–11; terminology in 11–12
equine-assisted counseling (EAC) 11, 43
equine-assisted counseling and psychotherapy (EACP): for adolescents 106–109; for adults 109–111; benefits for the equine 9; benefits of the natural environment in 51–53; counseling environments 50; counseling and psychotherapy formats 112–113; couple and family EACP 113–115; different client populations 118–128, 130–137, 140–141; the EACP team 179–180; ethical considerations 142–148, 151, 154–158, 161–162, 165; facilitating Relational Equine-Partnered Counseling 75, 80–84, 86–88; formal training 66; group EACP 116–117; integration of counseling theory 89–91, 93–94, 97–100; partnering with equines 7, 10–12; philosophical domains 23, 27–28, 30, 34, 44, 48; practice across lifespan 102–104; program design 174–175, 177–178, 180–181; research issues 182–185; risk management considerations 167–174; the treatment team 58, 61–65, 67–68, 70–71, 73–74; working areas in 53–57; working with injured, abused, or neglected equines in 59–61; for young children 104–106
equine-assisted learning (EAL) 182
equine behaviors 2, 14, 80, 84, 100; ethical considerations 145, 148–149; philosophical domains 34, 36; and the treatment team 63–64, 66–67, 69–70
equine facilitated psychotherapy (EFP) 10, 12
equine files 172
equine knowledge 62–63, 66–67
equine liability insurance 173
Equine-Partnered Play Therapy (EPPT) xii–xiii, 11, 51, 81, 104–106, 119, 157
equine specialist 28, 66–70; considerations for including 70–71
ethics 61–62, 81, 142; client physical safety 148–150; client screening 146–148; equine welfare 155–161; ethical knowledge 63, 67;

Index 215

in-session crisis 154–155; limit-setting 150–151; multicultural and diversity considerations 161–165; multiple relationships and therapeutic boundaries 142–145; termination 151–154; transference and countertransference 145–146; treatment team supervision and consultation 165–166
evidence 49
existential therapy 97–98
experiential domain 29–31

facilitative skills 68, 84–88
family counseling and/or psychotherapy; family EACP 113–115; family systems therapy 100–101
formal training 62, 66
funds 180–181

gender 161–164
Gestalt therapy 96–97
grief 118–120, 152–153
group counseling and/or psychotherapy 62, 71, 116–117, 132, 138, 174

HART *see* Human-Animal Relational Theory
healing 3–4
hippotherapy 12
horsemanship 12, 43–44
human-animal bond xi, 4, 34, 62, 171
Human-Animal Relational Theory (HART) 75–77, 183
human-equine bond xiv, 3–5
husbandry 1–2, 66, 69–70

immediacy 87
indirect personnel 180
individual counseling and/or psychotherapy 112–115, 117
informed consent 168–169, 174
initial assessment 170
injured equines 59–61
injury report 172
insurance 172–173
intake 132, 169
intentionality 64, 68
interactive vaulting 12
interpretation 44–47
interspecies neurobiology 31–38, 75

knowledge domain 62–63, 66–67

liability 67, 169–170, 172–174
licking and chewing 18, 36, 76, 80, 93, 121
limit-setting 150–151

malpractice 173
meaning, enlargement of 87
MI *see* moral injury
mild traumatic brain injury (mTBI) 135, 137–138
military clients 132–141
military families 114, 118, 138–140
military sexual assault (MST) 93, 138
military veterans 60–61, 83, 93, 99, 144–145, 154; *see also* military clients
mirror 44
moral injury (MI) 110, 136–137, 140
MST *see* military sexual assault
mTBI *see* mild traumatic brain injury
multicultural and/or diversity considerations 63, 67, 142, 161–165
multiple relationships 142–145

Narrative Therapy 99
natural environment 51–53
nature and nurture 20–22
neglected equines 59–61
neurobiology 75, 185; of the human-equine bond 4–5; interspecies neurobiological domain 31–38
neurophysiological benefits 34–35
non-suicidal self-injury (NSSI) 108
NSSI *see* non-suicidal self-injury
nurture *see* nature and nurture

observation skills 84–86
oxytocin 4–5, 33–35, 109, 121, 126

paddocks 55–56
pandemics 173–174; *see also* COVID-19
parallels 48–49
pasture 56–57
PATH Intl. *see* Professional Association of Therapeutic Horsemanship International
patterns 48–49
pens 55–56
personality 20–22
personal values 70
person-centered therapy 92–93
physical safety xii, 44, 70, 73, 106, 115; ethical considerations 142–143, 148–150

216 Index

play therapy 62, 76, 88, 149, 151, 174; *see also* Equine-Partnered Play Therapy
posttraumatic stress (PTS) 129–130, 136; *see also* posttraumatic stress disorder (PTSD)
posttraumatic stress disorder (PTSD) 129–130, 132–141
practice settings 176–178
precautions 146–148
prey animal 15–16
privacy 167–169
privilege, therapist-client 167–169
Professional Association of Therapeutic Horsemanship International (PATH Intl.) 10–11, 43, 66, 70, 155–157, 174, 178
professional development 65, 70
professional liability insurance 173
professional values 65
progress notes 171–172
psychoanalytic therapy 89–91
PTS *see* posttraumatic stress
PTSD *see* posttraumatic stress disorder

questions, therapeutic 87–88

Reality Therapy 98–99
REBT *see* Relational Emotive Behavior Therapy
re-homing equines 153–154
relational domain 24–28
Relational Emotive Behavior Therapy (REBT) 95–96
Relational Equine-Partnered Counseling (REPC) xii–xiii, 11, 23–24, 89, 120, 128, 130, 183; client presentations 82–83; equine communication in session 78–81; experiential domain 29–31; facilitation skills in 84–88; general guidelines 41–49; and Human-Animal Relational Theory 75–77; interspecies neurobiological domain 31–38; relational domain 23–28; relationships in 27–28; session themes 83–84, **85**; spiritual domain 38–41; the team approach 81
Relational Moments (RM) 75–77
release *see* Voluntary Release and Waiver
REPC *see* Relational Equine-Partnered Counseling
rescued equines 59
riding 12, 43–44

risk management 63, 67, 167–174
RM *see* Relational Moments
round pen 54–55

safety 3–4, 53–54, 65–72, 117, 146–150, 176–178; *see also* emotional safety; physical safety
screening 146–148
self-directed clients 83
selling equines 153–154
senses 16–18
sentience 41–43
session themes 83–84, **85**
SHARM *see* Significant Human-Animal Relational Moment
Significant Human-Animal Relational Moment (SHARM) 75–77
silence 86
skills domain 63–64, 68–69
social behavior 18–20
Solution-Focused Therapy 99
specialized skill set 64, 68–69
spiritual domain 38–41
stalls 53–54
stress management 63, 123, 132, 149, 160, 166, 172
substance abuse disorder 131–132
substance use disorder 116, 131–132, 135, 148
SUD *see* substance use disorder
supervision 165–166

talk-focused clients 82
temperament 20–22
termination 60, 142, 144, 151–154, 180
themes *see* session themes
therapeutic boundaries 142–145
therapeutic driving 12
therapeutic horseback horsemanship and riding 12
therapeutic questions 87–88
therapeutic relationship 58, 84, 107, 131; ethical considerations 143–146, 153, 162; integration of counseling theory 91–92, 94–95; philosophical domains 23, 25–27, 33
therapeutic riding xii, 9, 12, 145, 161, 178, 182
therapist-client privilege 167–169
therapy animals 7–9
training, formal 62, 66
transference 25–26, 28, 39, 67, 90, 145–146, 166

Index 217

trauma 37–38, 75–76, 102–104, 127–133, 147–149
treatment plan 64, 131, 171
treatment team 7, 12, 58; AATC Competencies Framework 61; client physical safety 148–150; client screening 146–148; considerations for including the equine specialist 70–71; counseling environments 51, 53–57; counseling and psychotherapy formats 112–113, 115–117; different client populations 121–124, 129, 132–134; the equines 58–61; the equine specialist 66–70; equine welfare 155–157; ethical considerations 161–162; facilitating Relational Equine-Partnered Counseling 76–77, 80–84, 86, 88; in-session crisis 154–155; integration of counseling theory 92–94, 96–97; limit-setting 150–151; multiple relationships and therapeutic boundaries 142–145; philosophical domains 23, 27, 30–31, 36–38, 40–41, 43–49; practice across lifespan 103, 105–110; program design 175–176, 178; risk management considerations 167–168, 171; supervision and consultation 165–166; termination 151–154; the therapist 58–65; transference and countertransference 145–146; the treatment team relationship 71–73; volunteers 74

values, personal 70
values, professional 65
verbal skills 86–88
Voluntary Release and Waiver 169–170
volunteers 74

waiver *see* Voluntary Release and Waiver
welfare xii, 48–49, 53–54, 64–73; ethical considerations 142–143, 148–150, 155–161; program design 176–178
working areas 53–57

yawning 36, 76, 79, 88

zoonoses 147